Collecting
MILITARY ANTIQUES

Collecting

MILITARY ANTIQUES

Frederick Wilkinson

Bracken Books
LONDON

This edition published 1984 by Bracken Books,
a division of Bestseller Publications Ltd,
Brent House, 24 Friern Park, North Finchley, London N12,
under licence from the proprietor Ward Lock Ltd,
82 Gower Street, London WC1.

Copyright © Frederick Wilkinson 1976

ISBN 0 946495 07 6

Printed and bound in Yugoslavia by Grafoimpex.

Contents

Acknowledgments

The thanks of the publishers and author go to so many people who, often at great personal inconvenience, generously opened their collections and stock to them. They gave their time, much information, and helped to ensure that most of the items in this book are illustrated for the first time. Special thanks must go to: L. Archer, G. Bennett, Collectors Arms Antiques, D. Davies, K. Green, Hayward & Son, J. Hobbs, D. Jeffcoat, K. Kearsley, E. Kempster Ltd, E. Kenten, A. Miller, M. Morrison, National Army Museum, R. Perry, H. L. Peterson, Sotheby & Co, Ormond Stamps, Wallis & Wallis and the West Point Museum, USA

The author would like particularly to offer his personal thanks to Paul Forrester, who took so much trouble over the photographs, and to Miss Sue Unstead for her support and forbearance. One thing is certain; without the efforts and hard work of Teresa this book would never have been written.

Introduction

It is perhaps ironic that this era, which has seen what is probably the world's greatest manifestation of pacifism and hatred of war, has also seen the phenomenal growth of interest in all things military. Following the 1939-45 conflict, interest in arms, armour and militaria has shown a steady and constant rise, a trend which is, unfortunately, reflected in the prices that such articles now fetch.

One great joy of this particular field of collecting is its enormous diversity and with this diversity comes the opportunity to suit almost any pocket or taste. Even the small collector with a very limited amount to spend still has a chance of acquiring pieces of quite considerable interest. For a comparatively small amount it is possible to start a collection of military buttons, badges, documents, postcards or stamps. For the fortunate collector with more to spend there are the less rare medals, odd pieces of equipment, belts, buckles, older documents, newspapers and odd pieces of uniform. It is possible to go through the whole range rising to rarer items, such as the Victoria Cross, fine weapons, early uniforms and rare helmets, which are likely to cost very large sums indeed.

Collecting also places certain obligations on the collector other than just amassing a vast number of specimens. A true collector will always want to know as much as he can about any piece he owns and this search for information can be both the joy and the frustration of collecting. One piece which should, on the face of it, be very easy to identify and record, can prove to be baffling and elusive, whereas another piece, which seems to be totally obscure, may suddenly be identified and prove to be of immense interest. For the collector with an enjoyment in researching, military antiques offer tremendous opportunities. From the seventeenth century onwards few topics have been covered so extensively in writing, drawing and photography.

This coverage varies from country to country; some, such as Germany, are particularly well covered and there are catalogues, detailed uniform guides and a whole host of documentation stretching back to the beginning of the German Empire in 1870, as well as numerous prints, memoirs and other material.

France, with its martial tradition, is also quite fortunate and its military history has been well covered in most media. On the other hand Britain and the United States are less fortunate and in some fields, such as British army badges, there are serious gaps in our knowledge. There are, however, opportunities for the serious collector-researcher to ferret out much information for himself.

Within the limits of a volume such as this it is impossible to do more than skim the surface, indicate some possible lines of approach and endeavour to give some guidance on possible sources of supply and information. The collector will probably find that he gradually develops a special interest which may well lead to any number of fascinating and previously unexplored paths. The stimulus for this interest may be totally unexpected; few collectors can recall just what it was that turned their interest in any special direction.

For the greater part of the 4,000 years of man's recorded history, somewhere in the world there has been war. Man has an aggressive nature and, unlike most of the animal kingdom, will fight to the death. War and combat of all kinds have consumed so much of his time and energy that to ignore their existence is futile. In the beginning the fighter was the hunter who matched his strength and courage against animals or against other hunters. It is, therefore, not surprising that military matters have always figured large in man's interests and activities, for often they were matters of survival.

Although in the past war was remote, there was, none the less, a great interest in military matters. From the seventeenth century onwards newspapers, magazines, books and today radio, television and film, have all been pressed by demand into supplying plenty of information about war. The soldier was, for centuries, an object of fear and suspicion, for he was so often a man apart. Even in those countries where some form of military service was obligatory the man in uniform was somehow different from the rest. This attitude began to change in Britain from the mid-nineteenth century, and throughout the whole of the British Empire during the South African War, when thousands of ordinary men volunteered for service. Until the 1914-18 conflict war tended to be something that only soldiers were directly involved in, apart, of course, from the luckless people who happened to live or work in the path of a marching army or near the scene of a battle. With the advent of aircraft, long distance weapons and the growing concept of total war, this separation was no longer valid and war involved soldier and civilian alike. World War I swept the great majority of men into some form of war service and the old idea of 'civilian' and 'soldier' being very different was largely forgotten. Soldiers and civilians found that war was degrading, debasing and terrible but at the same time it evoked a response from man which, while it was generous, heroic and selfless, was also cruel and mean. This contradiction is yet another reason for the absorbing interest of the subject.

It must also be agreed, reluctantly perhaps, that there was a glamour about warfare. Until the adoption of utilitarian uniforms in the twentieth century, war was colourful: the uniforms, the flags, the tents, even the weapons all combined to produce a picturesque gloss which obscured the squalor, boredom, misery, agony and filth which was the real war.

Military enthusiasts are often accused of liking violence, but the collecting of military pieces in no way suggests approval of the horrors of war. Most collectors see in their pieces only their finer association. They are certainly not violent, though they may, with more justice, be accused of being escapists.

1 The Mechanics of Collecting

'Military antiques' is a useful label but many of the items described as militaria do not, in a strict sense, qualify for this description. Legally an antique is usually understood to be over one hundred years old and many of the items discussed are nowhere near as old as this and so should not strictly be described as antiques. This is a rather pedantic approach: the important point is that everything discussed has some connection with the soldier, and he is certainly much older than one hundred years. Armies, in the sense of uniformly dressed and equipped bodies of men, were generally a product of the seventeenth century, but soldiers, or warriors, have been about as long as man himself. The field then is large, varied and exciting.

To the question of 'How did you start?' you will almost certainly get as many answers as there are collectors. However, it would probably be fairly safe to suggest that most begin in a casual way. A single piece will act as a catalyst which may well generate an

A group of Imperial German steins and flasks.

Group of US military items: pair of shoulder scales worn by light artillerymen; sling belt for the Sharp's carbine; American peace medal; trade knife made in Sheffield; beadwork scabbard of Plains Indians; Heavy Cavalry (Dragoon) sabre, 1840 pattern; holster for Colt Army single-action revolver, *c.*1880; stone bowl of Indian pipe; canvas cartridge belt.

enthusiasm and interest. It may be an odd relic left by grandfather, it may be something seen on a junk stall, but once the interest is there it will almost inevitably blossom. It may change direction but it will certainly expand. The possibilities of military collecting are very great and each branch has its own peculiarities: but there are certain procedures which apply to almost every field.

Where to find the material? This is one of the many joys and frustrations of collecting and the only real answer to this question must be anywhere, at anytime, and the only guarantee of success is persistence helped out by some luck. Auction rooms are often the most obvious and readily accessible sources of supply. The number of auction rooms which now hold sales of military and associated items increases steadily; in London all of the major houses hold sales of medals, arms and armour, costume, and prints, and in many cases their associates in the United States and Canada hold similar sales. Many Societies hold local or postal sales and a number of dealers are setting up their own auctions. France, Belgium, Switzerland and Germany have fairly frequent sales.

Buying at auctions has certain advantages; firstly the items hold some guarantee of authenticity, for although the laws governing auctions vary from country to country, most houses offer some form of guarantee that the item is as described. Any reputable house will take back a lot which can be shown to have been misrepresented in the catalogue or to have some serious fault. On the other hand the very probity and prestige of the auction house may well push up the price; but this is by no means inevitable. It has been known for pieces to pass through the sale room in clear view of any number of experts and dealers at a price which was far below its true value. Sometimes this happens because it has not been recognized for what it was; sometimes some well known dealer decides not to bid for it and this may well persuade others into letting it pass simply because they respect his judgment.

It is most important when bidding to decide exactly what your ceiling price is to be. The true professional decides on this figure and will, with rare exceptions, stick rigidly to it. It requires a great deal of experience to get the feel of the room and decide whether it is perhaps wise, or worthwhile, to go one bid on. It is fatally easy to think that one more bid will be enough, for this may be followed by another and another until suddenly, in the excitement, the pre-determined value has been left far behind. This raises one of the most difficult questions to answer. What is the piece worth? This is the perennial problem of the collector! Leaving aside such problems as how much money is available, the simple and only true answer is that any item is worth precisely as much as the collector is prepared to pay for it. There is a general market value which can be used as a guide, but it is only a guide. For example, at the time of writing the going price of a British Light Dragoon Sword, pattern 1796, is around £30-£35 (approx. $60-$70). However, this is the price of an average run-of-the-mill example; if there is some special feature, if it is in exceptionally fine condition, if it has some peculiarity of pattern or some association, then the value could rise to two or three times this figure. Equally well, if the condition is perhaps a little less than one might like then its value will be less. The collector must simply decide how much he wants the piece and how much he is prepared to pay and this is the only true figure. The values of certain groups may fluctuate slightly over the years but only in a relative sense, for it is reasonably safe to say that although prices will rise in the field of military items they have never, so far, fallen.

Major auction houses have another use besides being a source of supply, for they issue catalogues which are almost invariably of a

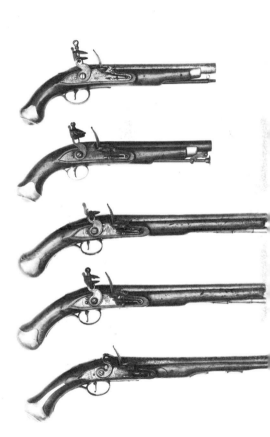

Group of British military flintlock pistols: Dragoon model, dated 1800; New Land model, the lock plate bears the cypher of William IV (1830–7); pair of Sea Service pistols, c.1800; early Heavy Dragoon pistol made by Edge and dated 1760.

high standard of research and scholarship and they also issue lists of prices realized at sales. Both these can be of great value to the collector whether he plans to bid or not. First of all the illustrations and information in the catalogue are a very useful source of reference and obviously the prices realized at auctions are one, though, it must be stressed, only one, indication of general figures across the whole market. Auction houses, then, are a reliable and useful source of supply, although, of course, the chance of acquiring a real bargain is fairly small. All the big dealers regularly receive the auction catalogues and are consequently very familiar with the market. Personal bidding is best but for collectors unable to attend the sales it is still quite possible to buy at auction. Auction houses will handle postal bids and normally undertake to acquire the item at the lowest possible figure. Collectors in Canada, Australia, New Zealand and the USA can make special arrangements to receive their catalogues by airmail, which gives them time to bid by post. The alternative is to use an agent who will vet and bid on any article when instructed by his client. In return for this service he will charge a commission, which is usually a percentage of the price paid. It must be remembered that the commission and shipping charges will be added on to the buying price and this is an important point when deciding on the bid to be made. A good, reliable agent is a valuable asset and once found should be guarded and cherished, for trust between client and agent is essential.

Next in importance are the antique dealers, but it is difficult to generalize about dealers. The vast majority are trustworthy, reliable and perfectly scrupulous tradesmen but there are some whose practice is, to say the least, somewhat sharp. Fortunately they are in a minority so that whilst not forgetting that they exist, one can, for the purposes of this discussion, ignore them. But the buyer should always beware. A dealer naturally purchases items from auction rooms but he also acquires his stock from other dealers. The whole antique trade is a rather closed shop and items will pass from hand to hand without ever leaving the trade. Dealers, as far as the military collector is concerned, fall into two obvious groups, the specialist and the non-specialist and the latter can prove to be a veritable gold mine. If the dealer is adventurous he may well pick up articles about which he has no knowledge but his trade 'feel' tells him that he will probably have a sale for it. In consequence it may be quite possible to purchase from him a military item at a price far below its market value. The non-specialist may also well be led by appearance or hearsay into asking a figure far in excess of the true value of a particular item. The fact that he does not sell it within a certain period, however, is usually a good indication to him that he has overpriced and he will consequently drop to a more reasonable figure.

The specialist dealer is far better equipped to offer goods at a more balanced and accurate price. He has a deeper understanding of the item and the trade and will, if he is well known, frequently be offered pieces that will be of interest. The best policy with all dealers is

Opposite Group of cap badges: bronze, US Army; Maryland National Guard, the part-time reserve forces; plastic version of officer's cap badge; gilt version of officer's cap badge, screw fitting; gilt and silver cap badge of officer in US Coast Guard Service; (*below*) brass shako plate, Maryland Volunteer unit.

Badges of the Royal Air Force: cloth arm badge, electronics, radar and wireless technicians and wireless operators in aircrew; cloth arm badge, leading aircraftman; brass arm badge, PTI (Physical Training Instructor); eagle flash, red on khaki, worn on desert uniform; VR patches worn by members of Volunteer Reserve.

persistence; gentle, firm persistence with regular visits, making clear one's own particular interest. The dealer, when he realizes that the collector is serious, will then probably keep an eye open for his special items and will reserve and put to one side pieces for which he knows there is a potential buyer.

Persistence in another field can prove very satisfying, for it is quite surprising what pawn shops, junk dealers, scrap merchants, house clearers, small transport concerns and general dealers will pick up. This is particularly true in Europe, possibly less so in the United States, but even so it is always worthwhile visiting any church bazaars, jumble sales, community function or street market because one just does not know what 'treasures' they may produce. Many a choice possession has been turned up under such circumstances.

A new development in antique collecting has been the growth of the so-called, super- or hyper-market or arcade. Here a whole group of dealers gather together, either outside, as in the famous Flea Market of Paris, the Portobello Road and Bermondsey Markets of London, or in a rather smart boutique. It is to these obvious places that visiting collectors flock and, whilst accepting that there is always a chance of finding a bargain, it must be realized that most of these markets are swept early in the morning by the dealers. It is, however, quite possible that during the course of the day late-comers may arrive with items for sale. But, in general, the bargains have gone first thing in the morning, around five or six am. This is not to say that such places are not worth a visit for the antiques may still be on sale there, but by the time the visitors arrive the piece may well have changed hands two or three times with a consequent rise in price on each occasion. Another area worth exploring is that of advertizing, for pieces in local newspapers, collector's magazines, Society journals, trade and professional journals. In these days of specialized robbery it is an unfortunate necessity, but a wise precaution, to use a box number in the advertisement.

Finally there are the specialist antiques exhibitions, shows or fairs which are now a fairly regular feature of the market. Such events may specialize in coins and medals, arms and armour, or firearms, or cast a wider net, like the London Arms Fair, which includes books, armour and arms, medals, model soldiers and all forms of militaria. Arms fairs are now an established feature of the antique market. In the USA the number is very considerable and specialist magazines will list dozens each month.

Membership of relevant societies is a tremendous help. Their journals offer articles of interest and practical use as well as providing opportunities for private trading and exchange–details of some societies will be found at the end of the book.

Every collector hopes that one day he will come across a 'sleeper'. This is collector's jargon for a piece which appears on the market untouched and without having passed through too many dealer's hands. It is unlikely to happen to everybody but it happens just often enough to keep alive a spark of hope in every collector's heart!

2 Care, Display and Research

Few collectors start out with any clear idea of their final objective. The usual sequence of events is a casual interest, stimulated by the acquisition of a piece or two, which grows and is eventually channelled into some specialist study. Few people begin to count themselves as collectors until they have a number of pieces to their credit. When this point is reached it is time to give some serious thought as to how best to deal with the collection.

Most collectors would accept that they have a duty to pass on their pieces to posterity. This may sound pretentious but it is surely no more than the truth. If a piece has survived for 200 years, fifty years or even twenty years then surely it is the collector's duty to see that it continues to survive and that it should be handed on in as good a condition as when it was first acquired. There are other considerations which should ensure that the collection is well cared for—present day costs alone are sufficient justification for taking very good care of it!

Most important of all must be the preservation of the item, for it should be looked after and displayed in such a way that it will suffer no deterioration. If the piece has to be handled then this point is even more important. Security must be considered, since, in these days of rising prices, almost any piece worth collecting is sufficiently valuable to make it attractive to a thief. It is therefore important to ensure that not only is it made difficult for the criminal, but, if something is stolen, then the law enforcement authority should be given every assistance to recover the piece with the minimum difficulty. Ideally the safest place for all items would be in the vaults of a bank or in some strong display case. Safely locked away in the vaults the collection gives little satisfaction and pleasure to anybody except the bank, and expense will probably preclude extreme security measures and special display cases. However a glass case does help to preserve the smaller item from the ravages of dust and damp and the fingers of a petty pilferer.

Some thought is required as to the possible future development of the collection. For instance, having acquired twenty-three badges, these could be very attractively displayed, but if, within two months, three other pieces which fit into the sequence have been acquired, then the whole display will have to be altered. Before anything approaching a permanent or even semi-permanent display is planned this fact should be borne in mind.

It would probably be of most use if each category of militaria is considered separately and some suggestions offered as to their care and recording. There are, however, some basic principles which most collectors will agree apply to all antiques. First and foremost the

Selection of American items, including daguerreotypes, belt plates, shoulder straps and peace medals.

Opposite Coat of hospital staff, *c.*1815, with typical high collar and flat gilt buttons; a single braid epaulette is fitted on the right shoulder.

piece should be very fully recorded. In these days of cheap cameras photography is no longer the expensive and complicated business it used to be. Modern cameras can cope with flash and artificial lighting and will produce very reasonable photographs even in the hands of a complete novice. Polaroids, although somewhat expensive to use, can give the collector a finished print in seconds so that he knows immediately if the photograph is satisfactory. The photography, of course, is probably best carried out after any cleaning or restoration has been undertaken. Photographs of front, back and sides of the piece may be necessary on one or two occasions but in many cases a front and perhaps a rear view will suffice.

Photographs can play a very important part but are not necessarily the only means of recording and some thought must be given to the written details and how to present them. Some collectors keep their

records in some form of book, others prefer loose-leaf folders or files, or record cards. Each system has something to offer. Details to be recorded will very obviously depend on the particular item but information concerning the acquisition and value of each piece should be included. It may be extremely useful if a note is made of the supplier and the price and date acquired. The recorded value will probably need to be revised at intervals and this figure will not necessarily bear any relation to the price paid. Many collectors dislike recording prices in open figures, but some simple code can be used. Dealers and collectors usually choose some easily remembered code word and allocate a number value to each letter. The word or phrase must have at least ten letters, all of them different. The price will then appear only as a sequence of letters incomprehensible to any outsider. At least one other person in the family or somebody connected with the collector should know the code word so that should any problem arise when the collector is not available the value can be discovered.

Every entry should also list any printed references, in word or pictures, relevant to the item. This may be no more than a picture in a book or a note of a similar piece held in another collection or museum, but references should be entered fully. It is very obvious at the time of writing that C.B. stands for Charlie Brown but in three years time one may not be quite so certain whether it stood for Charlie Brown or Carl Bacher. The entry should be as full as possible giving the source, page, illustration, title of book, in fact anything that may identify the piece with certainty.

If at all possible it is recommended that some form of identifying mark be placed on the piece, but it is very important that this mark should in no way detract from the value of the item. In some cases this is just not possible but in others the mark can be very easily put on in some inconspicuous place and will prove invaluable in identifying any particular piece. Again some suggestions as to the best places will be found under the various categories. Obviously a note should be made of any such mark placed on the piece.

Detailed information about the care of the various items is given in the supplement to each chapter but some general points apply to almost all antiques. Rust is the biggest enemy of all metal work, which should never be hung in a damp atmosphere. If this is not possible, then oiling and frequent inspections are essential. The new silicone-impregnated dusters are extremely useful and will deposit a thin protective film on a surface which will certainly help to protect it. Fingers sweat, so whenever a metal item is handled it should be wiped clean before it is put away.

Leather covers, scabbards and belts may be very dry and powdery, cracked, or in some other way require attention. There are a number of proprietary compounds available but most would agree that one of the best is the British Museum leather dressing described by H. J. Plenderleith in *The Conservation of Antiquities and Works of Art*. It produces a really miraculous improvement and offers long-

Opposite Selection of military items including: Victorian tunic of 1st Volunteer Battalion of Highland Light Infantry; Colt Army revolver, Model 1861; Sea Service flintlock, *c*.1800; German dagger; bayonets; badges; photographs and postcards; headdress and medals.

A small collection of pewter buttons of British Army, mostly dating from late 18th and early 19th centuries: (*top*) 49th (Hertfordshire) Regiment of Foot; (*middle*) 8th (The King's) Regiment; 89th Regiment of Foot; 43rd (Monmouthshire Light Infantry) Regiment; (*bottom*) 60th (Duke of York's Own Rifle Corps); 60th King's Royal Rifle Corps (post 1830); 41st Regiment of Foot.

term protection. Plenderleith's book contains a tremendous amount of expert advice on the treatment of a whole range of materials.

Insurance is another point to be considered and the collector may have difficulty in finding a firm which will insure him. Some companies are not very keen on taking on such uncertain liabilities as antiques. Practically every firm will require a fairly detailed inventory together with some authentication of the stated prices. It can come as a great surprise when the present day value of a collection is computed, for prices rise so quickly. Since the premium is related to value the collector is faced with a premium which may run into a considerable sum. Is it worth insuring? The answer, unless the premium is so high as to be totally out of the question, is yes, it must be. If the collection is lost it is irreplaceable, but at least some part of its value can be saved and a fresh start made. Values rise over the years and a periodical revision of the given figures and insured total should be carried out. At the time of writing an increase of, at the very least, 20% a year seems a reasonable working figure.

3 Uniform

Uniform, in the sense of a standardized dress for all members of a group, was not worn by the British Army prior to the seventeenth century. Some standardization had been achieved at an earlier date, as many nobles of the Middle Ages dressed their retainers in clothing decorated with part of their coat of arms. When a medieval sovereign summoned his army certain contingents might be dressed in clothing of a standard colour, for there are references to some towns giving their troops coats of a particular colour. However, there was no standardization throughout the army as a whole.

During the seventeenth century the troops on opposing sides often wore virtually identical clothing and often the only method of distinguishing friend and foe was by means of a field mark. A piece of cloth, a twig, a bunch of straw was pushed into the hat band or tucked into a belt and on this precarious identification might depend the soldier's life. After the battle troops escaped capture by removing or snatching up a field mark.

During the Civil Wars (1642-9) there were moves in the direction of a general issue of uniforms for the ordinary soldiers, although officers of all ranks were left free to indulge their personal taste. Red and blue seem to have been the most popular colours for coats and there is evidence to suggest that the trousers were commonly red.

In 1660 Charles II returned to take up the English throne and one of his first tasks was to reform the army. Many troops were demobilized but a number were retained and these, in effect, became the first British Standing Army. There were changes in the formation of the army: the number of pikemen was reduced to one third of the regiment so that the musketeers were now in the majority. The musketeers wore a short jacket at first but the length was later increased and by the beginning of the eighteenth century it reached nearly to the knees. This jacket was shaped to the body, with wide skirts and numerous buttons, which in some regiments, were made of brass. One feature of some uniforms during the Civil Wars was the use of lining of a different colour to that of the jacket. This lining showed when the cuffs, skirt and lapels were folded back and the patches of colour were known as the facings. These played an important part in the regimental distinctions.

Red was probably the most usual colour for the coats of the infantry although grey, black, blue and yellow were all worn. In addition to the facings the coats were also decorated with gold or silver lace.

During the seventeenth and most of the eighteenth century the regiment was still regarded as being rather the personal possession of the commanding officer, the Colonel. This officer was responsible for

Although executed in 1808, this print gives a very good idea of the 'shock' troops, the Cuirassiers, of the 17th-century army. Sir Thomas Fairfax was a leader of Parliament's forces during the English Civil War. He wears three-quarter armour and carries a pair of pistols at his saddle.

Engraving from a late 18th-century military book showing the typical British uniform of the period. The cross belts carry the 'breast plate' or shoulder belt plate, and the soldier carries a Brown Bess musket.

the clothing of the men and although guidance might be given the Colonel interpreted the regulations and made the arrangements for the supply of uniforms and weapons. If he chose to spend some of his own money in addition to his official allowance then his men might be better dressed than a regiment with a poorer or less generous colonel.

The man who did most to put the supplying of the army on a more controlled basis was John Churchill, Duke of Marlborough (1650-1722). He arranged for a Board of General Officers, all Colonels, to decide on and supervise the supply of uniform. Patterns were made and as contracts for the supply of uniforms were signed, samples were examined and then sealed so as to serve as a standard against which all future supplies could be judged.

At the beginning of the eighteenth century most British infantrymen wore a long, wide-skirted coat, reaching nearly to the knees. It had two, large side pockets and the sleeves had very large, fold-back cuffs. The front was remarkable for its many buttons and large buttonholes with the regimental facings. Legs were covered with breeches and with long gaiters, which buttoned up on the outside of the leg and tied at the knees. On the march troops wore brown gaiters but for parade these were replaced with white ones. The uniform was topped by a three-cornered hat although the grenadiers had their tall mitre caps.

During the first half of the eighteenth century there were more changes: cuffs were altered and the skirts of the long coat were hooked back to facilitate marching. The second half of the century saw more drastic changes including the wearing of epaulettes on both shoulders by Grenadier officers, whereas other infantry officers wore only one on the right shoulder. Waistcoats and linings were white instead of coloured although, as always, there were exceptions. The old, long-skirted coat was replaced by a jacket which reached down just below the waist. The long gaiters were replaced by boots, although shorter, half gaiters were still worn by some troops. This general trend towards simplification was probably at least partly due to the experience of the troops serving in North America against Indians and wily American colonists. By the end of the century the long-tailed coat had gone and the lapels, so much a feature of early uniforms, were abolished in 1797. The infantryman now wore a single-breasted red jacket, the shoulders fitted with stiffened, upstanding crescents of material known as wings. In place of his half boots and breeches he wore a pair of long trousers reaching to the ankles, although some troops still retained their half gaiters. In general cavalry uniforms were more elaborate than those of the infantry.

Although the British cavalry might have been rather glamorously dressed they seldom equalled the glory of the French forces. Swept along by their enthusiasm and military success in the revolution and by the leadership of Napoleon, never a man to avoid a little showmanship and glamour, the French army abounded in gorgeous uniforms. Loops, lace, feathers, plumes, frills, vivid colours, in fact nearly every accessory that has ever been added to army uniforms anywhere in the world, were all used. The expedition to Egypt in 1798 introduced Napoleon to the glories of the Orient and it apparently made its mark on his men as well. Many French units dressed their musicians with rather fanciful versions of the Egyptian costume.

The uniform of most European armies were now quite similar although they naturally varied in detail and colour. The Prussians generally favoured tall plumes; both infantry and cavalry wore them at the front of their shakos. Cavalry units of all armies delighted in extra frills such as a spare jacket, the dolman, which was slung from the shoulder of the Hussars and the elaborate front, the plastron, of the lancers' tunics.

Whilst the French enjoyed a great range of colours the basic colour of the British infantry was red. It was during the Napoleonic wars, in 1800, that green was first seen as part of the uniform of the British Army. Although it had taken twenty years the lesson of the American War of Independence finally got through and the commanders realized that the use of cover by soldiers was not cowardly but merely careful. In 1800 the 95th Regiment of Foot was raised and the men were given green uniforms. As riflemen they were expected to fight as individuals and use any means of concealment to get close to the enemy.

Following the Napoleonic wars one might have expected a lack of interest in all things military but it was not a period of quiet in Britain. The ruler at the time was the ex-Prince Regent, then George IV, a man with an abiding passion for clothes, who initiated several changes in uniform. Colourful accessories were added: the present day Household Cavalry owe their cuirasses and fine helmets to the Prince Regent. In 1822 during his reign the first set of Dress Regulations was issued. These regulations gave details only about the officers' uniforms and as they were frequently 'bent' it does not follow that every regiment and every officer adhered strictly to the guide lines set down.

Although Britain avoided any major conflict between the accession of Victoria in 1837 until the Crimean War which began in 1853, military life was not dull. Campaigns in which British troops were involved were taking place all over the world. Troops of the British army policed and guarded vast areas in Canada, Africa, Australia and New Zealand. They fought in minor actions against the Maoris and the men of the Indian frontiers and spent long boring hours guarding forts and stations in every climate. Since their opponents were usually lacking in everything except courage, British arms were generally triumphant, but this does not minimize the endeavour and courage of the troops involved. However, in 1853 the Crimean war broke out and for the first time since 1815, a gap of nearly forty years, the British Army was committed to a major European campaign. The results were pretty catastrophic; the Command was found to be ineffective and, even more important, much of the equipment and uniform proved to be badly designed,

Uniform of an officer of the 7th or Queen's Own Light Dragoons, c.1786. The Royal Warrant of 1768 stated that epaulettes were to be worn on both shoulders and the sash, previously worn over the shoulder, worn around the waist.

Helmet of the British Heavy Cavalry, pattern worn 1818–34. It was officially described as Roman style, with black glazed skull and peak, rich gilt laurel leaves, gilt chin scales and a lion's head at the comb. It was worn with an enormous crest of black bearskin.

defective and often totally useless. Major changes had to be undertaken and as a result much of the finery which had previously adorned the uniform was abandoned while the process of producing a practical, serviceable uniform was speeded up.

One big change which was already in hand was the replacing of the red jacket by a less obtrusive one. It was at last appreciated that the red offered an enemy an excellent sighting mark. Some troops had been dyeing their uniforms a drab yellow-brown colour known as khaki–a name derived from an Indian word meaning dust. In the first South African War of 1880-1 troops arriving in Africa from India were issued with khaki and in 1886 it was officially declared the colour for the active service uniform. The basic changes during this period all had one purpose in mind, that of producing a practical uniform suitable for active service. Dress uniform with all its fripperies was retained but was reserved for ceremonial use and parades. The final blow, if one was needed, to the impractical glory of war came in Britain with the Boer War of 1899-1902. When the British soldier went into the Great War his uniform consisted of a khaki general service cap, a khaki jacket with a number of pockets and a high neck, khaki trousers and strong boots. He was joined in this war by troops from all over the British Empire which was then at its peak. Nearly all had the same style of khaki uniform although they wore many different badges. The only part of the uniform that could be faulted as being perhaps less than practical were the puttees, introduced in 1902, which were long strips of khaki material, rather like a bandage, which were wound round the bottom part of the leg, covering the top of the boot. This was replaced in 1938 by a canvas anklet which was easily and quickly buckled on.

Following World War I the general development of British uniforms was again aimed at producing a really practical style. The general service uniform introduced in 1902 remained in use until 1938, when battle dress was introduced. This substituted a blouse type garment in place of the jacket, and the trousers had extra pockets in various places. The field service cap replaced the old general service cap and the beret became far more the fighting men's headgear. This trend was paralleled in almost every army in the world and there grew up an almost standard army dress.

This brief account of the development of British uniforms has dealt with the regular, full-time professional soldiers, but there were other troops. In addition to her Standing Army, Britain has often made use of numbers of part-time soldiers and these volunteers were often a law unto themselves as far as uniforms were concerned. The three great periods of volunteers were during the Napoleonic Wars, the mid-nineteenth century and the Boer War.

Napoleonic volunteers chose their officers and designed their own uniforms so that they might well incorporate features of several units. There were hundreds of these units dotted over the British Isles and their uniforms can be rather difficult to identify with certainty.

The second great wave of volunteers came during the 1860s, when it was thought that the military plans of Napoleon III could well include the invasion of these islands. The vast majority of units were Rifle Volunteers but there were Artillery, Engineers and, of course, the Mounted Infantry. Whilst the general style of uniform was orthodox some units experimented with their own style.

Volunteers of the Boer War were numerous and included many unusual units raised in South Africa. The two main groups from Britain were the City Imperial Volunteers and the Imperial Yeomanry. These units were armed by the Government but their equipment was mostly bought from funds raised. The uniform of the Imperial Yeomanry was fairly standard but contemporary accounts mention the variety of uniforms worn by the volunteers.

The tradition of 'volunteer' soldiers travelled with the migrants who peopled the British Empire; Canada, New Zealand and South Africa all developed their own part-time troops. In the early days regular British troops guarded the colonies but the expense alone was a strong enough reason for the central government to press for the formation of local forces. The first really effective volunteer units in Australia were the forces raised in Victoria, South Australia and New South Wales in 1854. These included a troop of cavalry and a battery of artillery as well as several companies of infantry. Inspired, to a degree, by fear of Russia, because of her involvement in the Crimean War, the colonists showed an enthusiasm which soon faded after the war ended. But in 1859 Tasmania, 1860 Queensland and 1861 Western Australia all boasted volunteer units. In 1871 the British Army was withdrawn and these colonies agreed to create their own Australian Armed Forces. Many volunteer units retained their separate identity but others were modified and became a militia.

The uniforms of these early Australian units often mirrored the British Army styles. When, in 1885, a contingent of New South Wales troops went to the Sudan, they wore a white helmet and trousers and a red jacket. Later other volunteers went to South Africa to serve in the Boer War. In 1901 the colonies were formed into the Commonwealth of Australia and among the alterations involved in this federation were great changes to the army organization. Some of the older State units continued under their old names but most units were given new titles and numbers. Calvary units such as the South Australian (Adelaide) Lancers wore uniforms very similar to those of British Lancers, with a coloured plastron for the tunic.

The move towards a practical uniform was repeated in most of the forces throughout the world and the history of the United States uniform in some ways closely parallels that of Britain. Until the creation of the new nation most of the forces serving in North America were, of course, regular British and French troops. Following the Seven Years' War the French were driven out and only regular British troops were to be seen, although there were some local militia units. During the American War of Independence or American Revolutionary War (1775-83), many of the colonists lacked any form of uniform and went into action in their civilian dress. The first regulations relating to uniform were issued in 1779, although as early as 1775 Congress was making plans for the supply of material.

Many of the Continental soldiers wore, as part of their uniform, a hunting shirt, which was loose fitting and reached roughly to the knees. The edges of the shirt were commonly fringed. Regimental facings were sometimes added to cuffs and collars and the garment was dyed a variety of colours. Apart from the hunting shirt the American military coat was very similar to that worn in Britain. Most units had coats of brown although some favoured blue, grey, green or red but in 1779 the regulations specified a blue coat with regimental facings. The general style of coat was very similar to the British pattern with turned back skirts and lapels. Beneath the jacket most soldiers wore a sleeveless, single-breasted waistcoat and a pair of breeches. Then about 1778 most units began to abandon the breeches and adopted overalls very like trousers.

Following their victories most of the army was demobilized or just went home but it was soon apparent that Congress would have to make arrangements for some form of standing army in addition to the many state militia units. By the 1820s the uniform of the United States infantryman was not greatly different from his British counterpart. He wore a waist length blue coatee with a high upstanding collar and greyish-blue trousers. For active service he had a short, pale blue jacket, trimmed with piping and white tape but still with the high collar.

In 1851 there were changes and in place of the old coatee a knee-length frock coat was introduced. The high collar was retained and for 'full dress' occasions very elaborate bullion epaulettes were fitted, but for normal wear the soldiers carried only small boards with rank insignia. The trousers were of dark blue cloth, the outer seam decorated with a narrow band of coloured material, white for infantry, yellow for dragoons and red for artillery. Coats for the other ranks were similar in shape and had nine buttons down the front.

When the Civil War broke out in 1861 the northern forces were mostly in the dark blue jackets and light blue trousers of the 'fatigue' or undress uniform. Men of the cavalry wore short 'shell' jackets coming only to the waist and trimmed in yellow. Light sky-blue trousers topped off a pair of boots or tucked inside a cavalry man's boot; down the outside of the leg ran a wide yellow stripe. It is of interest to note that like the British the United States army clothed its sharpshooters in a dark green uniform. Other bright colours were to be seen among the troops and these were mostly worn by militia volunteer units. Their uniforms often had French features.

If the North was in good shape as far as uniforms were concerned the South faced great problems from the very beginning of the war. Despite the existence of Dress Regulations very few Confederate units ever presented a totally uniform appearance. Grey was the predominant, but by no means only, colour worn and according to the regulations from the Adjutant and Inspector Generals Office in Richmond, the tunic was to be double-breasted, thigh length and with a high collar bearing the facings of the appropriate branch of the service. The same colour was to be used to trim the edge of the jacket and for the chevrons of rank. This was the regulation style but it was seldom seen in service. A short, 'shell' jacket was popular with the cavalry and was also worn by many infantry. By the end of the war the few fancy militia uniforms seen in the early days had long been forgotten and many of the troops were no longer even wearing grey. So difficult had the supply situation become that the uniforms were often home-dyed and the colours ranged from off-white to rich brown.

After the victory of the North in 1865 the armies, victorious and defeated, were gradually pruned: but the uniform was little changed. In 1872 a rather elaborate dress uniform was introduced, with a short blue tunic trimmed with the branch colour and with a variety of arm badges. A yellow stripe decorated the outside seam of the N.C.O's light blue trousers.

Engraving of an officer of the British Norfolk militia, mid-18th century. He has a large gorget at his chest and carries a cartridge pouch at his belt. The old gaiters have been replaced by half boots and the skirts of his coat are buttoned back.

Above US Army officer's cap worn by those above the rank of captain. This distinction is made by the two arcs of oak leaves on the peak or visor.

Right Jacket, technician (4th grade) in US Field Artillery with service stripe on left arm, member of 100th division.

In 1898 a field service uniform in khaki was authorized for tropical service which had canvas gaiters to cover foot and shin, with leather leggings for officers. The trousers for men and officers were all of the breeches style with wide tops, tight fitting from the knees down.

Olive drab uniform was authorized in 1902 and had a practical tunic, wide topped trousers, tight from the knee down, and canvas gaiters. It was in this uniform that the Doughboy came to Europe in 1917 and it remained largely unchanged until 1926, when the tunic became open-necked allowing, the wearing of a collar and black tie; all ranks received leather gaiters.

The service uniform was originally seen as a general purpose uniform but from 1941 onwards it was made a dress for formal and ceremonial occasions. From late 1941 the United States was involved in World War II and the rate of change in uniform accelerated and became far more diverse. Field jackets, rather like modern anoraks, first appeared in 1941, olive drab ties replaced the black one in 1942.

Shoulder straps: other ranks, Imperial German aviators; strap from leather jacket of 1st Flight Battalion; other ranks, Gross Deutschland Panzer Regiment, World War II; Italian General, World War II; Italian Colonel of Artillery, World War II.

As the forces became more and more engaged in combat there were calls for more practical styles and from 1942 onwards specialist uniforms such as one-piece and two-piece jungle suits, warm liners for jackets, wool field jackets, combined poncho-sleeping bags and white snow suits were just a few of the new issues of equipment.

The uniforms of most European armies went through this simplification process, although perhaps, in some cases, to a lesser degree. France and Prussia were two of the dominant powers and when they clashed in 1870 the results were disastrous for France. Prussia was jubilant and just before the signing of an armistice in January 1871 the new German Empire was established with William of Prussia as its emperor. All the forces of the German states were now united under the command of the Emperor although the individual states were still responsible for expense. Prussia dominated with nineteen army corps, Württemberg and Saxony had one each and Bavaria had two. The uniforms were varied with green, blue, black and red predominating for jackets; full dress uniforms were gorgeous with patches of colour at the throat, on the cuffs and on the shoulder straps.

By the beginning of this century most units had a dark blue 'walking out' uniform with a single breasted tunic, scarlet at the throat and cuffs, whilst the shoulder straps were coded in colour for various corps. This uniform was abolished in 1915, although the new style in field grey carried much the same regimental distinctions as the earlier form. It lacked some of the features of the earlier model. Litzen or braid which had been used on the 1910 pattern was either abandoned or modified.

Following the defeat of their forces in 1918 Germany underwent great hardships and the army was severely restricted. After great political stress and controversy Adolf Hitler became Chancellor in

Photograph of a typical infantryman of the Imperial German Army. His *Pickelhaube* has a cover bearing the figure 4 which was worn on active service. His rifle is the Mauser 98, and at his belt is an ammunition pouch and a case for binoculars.

1933 and soon the army was being expanded. In 1936 new uniforms were ordered. Members of the peacetime army were supplied with a dress uniform and service uniform but when war came in 1939 dress uniform was phased out, although it was still worn by certain personnel.

In 1943 economies were forced upon the *Reich* by the continuing war and new styles of uniform were introduced. The service tunic, model 1943, lacked refinements such as the pleats in the pockets, flaps were cut square instead of having three points and, possibly more important, the quality of the cloth was greatly reduced so that the jacket had a somewhat shoddy appearance. In 1944 there were further economies and the new style of field service tunic was, in fact, a blouse not dissimilar from the battle dress top worn by British troops. In colour it was more a grey-green, slate grey than the earlier patterns.

Special units of the German forces were often given uniforms which emphasized their importance by marking them out from the rest. A special uniform was issued to all members of the *Panzer* units serving in armoured fighting vehicles and this had long black trousers and a short, double-breasted jacket. Black was also the colour favoured by the dreaded SS or *Schutz Staffel* whilst the SA or *Sturmabteilung* favoured brown.

In addition to the basic clothing the Germans issued a great range of extras, some in the form of awards for skill and proficiency. Marksmanship carried a special lanyard of plaited aluminium cord with one flattened section bearing a badge. Like the lanyard the aiguillettes were also attached to the shoulder but the latter were purely decorative.

In addition to the standard army uniforms there are a whole range for parade and ceremonials and these picturesque items are often in the modified styles of past centuries. In Britain there are the fine dress uniforms of the Highland Regiments with kilt, plaid and feather bonnets, and those of the Household Cavalry with bright red jackets, white trousers and white gauntlets. In France the *Garde Républicaine* recalls the glory of Napoleon, and Greece has the *Evzones*. The West Point Academy in New York State was established in 1802 and its United States Corps of Cadets has a uniform which is rigidly archaic. Africa has many immensely picturesque units such as the Frontier Camel Guards of the United Arab Republic, the Tunisian Spahis or the Uganda Rifles.

Since the end of World War II there have been innumerable changes in uniform and the subject is so vast that it is imperative for the collector to arm himself with a good reference library. The variations in detail, between units, between battalions within a unit, between the uniform worn at home and abroad are so complex that it is virtually impossible to remember them and good references are essential. The collecting scope of uniforms has also widened considerably as the newly independent countries produce a whole new range of badges and uniforms.

COLLECTING, CARE AND DISPLAY

Uniforms are not the most popular items of militaria; they are difficult pieces to display and unless the uniform is complete there is a lost air about a single piece. Some collectors concentrate on one particular regiment; some will collect jackets or other pieces of uniform representative of one period, whilst others will seek to acquire one complete uniform of a particular campaign. The Boer War (1899-1902) is enjoying a certain vogue at the moment.

Complete uniforms, often with their japanned carrying cases, are not uncommon at auction houses which specialize in costume sales. Naturally a complete set of uniform may be expensive, especially if the owner can be identified, but it is a very desirable item.

The uniforms of the Third Reich and Imperial Germany are keenly collected and genuine pieces fetch high prices, but the problem with so much of this material is that it has been subject to the close attention of reproducers and fakers. The careful addition of a few shoulder or lapel flashes and extra buttons can convert an ordinary 'run-of-the-mill' officer's tunic into one belonging to an élite group and so multiply the price many times. Only knowledge and experience can guard the collector against the reproducer: there is very little real guidance that can be given, for there are so many clever ways of covering up modifications. The best hope is experience gained by examining genuine pieces, although it is appreciated that this is far easier said than done. It may be possible, through various specialist magazines and papers, to contact fellow collectors, who will be quite prepared to help with advice as well as providing the opportunity to handle and examine genuine uniforms. Some dealers offer a guarantee but it is not a common feature in this particular field since there are so many top quality reproductions.

World War II uniforms and occasionally those of World War I, can often be found in the surplus stores, one of the best supply sources, and prices are usually quite reasonable. Many of the items are second hand and consequently carry some form of guarantee that they are authentic. It is possible, with persistence and a degree of good luck, to build up a complete uniform of a GI, an airman of the RAF or some other member of the forces. It could well include all the accessories except the weapons—even these can be obtained as replicas.

Pieces pre-dating World War I are more likely to come through dealers or auction houses. Very early pieces are usually in need of some attention and cleaning, for dirt, tears and moth can easily ruin a piece and the care and restoration of the fabric are undoubtedly best left to the expert. However, all other things being equal, the price of most pieces is usually reasonable, even when the cost of restoration and repair is added to the basic buying price.

When deciding whether to buy or not there are one or two points which *may* help in deciding on the authenticity of an early piece. Prior to the 1840s all clothing was hand stitched: even the best seamstress produced lines of sewing which were slightly irregular and the size of the stitches was never quite uniform. Any item with very regular, even lines of stitching would therefore probably post-date 1840. If a uniform jacket carries facings then they should be consistent with the button holes and lapels and should correspond to the lists of facings given in the appropriate reference books. A dealer or collector may add any set of buttons to give a jacket a complete look so that buttons mean little or nothing when deciding the authenticity of a piece. The stitching, the method of manufacture and the material can all help in deciding, but it is still no easy matter to reach a firm conclusion.

If a complete uniform is being mounted then some form of wooden armature or tailor's dummy is needed. Dummies, even if made of modern glassfibre, are expensive, but quite a reasonable wooden former can be built up made of 2 in × 2 in (5 cm × 5 cm) timber, it need only be quite simple to form a basic shape. However, if such a wooden armature is used it is important that the wood should be as smooth as possible to prevent any snagging. If this is not possible then the wood should be covered in some way to ensure a smooth surface. If a dummy or stand is not desirable or available then the simplest method is, of course, to place the pieces on very well padded hangers. No matter how they are displayed it might be as well to cover them with a very thin plastic bag, which should hold the moth and dust at bay. A clearly marked label should be attached to the hanger so that the pieces can be identified with the minimum of trouble.

Identification marks are probably unnecessary on most of this material but if it is felt desirable to use one then a simple shape or letter can be stitched in some inconspicuous place, using a colour which is not immediately obvious.

The uniforms should be given periodic inspections to ensure that the moth has not attacked, and the piece should be gently brushed or vacuumed with a brush attachment at regular intervals.

The recording of the uniforms should be quite complete and in addition to the obvious details such as colour, size, button arrangement, facings, epaulettes, cuffs etc. attention should be given to the material and the way in which it is stitched. A colour picture is probably the easiest and best pictorial record. Failing that a simple water-colour sketch may suffice, for in both cases the accuracy of colour reproduction is likely to be about the same. A colour photograph does not record with total accuracy unless the lighting is very carefully controlled. As an alternative it is possible to build up a standard reference form for colour details by means of a square divided into sections. One section used to record the colour of collar, another for cuffs and so on—and if a standard grid is worked out it can be used for any variety of uniform. The entry should preferably contain reference to any prints, photographs or line drawings which show this type of uniform being worn. Identification can be a problem and is often a matter of looking at lots of pictures until the piece is recognized. Reference should be made to the appropriate books listed in the Select Bibliography.

4 Helmets and Headdress

Although uniform collecting is not one of the most popular fields that of headdress most certainly is. A solitary coat or tunic may look lost and forlorn but a helmet or shako can be mounted with an immediate appeal, and this may well be one of the reasons that they are so popular. Prices reflect this heavy demand and apart from fairly modern items most pieces are likely to be expensive.

Early helmets are extremely rare but examples dating from around the middle of the sixteenth century onwards do sometimes appear on the market. The close helmet is one of the more desirable and certainly one of the more expensive pieces. This type first appeared around 1500 and continued to be worn, in varying forms, until the early seventeenth century. A close helmet has a main part, known as the skull, which protects the top of the head and the back of the neck. Fitted to this is a pivotted face guard, the visor, which was made in a variety of styles. A third section, known as the bevor, pivots at the same point as the visor and protects the side of the head and the throat. To don the helmet both visor and bevor were raised. When it was in position the bevor was lowered and often locked into place by the action of a spring stud or hook and eye. Most helmets have a smooth surface but an attractive style, known as Maximilian, is immediately recognizable by the ridges which strengthen and decorate the helmet and armour.

During the fifteenth century the increasing use of firearms was making armour less and less desirable for the soldier and helmets of this period reflect the gradual lightening and simplifying of armour. Styles become less complex, so that by the late sixteenth and early seventeenth century many of the close helmets had little more than a rather crudely shaped piece of metal to guard the face. Light cavalry had become a common feature of many European armies and most wore little armour apart from a light form of helmet known as a burgonet. These helmets were open-faced with no visor.

The religious and civil wars of the first half of the seventeenth century saw a widespread use of the so-called lobster-tailed pot. This style was commonly worn by troops during the English Civil Wars (1642-9). It had a rounded skull, flared neck guard, two large cheek pieces and some form of peak. The face was protected against a sword cut by a sliding bar which passed through the peak. Another form had a more complex, three-bar guard, fixed to a pivotted peak. Large numbers of these helmets have survived and consequently they are not uncommon although prices are rising. For the foot soldier an even simpler style of helmet, known as the morion, was in general use. The commonest form consisted of a thick, conical skull, with a narrow brim, although another form, the pikeman's pot, had a much

Above French helmet and cuirass of Second French Empire. The breast plate which has an overlay of brass is dated 1865.

Above right French *Zischagge* helmet, *c*.1630, similar to the style worn by many troops in the first part of the 17th century.

Opposite Cap and Luftwaffe jacket of Oberleutnant, with belt of pattern authorized in May 1935, dagger of 1937 pattern, Iron Cross and pilot badge; jacket of 2nd Panzer Regiment officer bearing shoulder insignia of Hauptmann, with Iron Cross medal with bar, wound badge and tank battle badge.

wider, down-sloping brim. A common feature of many of the helmets of the seventeenth century is the method of construction for they are made of two sections of metal joined along the middle.

By the middle of the seventeenth century most helmets had been abandoned, although there was an exception in the case of siege helmets. These heavy pieces were usually of the burgonet type, with very thick crowns and very substantial internal padding. They were worn by the engineers and sappers who were obliged to work close to an enemy fortification and were, therefore, particularly vulnerable to missiles thrown from above. For most of the first half of the eighteenth century helmets were abandoned in practically the whole of Europe, but by the middle of the century a number of light cavalry units had been fitted out with fairly substantial leather helmets. These were more than decorative and offered some protection against a sword. However, a number of circumstances led the authorities to replace them with thin metal ones and the pattern was then established for the next century or so. Of all the Western Europeans the French were possibly most concerned with the protection of the head and many of their heavy cavalry units wore a quite substantial and very practical steel and brass helmet. British cavalry wore a number of helmets but essentially they were more decorative than functional. In 1812 the British Life Guards were issued with a peaked helmet with a very large, upstanding comb and a sweeping, black horsehair crest. It was thought that in addition to its decorative

function this horsehair would offer some protection against a sword cut to the neck. The helmet was varied in 1817, probably on the instructions of the Prince Regent, later George IV, who was certainly keenly interested in military costumes. The helmet was really rather impractical with a very high crest and a rather Roman style of decoration, but it was worn until about 1832. The next change came in 1842 when a simpler form of helmet, rather similar to that worn today by the Household Cavalry, was introduced, and this was worn until 1871. There were variations of this helmet but it was basically the same whether worn by the Heavy Cavalry or the Dragoon Guards. Light Dragoon helmets introduced about 1769 were of enamelled iron and had a brass comb. Some were decorated with fur crests and there were several varying patterns.

It was not until World War I that a truly functional helmet again appeared on the battlefield. In 1914 the French heavy cavalry wore their traditional metal helmet and many of the German troops wore a spiked leather helmet, but British and French infantry wore only a soft cloth cap. Despite optimistic predictions the war was not over by Christmas 1914 and had soon settled down to the demoralizing, slogging trench warfare which was to continue until 1918. In addition to all their discomforts the troops in the trenches were extremely vulnerable to head injuries and so serious did the problem become that there was a demand for some form of head protection. The French seem to have been the first to introduce the so-called Adrian helmet, which was rather light and consisted of a simple skull, small back and front peaks and a rather ineffective ridge comb running from back to front. Once the idea had been developed the other combatants followed suit and in 1915 the British developed their own steel helmet, which was not dissimilar from a very early style, known as a war or kettle hat. It was a simple, one-piece stamping, with a narrow, slightly downward sloping brim, and was fitted with a thick padded lining. The basic shape was to continue in use throughout two world wars although there were minor changes in the style and lining.

The Germans, too, experimented and produced their *Stahlhelm* in 1916, which was also a single piece moulding with internal padding and suspension, held in place by a leather chin strap. It was very functional with a slight forward peak and a deep, down-sweeping neckpiece, to offer maximum protection. Two ventilation lugs were fitted at the sides; these also served as a securing point for reinforcing plates, which could be strapped on by machine gunners and snipers, placed in particularly exposed positions. There were variations of the basic form including an extremely heavy one weighing 14 lb (6.35 kg), against just under 2½ lb (1.13 kg) for the standard pattern, which was intended for those who were at special risk. In 1931 a new style of padded inside, or liner, was introduced and in 1935 there were slight changes to the shape of the helmet, with the lugs removed and a less pronounced curve to the dome. During the next ten years there were a number of models but most had only minor differences, although that

Above British and French steel helmets, World War II; German *Stahlhelm,* World War I.

Opposite Pickelhaube, other ranks, with plate of the State of Baden; *Pickelhaube,* officer of the Prussian Infantry.

Grenadier's bearskin cap with silvered copper front plate and a backplate bearing the number 97. The name on the canvas lining and other facts date the cap to c.1795. The number identifies this piece as belonging to the 97th (Inverness-shire Highlanders) Regiment of Foot, which was disbanded in 1795.

of the parachutist—*Fallschirmjäger*—was very different. It had virtually no sloping brim and only a very small forward peak, and there were also differences in the liner. Variant forms of the Stahlhelm were made for the *S.A. Luftschutz* which was concerned with coping with air raids and the subsequent damage. The fire service also had a special pattern, with a strengthening comb running across the skull.

During World War I the helmet was usually painted with a camouflage pattern but following 1918 most Stahlhelms carried a state badge on the side. These were abolished by Hitler in 1933. In place of the state badge there were transfers of the national colours on one side and on the left side the badge of the service to which the wearer belonged. Various camouflage covers of cloth and wire were provided at different periods and these are not common. A very light plastic model was produced for high-ranking officers to wear on parade. Germany was not the only country to equip its troops with the Stahlhelm and the various models have seen service in at least twenty countries.

When the Americans joined the Great War they adopted the British steel helmet and continued to wear it until 1942, when a new style was introduced. The United States helmet was rather more elaborate than most for it consisted of two separate parts. There was a light plastic liner which had an internal system of straps, arranged to absorb the shock of a blow, and was held on the head by a narrow, leather, chin strap. This light helmet could be worn for parades or in areas of minimum danger, but a second, thick, steel bowl, of the same shape, could, if required, be used to cover the plastic liner and provide a very high degree of protection.

In addition to the standard infantry steel helmet there were others designed for special troops such as tank crews. Some were merely padded caps but others were quite complex helmets, designed to accommodate radio communication aids.

Such enormous numbers of helmets were produced during the two world wars that, fortunately for the collector, large numbers have survived. Collecting steel helmets is still a comparatively cheap field and there are so many variations that there are many opportunities. Those from Japan and some of the variant Stahlhelms are probably the most sought after.

Infantry were never very well protected and from the seventeenth to the twentieth century the majority of their headgear was almost invariably decorative rather than functional. During the seventeenth century most infantry wore a simple, broad-brimmed felt hat, although there were many differing styles. Some pinned up one brim, some two, until, eventually, it took up the traditional, three-cornered-hat shape. Towards the end of the seventeenth century a new style of hat appeared, worn only by a few of the strongest and tallest of the troops, whose job was to throw the crude bombs known as grenades. In order that their arm movement should not be hindered by the wide brim of the hat it was replaced by a tall cap. The early form had a long cloth bag hanging from the top but over the years the detail was modified and a clothing warrant of 1768 describes it as being of black bearskin with a metal plate at the front bearing the king's crest. This was worn until well into the nineteenth century.

The experiences suffered during the American War of Independence forced a number of alterations on to the British authorities. The old style of uniform was found to be rather unsatisfactory for the changing style of warfare with its more rapid movement and greater physical demands on the soldier. There were many changes in uniform and equipment of the troops particularly in headdress. Scottish troops were still wearing their traditional feather bonnet, while Marines and others had a form of top hat. But in 1800, during the Napoleonic wars, the British infantry made a complete break and introduced a new form known as the shako. It was a tall cylinder of leather with a small peak and a flat top. Mounted on the top, centre front, was a tall coloured plume. But the troops found this shako heavy and uncomfortable so in 1812 the so-called Waterloo shako made its appearance, and this model, being made of felt, was much lighter. It had a lower crown, although this was not obvious since a tall false front was fitted. The plume was retained and a plaited cord, white for the men, crimson and gold for officers, was draped across the front, which sported also a large metal badge. This form of shako, with variations, continued in use until 1815, when it was replaced with a rather peculiar form known as the bell top. In some respects it was not dissimilar from the Waterloo pattern except that the body widened towards the crown. The old feather plume was retained until 1835, when it was replaced by a worsted ball. The bell top shako was varied in 1839 and replaced in 1844 by the Albert shako, which, in some ways, reverted to the old Waterloo pattern. It had a leather top, small front and back peaks and stood some seven inches tall. The style of badge was very different from that of the Waterloo shako. The Albert shako continued in use until 1855 when a new style was introduced which had a lower crown and, instead of being cylindrical, the body tapered slightly towards the crown, but still retained its back and front peaks. In 1861 there was another change and the crown was lowered even further, while the outer lining was stitched on to a cork body. This was known as the quilted shako. In 1869 it became obvious to the authorities that the old quilted shako had an unfortunate tendency to disintegrate and a simpler but very similar version was introduced, in which the old black chin strap was replaced by a gilt metal chain. This style of shako continued in use until 1879, when a completely new form was introduced.

The Prussian Army had impressed the rest of Europe with its efficiency and, imitation being the sincerest form of flattery, many countries adopted variants of its famous spiked helmet. In 1879 the Home Pattern Helmet was adopted by the British Army; the cork body was covered with dark blue material and at the top was a decorative cross-piece base into which screwed a spike nearly three

Bell top shako of an officer of 76th Regiment of Foot, 1829–44.

inches tall. The officers' pattern had the front peak edged with brass whilst other ranks merely had a leather edging. The chin chain could be looped across the front of the helmet up to a hook fitted at the back of the spike, or worn under the chin. Light infantry wore the same helmet but it was then covered with a dark green cloth, and the pattern for the Artillery, Army Service Corps and Royal Medical Corps had a cup and ball fitting in place of the spike. This helmet remained as dress wear until the 1920s. For off-duty wear there were a number of cloth caps such as the Kilmarnock or 'pork pie' and the glengarry, originally worn only by the Scottish regiments. The latter became general issue from 1868, although it was some time before all regiments received it. Later there was the field cap of 1894 and the khaki, general service, peaked cap of 1905. In 1916 the beret appeared on the battlefield. It was introduced for the tank units as the only practical form of headdress possible inside the confined quarters of a tank.

Elaborate headdress never really returned to the British Army, although, at one time, there were a number of coloured field caps and coloured versions of the peaked, general service cap were used. In combat, during World War II, the beret replaced all hats, with distinctions only in colour; Commandos, during World War II, wore green, and paratroops maroon. The Royal Armoured Corps wore black and most infantry had khaki.

Although the hats described above were worn by the majority of infantry, special units, such as the Rifle Regiments and some fusiliers, had their own particular form of headdress. During the Boer War (1899-1902) the volunteers wore a slouch hat with one brim turned up, rather in the Australian style. There were, in addition to the standard headdress, a number of special styles peculiar to certain regiments. Highland regiments had their bonnets of ostrich feathers, the number of tails—the pieces hanging down at the side—carefully controlled by regulations. The Highland Light Infantry had a 'chaco', somewhat similar to those of the mid-nineteenth century.

Rifle regiments had a cap, which was known as a busby, although it differed from the cavalry busby pattern.

British cavalry headdress was far more elaborate than any of the infantry models. In 1812 the Light Dragoons wore a form of bell topped shako, fitted with a large plume and elaborate chin strap. There were distinctions between the various regiments of Light Dragoons, and some, in addition to the plumes and decorations, had heavy plaited festoons across the front. In 1857 there was a simplification and the new Light Dragoons shako was not dissimilar from that of the infantry, although still far more decorative. Some concession to necessity was made in that a foul weather cap was available for use in bad weather. This was originally an oilskin cover which fitted over the cap but some officers had a shako made in oilskin so that they merely changed their headgear in bad weather. Another glamorous form of headgear worn by some units of Light Cavalry was the busby. Known originally as the kalpak, it probably takes its name from Busby, one of the hatters who was well known in the early nineteenth century for making this particular form of headdress. It consists of a cylindrical fur hat with a cloth bag hanging from the top which normally draped on the right. In order to retain both the shako and the busby cap, long cords, called lines, were fitted, which looped around the body and were clipped on to the hat. There are variations in the style of these busbies, the bag pattern and the plume, all strictly controlled by tradition and the Dress Regulations.

Even more exotic was the headgear of the Lancers. The lance had been abandoned as a serious weapon during the seventeenth century but was reintroduced into Western Europe by Napoleon who was fascinated by the Polish Lancers. He believed that the lance was useful for attacking infantry. The British Army did not form any lancer units until 1816, but with them came a form of the traditional Polish *czapka* or *tschapka*. The style of this was still to be seen in the hats worn in World War II by the Polish infantry. It had a coloured square top fitted on to a rounded skull and most carried a cockade or plume of one style or another, as well as a chin chain. The most noticeable change over the years in both busby and tschapka has been reduction in height, and as a general guide it may be said that the taller they are the earlier they are likely to be. As with the busby and the shako a foul weather lance cap was also produced.

Since troops were so often on the move the officers' elaborate headdress needed some protection and they were purchased complete with a carrying case. The tins were shaped to fit the contents. Those for the great caps of black bearskin worn by the Foot Guards were tall and cylindrical; those for busbies were cylindrical but much shorter. The tschapka were in square boxes and the blue cloth in cylindrical ones with a special, tapered lid. Many of these cases carry the maker's nameplate and a brass plate engraved with the owner's name and regiment.

One of the most collected styles of headdress is the German spiked helmet, the *Pickelhaube*. The first model, introduced in 1842, was not

British officers' lance caps, early
20th century: 12th (Prince of Wales's
Royal) Lancers, with scarlet cloth
top; 21st (Empress of India's) Lancers,
with French grey top; 5th (Royal
Irish) Lancers, with scarlet cloth top.

quite the same as later ones. It had a high dome with a peak back and
front and, of course, its spike on the top. After various changes it took
on a lower crown and a round peak in 1867, and this is the form which
continued until the style was finally abandoned. There were many
variations of pattern but basically they were of leather, with small
peaks at back and front and a leather chin strap. Units were
distinguished by coloured rosettes which slipped over the metal strap
fitting at the side of the helmet. On the right the rosette was red,
white and black, the colours of Imperial Germany and that on the left
varied according to the home base be it Dukedom or State—black and
white for Prussia, black and red for Württemberg and so on for some
fifteen other combinations. At the front was a large plate which,
again, varied according to the unit or state and these are attractive
pieces for the collector. For ceremonial occasions horsehair plumes
were fitted and, of course, the officers' patterns were far more
elaborate. For field service a cloth cover was adopted in 1892. At first
these carried the regimental number but later versions were
quite plain. Because of the supply problems of World War I the
pickelhaube was produced in a variety of substitute materials
including felt and metal and these, despite the poor quality, are very
desirable for collectors. When the pickelhaube was worn during the
Great War it was modified and the spike was increasingly left off until
in 1915 a general order was issued for their removal. The pickelhaube
was not the only form of headdress worn by the Imperial Forces.
There were the tschapkas, rather like those of Britain, worn by the
Uhlan cavalry units and the shako worn by *Jäger* and *Schützen*
battalions, as well as the police. Hussars wore the *Pelzmütze,* which
was a form of busby.

Probably the most striking of all Imperial headress were the parade helmets of the bodyguard, Garde du Corps, with their great eagle in place of the spike, and the parade helmet of the Saxon Guard Cavalry Regiment which had a crouching lion. Another curiosity was the parade helmet of the 1st Guard Regiment of Foot. This was a metal form of the old mitre cap worn by Grenadiers in most armies, including the British, during the eighteenth century. In addition to the ceremonial helmets the Imperial forces had cloth field caps known as *Feldmütze,* which were the colour of the tunic, with a band matching the facing. Imperial and State cockades were also fitted on the cap at the front. The officers' pattern had a small leather peak which was lacking on the other ranks' pattern.

With the advent of Hitler in 1933 there was an increasing stress on the importance of the armed forces and a number of changes were introduced. At this time a uniform cap (*Schirmmütze*) was usual wear in the German Army. It had a field-grey top, a band of greeny-blue material and a small shiny black peak. Around the crown and the hatband narrow piping indicated the wearer's branch of the service. On the officers' pattern there was a silver cap cord running above the peak and for NCOs and ORs this was replaced by a black leather strap. At the centre of the band was an oak leaf cluster, encircling the cockade with the national colours. On the centre of the top section was the eagle emblem.

The usual pattern of *Pickelhaube* with its pointed spike, although this model with a silver-plated helmet plate was worn by a paymaster in the Prussian Infantry; *Picklehaube* of NCO of Prussian Guard Field Artillery, distinguished by the ball instead of the usual spike.

The famous parade helmet of the Cuirassiers forming the bodyguard, Garde du Corps, of the German Emperor. For normal wear the eagle was replaced by a spike.

There was also the field service cap of 1938, which was in grey material with flaps which could be pulled down to cover the ears. It carried the eagle and a right-angled piece of braid, enclosing a woven material cockade. In 1942 a new model was adopted and this very closely resembled the British 'side cap', being flatter and less round than the earlier model.

In 1943 a new style of cap was introduced and soon became the most commonly worn of all. It seems to have originated among German troops serving in North Africa and had a peak, semi-stiff, and a field-grey, cloth body. The two side flaps passed around the front and were secured by two small buttons at the front. It carried the material cockade and emblem at the front. Other German headdress included fur covered caps for use on the cold Eastern front, a sun helmet for the

Africa Korps and a black beret for the Panzer, although this also incorporated a protective lining.

In America the story of military headdress began with the colonists and as with their uniform they often had no military hats but resorted to wearing a civilian one. When uniforms were supplied the usual headdress was a cocked hat with a rosette on the left-hand side and a feather for officers. Cavalry units such as the Continental Dragoons wore a cap not unlike the British Light Dragoon helmet with its fur crest. By the early part of the nineteenth century the infantryman of the United States did not differ greatly from that of Britain, with a red coatee with facings and on his head a shako not unlike the British Waterloo pattern. In 1821 the Infantry were wearing a bell-topped shako with a coloured pompom, although other units, such as the Dragoons and Army Ordnance still retained the cylindrical tall shako. Whilst the tall shako might look impressive it was not a comfortable or practical hat and for campaigning many of the infantry wore a dark blue cap of woollen material with a leather peak and chin strap. Distinction of company and service were sometimes attached to the cap although it was by no means a general practice. A flap of cloth was fitted at the back so that the neck could be covered in bad weather.

In 1851 a set of uniform regulations was issued and there were numerous changes in headdress. Until 1854 a new type of shako was worn by all the branches of the armed forces. It was tall, tapering slightly towards the crown, and had a flat leather peak and a black chin strap. It was dark blue with a broad band of coloured material encircling the body above the peak and a pompom at the top of a yellow metal badge fitted at the front. The officers' pattern lacked the coloured band.

Ten years after these regulations the great Civil War (1861-5) broke out: the United States Army was split and the North and South followed different paths. Despite their political and military differences the two sides wore much the same style of headdress. The most common form of Northern hat was a soft sided, low-crowned kepi with a flat leather peak. Most were in blue, but some rifle regiments had the same pattern in dark green and a few of the colourful militia in their Zouave uniforms had kepis of red and blue.

On the Confederate side the kepi was normally of grey but very similar in shape and style. Another popular style of felt hat was known in the North as a Hardee or a Jeff Davis. It had the left side of the brim turned up. A modified form of this was known as a 'Burnside Pattern'. These hats were most often reserved for formal or 'dress' occasions.

When the war ended the campaign uniform was left unaltered for some time, although, as the North was victorious, the standard colour was blue. In 1872 a number of changes were made and a new hat was introduced for the infantry, a shako, not unlike the British pattern, with tapering sides and flat peak. For the cavalry there was the wide-brimmed, campaign hat, which was apparently unpopular,

Cap of Bavarian officer of the line, with red band, red piping and grey top; cap of transport officer, with light blue band, dark blue top and light blue piping.

for it was too soft and in rain drooped all round like a miniature umbrella. The old, kepi-style forage cap was often worn in its place and a new dress helmet was introduced in 1872. Like the British the military fashion designers were apparently influenced by the Prussian victory for the new helmet was spiked. It was lighter than the British equivalent, being made of black felt; it was worn by cavalry and then in 1881 a very similar pattern was made official for the infantry, replacing the shako; the cavalry pattern was altered at the same time. A cork pith helmet to keep off the sun was authorized in 1884.

In 1898 the khaki uniform was adopted for tropical wear and with it went a campaign hat of the same colour. Judging by the photographs of the period the men wore these hats in almost any style they fancied. In 1902, when the olive drab uniform came in, the campaign hat was standardized, with a stiff flat brim and the crown pinched in to a point, very much like a boy scout hat. Around the hat, resting on the brim, was a cord, the colour of which varied according to the wearer's branch: scarlet for artillery, maroon and white for medical and so on. Instead of the campaign hat many wore the overseas cap, which was very like the side cap, although it was worn more on the top of the head rather than to one side. It was piped along the edges with the colour of the branch of the services; infantry was light blue.

Campaign hats survived World War I and were still being worn in the 1940s, but a peaked cap was worn by many, as was the overseas cap. When the United States entered the war in 1941 there were many different styles of hats in service, including a knitted toque, known as a balaclava in the British Forces, winter hats and fatigue caps. In 1943 a combat suit was adopted and this included a light material cap with a comparatively large peak, and a back section which could be folded down to give the neck some protection.

Peace did not follow World War II and battle experiences in Korea and the East led to further changes. Late in the 1950s a new, dark green, service uniform was adopted in place of the khaki brown. The cap was round, with a patent leather peak and strap and for full dress wear there was a blue cap to go with the new dress uniform. During the 1950s the famous green beret was adopted by the US Special Forces, a somewhat mysteriously organized force.

Campaign hats like those of the United States forces were favoured by some of the New Zealand and the Australian forces also, and those serving in Malaya and Burma during World War II wore the campaign hat with the brim turned up on one side. Jungle warfare in Malaya, Vietnam and other areas led to changes in headdress. Many armies adopted soft, rather shapeless hats, often in camouflage colouring and with a narrow brim.

In addition to the standard, army issue headdress there are other interesting pieces, such as flying helmets, of which several patterns were issued during World War II. There were comparatively thick ones for European theatres of operation and lighter versions for the Middle and Far East. There are also helmets and caps worn by such units as military police groups, although, in most cases, they wore specially painted steel helmets or coloured caps. There were also variations of the standard pattern for officers of various ranks, all of which increase the great range of material available for the collector.

COLLECTING, CARE AND DISPLAY

Most of the larger auction houses include helmets and headdress in their arms, armour and militaria sales, but one or two hold costume sales, which may well include some headdress. Specialist dealers will obviously carry stocks but general dealers are not very inclined to handle them, except, perhaps, the metal helmets which look attractive.

Prices have climbed consistently over the past few years, so that everything except the commonest of items is likely to prove fairly expensive. Close helmets of the sixteenth century are rare and expensive but the military style burgonets and other helmets of the seventeenth century are far more reasonable, although by no means cheap.

Apart from the early helmets the most expensive items of military headdress are likely to be those of the early nineteenth century and again, as a general rule, the older the piece the more expensive it is likely to be. Genuine Napoleonic headgear, Waterloo shakos and similar items will certainly run into very large sums. Later pieces such as the British, blue cloth helmets, in good condition and with a tin case, are much more likely to cost less but will still not be cheap.

Many of the headdress and helmets of the British, German and American armies have been copied at various times for theatrical purposes. Some of these copies are obvious and would fool no one, but others are of superb quality and require a close examination before any opinion can be given. In some cases modern caps which are similar to the earlier models can be altered and again may prove difficult to distinguish from the original. Hats of the Third Reich have been especially subject to this kind of attention, and here it is very much a case of the 'buyer beware'. American Civil War kepis have been reproduced in bulk over the years for films and for the many groups who enjoy dressing up and acting out the drills and events of the war. Some of these reproductions are of such high quality that any kepi apparently of this period which appears on the market should be treated with great caution.

It is not easy to give advice on how to detect a modified item but as with every antique there is no substitute for experience. Close attention should be given to all individual features such as buttons, lining, maker's name, wear, extra holes suggesting a change of badge and, if possible, the condition of the material normally covered by the badge. It may be possible to draw some conclusion from the colour and wear on this particular piece of material, for if the badge has been long in place it could well mean this material will possibly be brighter in colour and less worn than the surrounding area. However, this is not necessarily so and it is just one factor to be considered in conjunction with all the others. If the headdress has any brass fittings then their colour can be another pointer, for modern cast brass usually has a slightly different colour from the older materials. The markings inside headgear are often of interest and many pieces of the nineteenth and early twentieth centuries carry makers' labels. In the case of British pieces the type of crown which is sometimes found on these labels may indicate whether it is a Victorian or Edwardian piece. Many British hats and helmets have appeared on the market over the past few years which bear a stamp on the inside of the crown reading 'Aldershot Tattoo'. These are perfectly genuine pieces which were held in store for this particular military spectacular, so popular during the first part of this century.

German pickelhaubes have come in for their fair share of restoration and alteration and it is important to know which patterns were in use at various dates. Some glassfibre facsimiles have been produced, and they are remarkably accurate, although they would fool no one once they have been handled, for they are much too light.

With the exception of many German patterns, examples of the standard 'other ranks' issue hats of World War II are fairly common. In Britain many of them enjoyed a vogue with those who liked 'off beat' dress and they are still to be found on market stalls at very reasonable prices. Less common items such as New Zealand or US Campaign hats are likely to prove difficult to acquire.

Steel helmets of the British, American and French standard patterns are still common and cheap. The famous Stahlhelm of the German forces is a little more highly prized and special patterns such as the parachutist model are quite expensive. Standard World War I models are less common and those of shapes differing from the standard form are sought after.

Researching helmets and headdress is fairly straightforward; most of the standard patterns have been well recorded and the results published. Photographs, engravings and prints are all likely to prove useful in identifying and dating any particular pieces. It should be remembered, however, that the badge on the cap or helmet is not necessarily the original and this fact may explain apparent discrepancies in fittings and other features. It must also be stressed that although the regulations may give a date for the adoption of a new style this did not mean that it was at once issued to every man in the army. It was possible for a superseded style of hat to be worn for years after it had been officially replaced.

Metal helmets of the seventeenth century are, of course, very susceptible to rust and the prime concern of the collector is to remove and prevent it. The procedures are the same as for armour (see page 82). Brass and white metal helmets of the nineteenth century require a different treatment and the first step should be to strip them into their component parts. Usually this is simple but if, through corrosion or deformation, the pieces will not unscrew and it is necessary to use some leverage it is very important to exercise great

The crested helmet was popular with cavalry units of many countries during the 19th century. This example was worn by an officer of the Bavarian Cuirassiers. It has the cypher of Ludwig I (1825–48) and has a skull of steel and fittings of brass.

care, for the metal is usually thin and not very strong. If a piece is gripped with any form of mechanical aid the jaws of the grip must be padded to prevent any marking. Dents can be knocked out but it is a job that requires some skill and great care and both the anvil and hammer need to be padded. The amount of cleaning will vary but in most cases a very careful wipe over with a damp, soapy cloth will often remove an amazing amount of dirt. Care needs to be taken to ensure that all parts are thoroughly dried to prevent rusting. Polishing is best undertaken with the gentlest polish available, impregnated wadding is possibly the best but stubborn patches may require something a little stronger. The various parts can be cleaned, the helmet reassembled and then wiped over with one of the silicone-impregnated cloths.

Cloth and leather headdress presents more problems and probably requires even more care than the metal helmets. Fittings on pieces such as the blue cloth helmet can be removed and the material can

Mexican army cap, maroon with braid decoration and an embroidered badge of an eagle holding a snake in its talons.

then be brushed and possibly wiped over with a damp cloth. The metal pieces can be cleaned and the whole hat reassembled. Leather parts such as the peaks can be treated with an approved leather dressing or given a polish with a soft cloth.

Dust and dirt are hard to avoid in town and if the hats cannot be kept under cover they need constant checks. To remove dust a vacuum cleaner with a soft brush attachment is very satisfactory or, failing that, a firm but careful brushing will suffice. If it is desired the hats can be covered with glass or plastic domes but these can be expensive. Transparent plastic bags are very much cheaper although they tend to look untidy and detract from the beauty of the hat.

Obviously the displaying of headdress is dependent on space and facilities available but they can be set up in various ways. Most will need some form of internal support. It is unwise to let them stand flat as this may put undesirable pressure on the peaks or sides. If they are mounted then the support should be such that the weight is evenly spread and not concentrated at one point. A simple but effective stand can very easily be constructed from a base, with a section of broom handle or dowelling mounted at the centre. On the top of the centre support a piece of polystyrene can be mounted, of such size and shape as to engage with the sides of the hat without touching the crown. The stands can be free standing or they can be fixed to the wall as an L-shaped bracket. They also have the virtue that they can be constructed to take almost any style and size of helmet or hat.

There is no doubt that the appearance of the headgear is greatly enhanced if it is mounted on some form of head. The cost of commercially produced heads is likely to be high but with some ingenuity it is possible to construct a reasonable head. Polystyrene wig blocks can be used either as they are or as a former on which a papier mâché head can be built up.

A photograph is the obvious way to record a helmet but a full written description is necessary. Material, lining, badge, fittings and full details of regulations concerning the style should be recorded, together with reference to any photographs showing it being worn.

Very occasionally a British helmet or cap will be found, with a label and red sealing wax attached by a ribbon. This is one of the few sealed pattern hats produced for each new style. They are uncommon and therefore very desirable to the collector.

If it is wished to put on some identification mark this can take the form of some small Indian ink letter on the inside of the internal leather hat band or in the crown.

It is always worth acquiring any odd accessories and fittings for headdress such as chin straps, and chains, bosses, plumes, spikes and pompoms. They are difficult to obtain and may well complete a newly acquired piece; ideally the piece should be totally original but often one small item, which may be missing from the original or damaged, will complete the piece very satisfactorily.

5 Badges

The origins of the soldier's badges go back to the Middle Ages, by which time the science and art of heraldry had been fully developed and a part of the coat of arms was often used as a means of identification. Badges in the modern sense of a separate item do not really appear before the eighteenth century.

Armies of the seventeenth century marched into battle wearing some kind of uniform, but it was usually devoid of any badges and often the only means of distinguishing between friend or foe was the field mark. In the British Army the Royal cypher was used in the sense of a badge from the time of the Restoration but it was usually embroidered or painted on to the equipment. It was also engraved on the locks of military firearms. It seems most likely that the first headdress badges, and these are the ones which mainly concern the collector, appeared during the seventeenth century, when the grenadiers had an embroidered royal cypher, a grenade or some other appropriate symbol, on the front of the mitre cap.

By the beginning of the eighteenth century this practice had spread to other regiments including the Foot Guards, and it is highly likely that by this period a number of embroidered badges were in use. It is fairly certain that the Colonel of the Regiment, almost invariably a man of title or position, often used part of his own coat of arms as the regimental badge. This is confirmed by a Clothing Warrant of 1751 which states categorically that 'henceforward no Colonel will be allowed to place any part of his personal coat of arms on the appointments of the regiments'. This same warrant also details the Grenadier cap badges: on the front of the mitre cap there was an embroidered white horse of Hanover with the Royal cypher, whilst the number of the regiment was on the back of the hat. The regimental badge was also painted on the pieces of equipment.

The first positive evidence of metal cap badges occurs in another Clothing Warrant of 1768, which specifically mentions that the Grenadiers are to wear a black bearskin cap (originally granted to the Highland Grenadiers in 1747) on the front of which was to be the king's crest, silver plated on a black background with the motto *Nec Espera Terrent*. The wording of the warrant would seem to suggest that this practice was limited solely to the grenadier's bearskin cap.

Around 1760, the Light Dragoons were issued with a leather cap on the front of which was a metal cap badge consisting of a crown with the Royal cypher and the initials of the particular regiment. Again the ordinary infantryman apparently had no badge on his headdress. It was with the introduction of the tall, japanned leather shako in 1800 that the use of metal hat badges became an established practice. The badge was a large, near-rectangular, brass plate embossed with

Helmet plate for Royal Marine Artillery, 1879-1923.

Above Brass plate from a British shako, 1800–12.

Above right Large gilt and silver shako plate worn by officers of the Indian Madras Light Cavalry, 1846–57.

Opposite Insignia, mostly of cloth, of many countries and forces, including: nationalist Chinese navy hat band; Polish cap badge; Russian shoulder board for a captain of engineers; divisional signs of World Wars I and II and German rank badges.

the Royal cypher and some form of the regimental number or name. In 1812 the Waterloo-type shako was introduced and a smaller, plainer, pressed brass plate, basically oval but with baroque-style edges, was introduced. This plate was worn by most of the infantry, although the Light Infantry had their own special design.

With the introduction of the bell-top shako in 1835 came another change and variants of this new basic pattern were to be worn for a very long time. It was a large plate of an eight-pointed sunburst or star, surmounted by a crown and with a regimental device superimposed in the centre. This badge was of gilt for officers and brass for other ranks.

When the Albert shako was adopted in 1844 it was fitted with a smaller version of the earlier pattern. It had more clearly defined points, but was basically of the same construction, with a centre piece and a surmounting crown. This style continued in use until the smaller shako appeared in 1855, when a new badge was introduced consisting of a wreath surrounding the regimental insignia and surmounted by the crown. When the blue cloth helmet was adopted by the British Army in 1879 the badge reverted to the basic, eight-pointed star, with a regimental centrepiece.

In 1868 a new type of badge made its appearance; this was the glengarry badge worn on the Scottish-type, side cap introduced to the infantry in that year. These badges vary from regiment to regiment but the majority consist of a garter, with the regimental number

and/or badge at the centre. With the adoption of the field and general service caps smaller badges were introduced which, for other ranks, were of stamped brass, or brass with superimposed white metal insignia. Officers' badges were normally gilt and white metal. Until the introduction of this Field Service cap most badges were attached to the headdress by lugs, which were pushed through the material of the helmet and then secured on the inside by a small leather wedge or brass split pin through the hole. When the smaller badge was introduced many retained their lugs but some were fitted with a slider, an L-shaped bar at the back of the badge, which engaged with an appropriate slot in the cap material. During World War I a number of British cap badges, normally of two metals, were produced in solid brass, in order to conserve materials and time. Similar economy measures were undertaken during World War II and in 1941 it was decided that many badges were to be produced in plastic. They were adopted, reluctantly, by many regiments as well as the Royal Air Force and various corps. Later anodized plastic badges were issued which have a shiny coating on top of the plastic.

Smaller versions of the cap badges were made; some were worn on the beret and others on the lapels of the tunic, when they were known as collar dogs.

A third form of metal badge was the title, which was worn on the shoulder strap. The usual pattern was of brass but the designs varied considerably from regiment to regiment; some carry the full name of the regiment and the number of the battalion, others have simply a number and the initials of the unit. One may have an obvious and full identification such as T, Cyclist, City of London, in three lines, or more cryptically IXL for the 9th Lancers.

In the British Army a distinction was made in the badges worn by the local militia, which was a form of reserve force, and the regular army. Regular army badges were of brass, or at least some form of yellow metal, whereas the militia or volunteers normally had their badges in white metal. This is not the case for Scottish regiments since most of the regular Scottish units had white metal badges, although some were made in brass or bronze. When a regiment played a particularly distinguished part in a battle or a campaign then it might be granted the right to carry the name of the battle on its colours and on its badge. In the case of the Royal Artillery so many battle honours were acquired that they were dispensed with. In their place the corps was given the simple but eloquent *Ubique*, meaning everywhere. Another distinction indicating whether a regiment belonged to the regular or volunteer battalion was that the militia and volunteers did not, as a rule, carry the battle honours held by the regular battalions.

In addition to those badges worn on caps and uniforms others were fitted on various pieces of equipment. Pouches and harness were often fitted with the metal badge of the regiment but these can usually be distinguished from cap badges by their means of construction. If the badges have a threaded fitting or fold over lugs on

Above Helmet plates of British rifle regiments: Queen's Westminster Volunteers, *c.*1880–1902; King's Royal Rifle Corps, 1884–90.

Opposite Hilt of an English mortuary sword, early 17th century; it has an unusually wide blade for this type of sword but the screws securing the guard to the pommel are typical.

the back then they are probably off equipment of one kind or another.

Most early badges of rank were incorporated into the uniform, but later on chevrons and 'pips' were introduced. In addition to badges of rank, normally of cloth, worn on the arm, there were arm badges which were worn by many of the NCOs of the cavalry regiments. These attractive pieces were usually made up of part of the regimental badge and were worn above the chevrons on the right arm. In the infantry there were large, embroidered badges which were worn on the arm by senior NCOs. The design varied according to the rank and regiment but their equivalents are still to be seen today. There were also a variety of cloth or metal arm badges worn to indicate trade or proficiency. These are readily available and still quite cheap.

The regimental emblem was usually repeated on the army buttons, which came to play quite an important part in the uniform of the British Army. At first the design appears to have been a matter of individual choice, probably by the Colonel of the regiment. It is known that in 1767 regulations stipulated that the number of the Foot Regiment should appear on the button, and in the same year it was decreed that the Dragoon Guards should have buttons bearing the initials of their regiments. Until 1855 the men's buttons were of pewter and were normally made in one piece, with a slightly dome-shaped front and a simple shank at the back. The officers' buttons usually had wooden or bone formers, covered with thin gilt or silver foil, but later these were replaced by single-piece, metal buttons. Early in the nineteenth century the conventional buttons with a back, a domed front and a loose shank were adopted. In 1855 the tunic became part of the uniform and the size of buttons was changed; the officers' were still of gilt but brass was the new material for other ranks' buttons. Most of the line regiment buttons had a fairly simple design which incorporated the regimental number, for until 1881 all British line regiments were known by a number in addition to any name that they might have. The designs of the buttons changed very little over the next few years, until 1871, when the old regimentally distinguished buttons were replaced by a standard brass pattern, carrying only the Royal Arms. There were one or two exceptions to this rule but this was the standard button for the whole army until 1924, when the regimental buttons were re-introduced. The distinction of colour in the regimental badges also applied to the buttons so that in general militia buttons are silver or white metal whilst those of the regular army are of gilt or brass. There were

different sizes of buttons depending on which part of the uniform they were to decorate. The large ones were about 1 in (2.5 cm) in diameter, the small about ¾ in (1.9 cm). On the front of the field service cap there were two cap buttons just over ¼ in (1.5 cm) in diameter. In addition to those worn on the tunic there were special ones for mess jackets. These were flat, with the pattern engraved into the face instead of being embossed on the dome. In the 1950s anodized buttons were introduced but, as always, there was a considerable time lapse before they were in general use.

Many of the buttons are stamped on the back with the maker's name and often his address as well. The well-established firms such as Nutting, Sampson and Wright and Gaunt changed their titles and addresses, and since these changes have been reasonably well researched it is possible to use this information to obtain an approximate dating of the buttons.

In addition to the metal badges and buttons on the soldier's uniform there were many cloth badges of rank, chevrons or stripes, proficiency and trade badges and various formation badges. The practice of using cloth divisional signs was started in World War I and was revived in World War II. These patches were worn on the sleeves and from 1940 onwards they included a strip of coloured material which identified the particular branch of the service—infantry was scarlet, signals blue and white and so on. In addition to the unit badge there were cloth titles of the regiment, specialist badges—parachute, tank badge, and so on, and tartan patches for the Scottish regiments. Cloth insignia were a very notable feature of the United States Forces uniform, where they are large and colourful.

Above and opposite Selection of British, Irish and American buttons and lapel badges, dating from the late 18th century.

The young army of the American colonies was so short of time and material that badges were a luxury as were regimental buttons. Some official pattern buttons were worn; they were usually of pewter and carried a device such as the number of the unit—25th (Continental Infantry). Some had the initials USA and from 1779 it was decreed that this type was to be worn on the coat, with a State button on the hat.

During the Civil War (1861-65) the majority of United States buttons were yellow, with the eagle at the centre and an identifying letter on its chest, A for artillery and C for cavalry. Some of the Confederate buttons also carried the eagle but others were marked CSA or merely carried an identifying letter.

During the two World Wars the United States forces made use of small circular metal badges which were fitted to the coat lapels. In yellow metal, they carried representational insignia including crossed swords for cavalry, crossed rifles for infantry and crossed cannon barrels for artillery. Particular units were identified by attached letters and numbers. Similar badges were fitted to the dress cap, but this practice was abolished in World War II when a standard cap badge was worn. Enlisted men wore standard buttons which carried a device such as the number of the unit—25th (Continental arm of the service.

Whilst the US forces may not have been so diverse in their use of cap badges they have made very full use of a multitude of other insignia and badges. In the Navy, distinguishing marks were first introduced in 1841, and since then over 130 different ones have been used. Army cloth insignia first appeared in the 1880s and there are many types of these. Like the British the Americans also made use of special proficiency and qualification badges, although they favoured metal ones worn on the left breast of the tunic. US Army Air Corps and Air Force flyers had a variety of wings in greyish silver to indicate their position, pilot, navigator, bombardier and others. For the army there were Infantryman badges of various grades, shooting badges and marksmanship badges as well as a range of corps badges and shoulder insignia. It is usually believed that corps badges were introduced as a result of a case of mistaken identity by General Philip Kearney. Tradition has it that he berated some officers believing they were under his command, only to be told politely that they were not. The mistake arose because there was no way of distinguishing members of one command from another. As a result, in 1862, it was decreed by Kearney that all his officers should wear a piece of red cloth on the front of their caps—an interesting revival of the seventeenth-century field mark. The practice spread to his troops as well, and by March 1863 a plan to introduce corps badges was issued. There were some thirty-two corps and most used a simple shape, a star (14th), a double star (22nd) or a heart (26th). During the Civil War the troops also wore on their caps a metal badge which indicated their branch of service, a curly bugle for infantry, crossed sabres for cavalry and crossed cannons for artillery.

It was in the area of cloth patches that the US forces excelled. From October 1918 they have been an official feature of the uniform, worn on the left sleeve just below the shoulder. Their number was very great as was the range of designs and patterns and the idea has been extended to cover such events as the Apollo missions in space.

The conflict in Vietnam was responsible for a whole range of new designs and patterns including the so-called 'beer can' badges, hand done by local artists on any piece of suitable metal, including flattened empty beer cans.

Another country which made great use of badges and insignia was, of course, Germany. The pickelhaube had a large decorative plate and the pattern varied from unit to unit; those of the Prussian line

Opposite Group of American badges: (*top*) Long Range Reconnaissance Company of 7th US Corps; 325th Parachute Infantry Regiment; 456th Airborne Field Artillery; (*middle*) 188th Parachute Infantry Regiment; 544th Airborne Field Artillery; 327th Infantry Regiment, a beer-can badge, hand made and painted in South Vietnam; (*bottom*) HQ of United Nations Command in Korea; large White House Service badge worn only by personnel serving in the President's Washington home.

Right German arm shields awarded for action in certain campaigns: (*top*) defence of Cholm in Russia; landing at Narvik in Norway, silver for Army and Air Force and gilt for Navy; (*centre*) defence of Demjansk in Russia; (*bottom*) Crimea Campaign; Kuban Campaign.

Opposite (*top*) gilt, Imperial German U Boat badge worn on the left breast; (*middle*) Imperial German pilot's badge; Imperial German Observer's badge; (*bottom*) wound badges, black silver and gilt. The black and silver are a little unusual in that they are not solid. The smaller is a lapel or tie pin.

regiments were based on the heraldic eagle with wings outstretched and claws holding orb and sceptre while Baden had the griffin: each carried variations of the state arms. The Imperial German Air Force issued flying personnel with breast badges. Most German units were identified by embroidered numbers on their shoulder straps.

When, in 1933, the German Third Reich began to expand its armed forces there began a flow of badges and insignia which was to continue for the next twelve years. Many of these badges were political rather than military but as the distinctions were often blurred they fall within the scope of this section. Rank in most units was indicated by collar patches and shoulder straps and these were varied in pattern and colour. There was a range of Party and State insignia for all manner of units and associations. After war broke out in 1939 the various campaigns were commemorated by Arm Shield badges which were pressed out of thin metal; they were awarded for campaigns in Norway, Poland, France, Russia and the Balkans. Embroidered cuff titles were also issued as campaign awards.

War badges were given to men who saw action, whether in an infantry or in a tank assault, and there were similar awards for navy personnel. Aircrew members wore breast badges and could also be awarded war badges for their part in various actions. In addition there were Operational Flying Clasps which were granted for those

(*top*) Gilt beret badge of Netherlands Bewakingskorps, 1950–5. This unit provided guards for military installations; (*middle*) lapel badge of the Netherlands Field Artillery, brass on a black backing with red edging; lapel badge of Netherlands Infantry, gilt on red cloth; (*bottom*) brass shoulder badge of Netherlands anti-aircraft units; Bulgarian officer's cap badge, silver lion on white, green and red background, gilt shoulder badge of Netherlands Pontonniers, 1947–63.

who saw combat. There were also innumerable political, commemorative and donation badges.

Every country has issued a variety of badges for its forces and the range is very extensive. British Commonwealth countries have often based their designs on those of Britain. In Canada, militia units date back to the seventeenth century. The number of regiments grew as the new areas were settled in the vast country. The strong British connection was reflected in the number of 'Highland' regiments and those with titles incorporating English names, The Essex and Kent Scottish Regiment for example. New Zealand, Australia and South Africa have all followed similar paths.

European countries, France, Belgium and Holland, for example, all have a fairly well-documented series of regimental badges. In the case of France those of the Napoleonic period are highly prized and comparatively scarce. In addition to all the older countries there are, of course, many, newly-formed, independent countries creating their own tradition of badges and buttons—the field is enormous.

COLLECTING, CARE AND DISPLAY

For many years badge collecting was regarded as rather the boys and 'poor man's' military hobby. Until about ten years ago the prices of any but the rarest badges were low. Today the situation has changed, so that one blue cloth helmet plate can now cost as much as the complete helmet did a few years ago. Interest in this field, and consequently, demand, has grown. This has encouraged the supplies of 'reproductions', 'fake' or 'replica' badges—the description is one of personal choice. The metal badges were made from a pair of steel dies and today some of the original dies, as well as castings, are being used to produce 're-strikes'—modern examples of an old badge. At one time any badge that a collector acquired was virtually certain to be genuine. Today, for a large number of the rarer items, the odds are against this. New and accurate casting methods can produce badges that are so good that it takes a great deal of experience to detect the new ones.

Dealers will sometimes indicate which pieces they consider to be copies but it is very difficult to be sure. Other dealers will simply list the badge for what it appears to be; yet another case of 'buyer beware'. If rare badges appear with regularity in a list then one is entitled to ponder and ask whether the dealer is extremely lucky, or merely selling re-strikes.

Trying to decide on the authenticity or otherwise of a badge can be extremely difficult. As with every antique, experience is most important, so no chance of examining genuine pieces should be missed. Membership of a society helps, for it encourages contact and the gaining of knowledge from more experienced collectors. The back of the badge is often as important as the front, sometimes more so. Genuine British badges were die-stamped. The back should be as clearly marked as the front and variations of thickness or roughness may suggest that the badge is a casting. Some regiments in India did have badges cast so this single fact does not necessarily condemn a piece. Colour is another guide, for brass, being a compound, is not a consistent colour, but older badges lack the rather garish look of modern brass. The lugs and slider can also give some guidance, for the method and quality of the soldering should be good and inconspicuous. Large blobs of solder or brazing must raise suspicions but the standard of re-strikes improves constantly, and it must be admitted that it is becoming harder and harder to discriminate with certainty.

Badges of the Third Reich were among the first groups to suffer the attention of the reproducer and all the most popular and, later, the rarer badges and items of insignia have been produced in bulk. The quality of these copies ranges from first-class to obvious and after discarding the cheap and nasty, one is left with a number of items that are often difficult to decide on. Since many of the originals were cast the only guide may be in the quality. The detail should be clear and sharp and there should be no tiny air bubbles showing. The pin,

Above Combat badge of German Third Reich for service with E Boats.

Left Large brass badge for the shako, French Infantry 2nd Empire.

commonly fitted on German badges, and its method of fitting may also help in deciding. Makers' marks are not of much help for the reproducers have copied these. Weight and texture of metal are features worth examining but all these guides are of little help if one has no yardstick gained by examining genuine pieces! The appearance of the reproductions on the market has depressed the demand for badges of the Third Reich and there has been a pronounced falling off in their value as a result.

Badges of the United States Civil War and the following years have been extensively reproduced for the many groups who delight in taking part in mock-battles and parades in period costume. Most are obvious but all items of this period should be treated with reserve.

Buttons have been less extensively copied although the manufacturers have, in the past, supplied re-strikes or copies of the older brass buttons.

Cloth insignia have not been reproduced to the same degree as the metal badges but nevertheless copies of the German cuff-titles and qualification badges are available. Some study of the construction of these copies has been done and details of the method of stitching and quality of work recorded.

Despite this rather gloomy assessment of the present situation, badges and button collecting can be very satisfying; it is still possible to find the odd treasure amongst the 'junk' boxes. Never miss an opportunity to dig through the odds and ends box.

Few auction houses specialize in badges but many carry the odd lot in their arms and armour or costume sales. There are many dealers

Opposite German silver wound badge introduced September 1939; German Infantry Assault badge awarded for participation in three separate assault actions; German Destroyer War badge introduced June 1940; (*middle*) German eagle of pressed aluminium; machine gunner's badge of Imperial Army worn by members of *Württembergische Maschinen Gewehr Scharfschützen Abteilung N.53*; German Coastal Artillery badge introduced in 1941; (*bottom*) Imperial German U Boat tie pin; German Close Combat badge introduced September 1942 and awarded for taking part in thirty actions.

who handle them mostly on a postal basis, and this method of collecting has the advantage that most dealers offer some limited form of guarantee and will take back any suspect pieces.

Condition and material must determine the best method of cleaning a metal badge. If a piece is delicate then a gentle wash in a strong detergent will probably suffice. The piece should be gently agitated and then rinsed in clean water and thoroughly dried by gently patting with soft tissues. Some collectors prefer to use the various proprietary solutions and dip their brass, silver and gilt badges and certainly this method is very effective. However, these solutions should be treated with caution for they can etch the surface if the badge is left in too long. As always the solution should be tested on some unimportant piece before risking any prize items. Helmet plates such as those on the British blue cloth helmet should, if at all possible, be stripped to their component parts and each piece cleaned individually. On the whole metal polish is not recommended since it may well dry and leave deposits in cracks and crevices. Vigorous rubbing, unless carefully done, may damage the surface or snap off the odd thin projection.

Plastic and anodized pieces should not require much more than a careful wash and dry.

Buttons will respond to the same cleaning methods as recommended for badges. Early pewter ones are probably best left as acquired apart from a careful wipe over with a clean cloth.

Cloth insignia can prove rather delicate and in many cases it is better not to clean it at all and keep the piece dirty but intact. Gentle washing may do for the modern robust examples or the use of dry-cleaning fluids may be better—in every case always check the effect on less important pieces first.

Identification of the multitude of badges and buttons can be difficult and may necessitate long periods of looking through reference materials. Some will defy all efforts to label them and in such cases the only course open is to put the badge away and just keep looking and hoping. In most cases someone will come along with the answer. With British badges approximate dating can often be made from the style of name of the regiment, which, over some two centuries, has naturally changed. If a regimental number appears on an infantry badge then this suggests a pre-1881 dating, for such numbers were dropped during that year. However, it must be stressed that not every regiment discarded the number, so a numbered badge may post-date 1881. If the regiment is known then it is possible, in many cases, to consult the regimental museum, of which there are many, and the curator may be able to help. British badges may also be dated by the style of the crown, if it appears, since each monarch has used a different shape. Victoria (1837-1901) had a crown with a marked, upward swing to the arms. Edward VII (1901-10) had a more angular shape. George V (1910-36) and George VI (1936-53) crowns had a less pronounced sweep and Elizabeth II (1953-) has one not greatly dissimilar from Victoria's.

Opposite Cloth badges of the Third Reich: (*top*) *Ski-Jäger*; standard bearer; *Gebirgsjäger* for tropical uniform; (*middle*) NFSK, worn above breast pocket by members of National Socialist Flying Corps; Don Cossacks Volunteers worn on upper right arm; (*bottom*) woman helper on anti-aircraft unit; Russian SD Volunteers worn on upper right sleeve; arm badge of *Sonder Verbande* worn on upper right sleeve.

Shako plates of the London Rifle Brigade. The differences in the pattern of the crown are clearly shown: on the left is the shape used during the Victorian period; on the right is the style adopted after 1901.

Records should include a full description of the badge; type, material, colouring, size, lugs or slider, officer's or other ranks and dates where known. Background information on the regiment, its past and present titles, illustrations showing the badge being worn, variations on the particular pattern, and actions in which the regiment served, all help place the badge or button in its correct context.

Displaying buttons, badges and insignia can present problems and certainly requires some thought and planning. Before setting up a display the collector might like to give some thought to the total number likely to be acquired and plan accordingly. Plastic envelopes or sheets are possibly the safest for delicate or rare pieces but for a longer and more permanent display some form of backing is required. Polystyrene, card, hardboard and fabric-covered material can all be used. The badges are mounted by piercing the backing, pushing through the lugs and securing them by a piece of wire or a matchstick. Slides may need a little extra care when trying to push them through the backing—too much pressure and they may snap. The completed board can be hung like a picture or stored in a cupboard with layers of material or plastic to separate them, to prevent scratching. Buttons can be mounted in the same way.

Cloth insignia can be mounted on similar boards although they will probably be best attached by using some inert adhesive, such as Blue Tac, which will not damage them.

6 Arms and Armour

It was only with the growth of technology that the armaments of an army could be said to have become full standardized. Prior to this period the weapons were hand made and inevitably varied slightly from the basic pattern. Before the seventeenth century there were virtually no standard patterns but they were gradually introduced during the century, as standing armies developed. Although there were differences the equipment of most seventeenth-century armies was basically the same.

At this time, firearms were acquiring supremacy on the battlefield and ousting the heavily armoured horseman, the archer and the swordsman. The musketeer was becoming the most important man on the battlefield and his equipment was quite elaborate. His musket was long and heavy and was fired by means of the matchlock mechanism. When the trigger, or a metal bar beneath the stock was pressed, a pivotted arm, the serpentine, swung forward and pressed the glowing end of a piece of slow-burning cord into a small pan of gunpowder. As this powder flashed the flame passed through a small touch-hole and ignited the main charge of powder, which then exploded and so fired the bullet. With its 4 ft-long (1.22 m) barrel the musket was heavy, so, to ensure a reasonably steady aim, the musketeer rested the barrel on a long wooden rest, with a metal U-shaped piece at the top.

Loading was a slow business, for powder had to be poured down the barrel, and followed by a ball, both being rammed down by a long wooden stick, the ramrod. When not required, the ramrod was housed in a groove situated beneath the barrel, in the wooden stock of the musket. In addition, the soldier had to watch the match to ensure that it was glowing satisfactorily and in no danger of igniting the powder before he was ready. During the time that he was reloading he was virtually defenceless: for his protection each regiment had a proportion of pikemen. These troops were armed with pikes up to eighteen feet in length with which they could hold off an enemy cavalry charge. The pikemen wore a fairly substantial breastplate, a thinner backplate and a skirt of armour which had the appearance of being made up of a number of strips but was, in fact, just one large plate. The helmet was known as a pikeman's pot and had a characteristically wide, down-sloping brim. Both musketeer and pikeman could well be armed with a sword, which might be a rapier.

Cavalrymen also had armour, usually limited to a breast and backplate worn over a buff-leather coat. The left hand, which held the reins and was therefore rather vulnerable, was often protected by a gauntlet, with a long cuff reaching up to the elbow. Most of these elbow gauntlets were for the left hand. Pairs were made but right

One of Jakob de Gheyn's prints showing the musketeer of the early 17th century with his impedimenta – bullet bag, powder flask, spare match, bandolier and rest, in addition to his sword and musket.

Above Helmet and armour of a 17th-century pikeman, standard for most armies of Northern Europe in the first half of the 17th century. Some helmets had a much wider brim.

Opposite Sword of the Cuirassiers, the French Heavy Cavalry, dated 1814, and poster of Revolutionary France exhorting all to serve 'La Patrie', June 1798.

hand ones are far less common. On his head the cavalryman had a burgonet, an open-faced helmet consisting of a basin-like skull with a sweeping neckguard, two large cheek pieces and some protection for the face. The most usual style had a single, adjustable bar, the nasal, which pierced the peak and could be locked into position. The other style, popular with the English Civil War troops, had a pivotted peak fitted with a three-bar guard.

Cavalry were armed with a sword and possibly a pair of wheellock pistols. These weapons were complex and were operated by a spring mechanism, which struck sparks from a piece of mineral called pyrites. They were not only a little unreliable but also expensive to produce. Consequently not all troops were equipped with them. The swords varied from country to country but most had a long, double-edged blade with a metal basket type hand-guard. In Britain a sword used by troops on both sides during the English Civil War (1642-9) had a round metal guard with a series of S-shaped bars, joining to a bar which reached up to the pommel—the weight at the top of the grip. Chiselled into the underside of the guard was a simple pattern incorporating a head, which is taken to represent Charles I. This type of sword is known as a mortuary sword, from its supposed connection with the executed king, but the connection is perhaps more romantic than factual. Other European cavalry favoured the Walloon sword, which had a guard consisting of two pierced shells, a single knuckle bow and a small, down-curving guard at the rear of the guard.

Officers, as a general rule, provided their own swords, which, naturally, did not conform to any standard pattern. During the eighteenth century the infantry carried a brass-hilted short sword, but in 1768 the sword was withdrawn from service. Officers still carried one, as did the cavalry, and these weapons were standardized. One of the earliest regulation Infantry swords was the 1796 pattern, a straight, thin blade with a simple gilt guard. The swords were often treated to give the top section of the blade a beautiful blue colour, which was embellished with a gilt design. Officers of the Flank Companies had a sword of a different pattern, with a curved blade and a slightly more elaborate hilt, incorporating the Royal Cypher, a bugle and a lion's head pommel. In 1822 a new pattern of hilt was introduced. This was the so-called Gothic hilt which had three bars sweeping up from the guard to the pommel. There were numerous other variations, many of which incorporated regimental designs in the metalwork of the hilt.

Cavalry swords were of two main groups, cutting or thrusting, although some attempted to incorporate both attributes, usually with limited success only. The 1796 Light Dragoon sword had a single-edged, curved blade and a very simple, stirrup-shaped hilt. This model was rather unusual in that it had a steel scabbard: leather was the normal material for scabbards. In 1821 the hilt was changed to something rather like the infantry officers sword. For general officers there was the Mameluke sword, with an ivory grip and a bronze cross-guard.

ÉGALITÉ.

DIVISION

PROCLAMATION

DU GÉNÉRAL DE DIVISION

LAUBADÈRE,

Commandant en Chef la 15me Division Militaire,

Aux Administrés du Département de la Somme,

Sur l'Arrêté de l'Administration Centrale, qui met à sa
disposition les Colonnes Mobiles de ce Département.

Amiens, 30 Prairial an 7.

CITOYENS,

Vos Administrateurs avaient pensé qu'à
la voix de la Patrie, il vous suffisait des
Loix pour les exécuter. Long-temps con-
vaincus qu'il suffisait de vous in...
pour vous porter à les rem...ent
s'est-il fait qu'une aussi ...ur la
durée d'un songe? P... nceivable,
méconnaissant to... qui vous a si
long-temps g... Département est-il
devenu l'a... cratie Sacerdotale et
Nobili... ngué entre tous ceux de la
Ré... insouciance et son apathie!
... dition ouverte contre les Loix du

... précises et positives appellent à la
... de la Patrie tous les Réquisitionnaires
... des Conscrits de première classe. Cent fois la
voix de vos Administrateurs vous a rappelé vos devoirs
à cet égard, et cependant, ô comble d'ignominie! ou
les Conscrits et les Réquisitionnaires sont restés im-
mobiles, ou, s'ils ont paru entendre un moment la
voix de la Patrie, s'ils ont paru un moment se ranger
sous ses bannières, ce n'a été que pour déserter lâche-
ment les Drapeaux de l'honneur et de la victoire!

Citoyens, un pareil ordre de chose est, tout à la fois,
une tache d'ignominie imprimée sur vos fronts, et une

...ation de guerre contre le Gouvernement. Investi
sa confiance, je jure par la Liberté, d'éteindre ju-
qu'au souvenir d'un pareil scandale; je jure que tous
les Réquisitionnaires et tous les Conscrits quels qu'ils
soient, quels que soient leurs Protecteurs et leurs
moyens de séduction, partiront tous sans exception,
pour se rendre au poste, ou le devoir et l'honneur les
appellent. Ils auront beau se cacher, en vain cherche-
raient-ils à se soustraire à tous les regards, la force
est là pour les contraindre, et guidée par des mains
éprouvées, elle frappera indistinctement et à coup sur.

Vous, braves Gardes Nationales, que je m'énor-
gueillis de commander en ce moment; vous qui, dès
l'aurore de la Révolution, donnâtes tant d'exemples
de dévouement à la chose publique; levez-vous de
nouveau, vos Magistrats vous l'ordonnent; prenez
vos armes, non plus pour combattre comme aux
premiers jours de la Liberté, les ennemis extérieurs,
mais pour arracher au sommeil de la mort et de l'infamie, cette jeunesse efféminée que des suggestions
perfides rendent sourde à toutes les sollicitations de la
Patrie? arrachez de leurs repaires ces êtres pusilla-
nimes, qui préférent la honte et l'infamie à l'honora-
ble prérogative de servir leur Pays? Qu'aucun n'é-
chappe à vos recherches, et déposez ces armes,
que la confiance de vos administrateurs remet entre
vos mains, que lorsque le dernier des lâches aura payé

sa dette à la Patrie. Il ne doit plus vous être permis
de goûter le repos que lorsque tous les ennemis de la
République auront été vaincus.

Et vous Magistrats du Peuple, dites à vos administrés, que fort de la volonté du Législateur, je marche à
la tête des Colonnes Mobiles, pour forcer les déserteurs
et les réfractaires à la loi à rentrer dans les rangs, et que je
ne leur donnerai de relâche que lorsque ce Département
se sera purgé de la lèpre honteuse qui le ronge, et qui
le deshonore aux yeux des Républicains.

L'Administration Centrale a remis entre mes mains
tous les moyens de parvenir à ce but, je n'en négligerai
aucun. Veillez de votre côté pour que tous les lâches
et tous les déserteurs soient signalés et arrêtés, et soyez
assurés, qu'il en sera fait une justice telle qu'elle portera
l'épouvante dans le cœur de tous leurs suppots, et de
tous leurs appuis.

Le temps de l'indulgence est passé; les ménage-
mens seraient un crime. Nous exécuterons la loi sans
craindre de heurter les intérêts ou les passions diverses
de quelques êtres qui veulent encore des Pri-
vilèges; nous ferons tous courageusement notre devoir,
et nous aurons tous bien mérité de la Patrie.

Signé de la main gauche,
G. F. LAUBADÈRE.

A Amiens, De l'Imprimerie
Imprim...

During the century the sword became less and less important in war and although retained for ceremonial purposes it was seldom seriously used in war after the nineteenth century.

In America the general style of infantry sword usually had a stirrup-type hilt, whilst the cavalry pattern tended to have a larger, more basket-like guard. Prior to the nineteenth century the style of the NCOs sword is not clearly defined in orders, but it was apparently fitted with a single-edged broad, curved blade. The grip was of horn and shaped to fit the hand whilst the knuckle bow was of brass, although in 1801 it was stated that those swords for infantry NCOs should have iron hilts, with brass being reserved for the artillery. In 1840 a new model was introduced and this had a long, straight, single-edged blade, with a cast brass hilt consisting of a flat disc-like guard with a flattened knuckle bow and cross-guard.

A variety of cavalry swords were used but the majority had a simple stirrup hilt, although in 1840 the War Department introduced a Heavy Cavalry (Dragoon) Sabre very similar to that used by the French. The blade was slightly curved and the hilt had a leather-covered, wooden grip with wire binding. A brass half-basket of two short bars swept up from the main guard to join on to the knuckle bow. In 1913 the American cavalry adopted a thrusting sword with a long, rigid blade and a solid basket to protect the hand. It was not dissimilar from the British pattern of 1908, the result of the efforts of a committee set up to determine the best cavalry sword.

In 1832 a strange style of sword was supplied for the use of the US Foot Artillery, not unlike a French sword. It was a rather fanciful copy of a Roman sword with a large, solid brass hilt and markings representing feathers which, in fact, look rather more like fish scales. The blade was nineteen inches long, wide, double-edged and elliptical in cross section. During the early part of the nineteenth century some officers purchased their swords from France. One popular style had a grip of mother-of-pearl and a pommel fashioned in the shape of an eagle.

Although most infantry troops discarded their swords around the middle of the eighteenth century they did not do without an edged weapon. During the seventeenth century the bayonet was evolved and it proved an important and effective weapon. At first it seems that the troops thrust the handles of their knives down the muzzle of the musket. This gave the infantryman a short pike but it rendered the musket useless for firing, so designers looked for ways of allowing the musket to be used when the bayonet was in position. The solution was the use of a socket bayonet which consisted of a tube, some two or three inches long, just the right size to slip over the barrel, with a slot cut to engage with a lug or foresight fitted near the muzzle. A curved arm projected from the tube and on to this was fixed the triangular blade, around 18 in (45.7 cm) long, which converted the musket into a short pike. Socket bayonets were used throughout the eighteenth century and well into the second half of the nineteenth century. A second type of fitting which was developed around the mid-

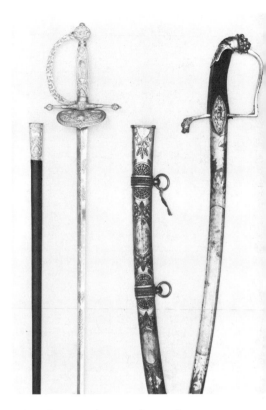

Above Presentation swords: small sword presented to Sir S. Whittingham for his services during 'his residence and government as His Majesty's representative in Dominica' in 1822; English sword made in French style, presented by NCOs and privates of C Troop of 1st Regiment of Life Guards to Lt Sullivan at St Jean de Luz, France, 24 March 1814.

Opposite Colt .36 Navy revolver, popular with both armies during the American Civil War, 1861–5. This example has a contemporary holster, a cap pouch and black leather belt with brass buckle.

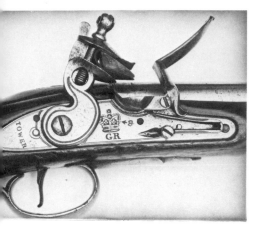

Lock of a Brown Bess musket, India pattern, showing Royal Cypher and Tower mark, c.1800. These marks are fairly typical, although the crowned cypher varies according to the ruling sovereign.

nineteenth century was the lug and slot method. A slot was cut along the back of the hilt of the bayonet and the cross guard, the quillon, was pierced by a hole the diameter of the barrel. Situated near the muzzle, usually underneath the barrel, was a lug shaped to engage with the slot cut into the hilt. As the bayonet was pushed home on to the rifle the lug engaged with the slot and the muzzle passed through the hole in the guard. There was usually a spring clip which locked the bayonet in place.

Many types of bayonets were produced during the nineteenth century for the various rifles and carbines which were adopted for military use. Some, like the Jacobs bayonet, were long—30 in (76.2 cm)—whilst others, like the spike bayonet for the Lee Enfield No. 4 rifle, were only 7¼ in (18.4 cm) long. Although many authorities have argued that with modern firepower the bayonet is useless it is still used and is even fitted to some modern automatic rifles.

It was in the field of firearms that the greatest developments took place during the nineteenth century. Wheel-lock pistols and matchlock muskets remained the standard weapons of the army until the middle of the seventeenth century, when the flintlock, first made popular in France, began to replace the older mechanism. Muskets and pistols were fitted with the lock which was to continue in use until the mid-nineteenth century.

Early in the eighteenth century there appeared the famous British Army flintlock musket known as the Brown Bess. The musket was to vary in detail and barrel length, 48 inches down to 39 inches, but it was a sturdy, reliable weapon, firing a bullet about .75 in (1.9 cm) in diameter. A socket bayonet was issued with the musket.

A variety of flintlock pistols were used by the British Army and, again, they conform to a basic pattern although varying in detail and barrel length—9 in-12 in (approx. 22.8 cm-30.48 cm).

The supply of firearms was the responsibility of the Board of Ordnance, who purchased the weapons from commercial gunmakers. The firearms were inspected and if satisfactory the locks were stamped with the maker's name and the date of manufacture. Unfortunately for collectors, from 1764 the date and maker's name were omitted, although the word 'Tower' was still stamped on the lockplate.

Early in the nineteenth century the Rev. Alexander Forsyth developed his own system of percussion ignition for firearms. He used the flash produced by the explosion of a very small amount of fulminate of mercury to ignite the main charge of powder. The fulminate was exploded by striking it with a metal arm, the hammer. Eventually the system was developed and the outcome was a small copper cap holding a small deposit of fulminate. The cap was placed on a small metal pillar, the nipple, with a tiny hole drilled through it to connect to the main charge. There was much experimenting and development before in the 1830s the British line regiments began to receive their new percussion muskets. It was some time before the flintlock was completely taken out of service.

Webley Mk VI .455 revolver. This sturdy weapon was used by officers of the British Army for many years. It was self-ejecting so that when the weapon was broken the empty cases were automatically thrown out of the cylinder.

The Crimean War (1853-6) exposed the shortcomings of the army and its supply system and as a result a government factory for the production of firearms was established at Enfield. The weapons from the factory bore the name Enfield and this name together with the initials like BO (Board of Ordnance), WD (War Department) will, from 1855, be found on many military weapons of this period. The Royal Small Arms Factory at Enfield produced a range of rifles and edged weapons.

The percussion cap opened the way for further development and experiments with a self-contained cartridge holding powder and bullet. After many tries the problems were finally defeated and a new cartridge facilitated the breech-loading systems. In 1867 the Snider rifle was adopted by the British Army. This was really the old percussion rifle adapted to take the metal-cased cartridge.

The Snider was not totally successful and in 1871 it was replaced by the Martini-Henry rifle. This was a single-shot weapon, loaded by operating a lever attached to the trigger guard. This opened the breech, allowing a large metal cartridge to be inserted into it. This rifle saw service in many countries despite its rather erratic performance, and it led to the development of the magazine rifle. In 1895 the famous Lee-Enfield rifle was adopted by the army and was to see service in both World Wars.

Officers of the armed forces often supplied their own weapons, usually a .45 or .455 revolver. Many were official issue weapons and bear the WD stamp on the metal frame. Webleys, the gunmakers, supplied several models of their famous revolver to the British Army.

In America the standard weapons of the early colonists were essentially British but when war broke out in 1775 supplies were cut off. The colonists turned to Britain's old enemy, France, and large numbers of French muskets and pistols were supplied to them. Some

Flintlock pistol .64 calibre made by Simeon North for the US Navy in 1808. This was fitted with a belt hook. A similar model without the belt hook was made for the army in 1810.

weapons were made by American gunmakers under contract to the Congress and these are usually known as Committee of Safety Muskets and were basically copies of the British Brown Bess musket differing only in details.

Although various French muskets were supplied, most conformed to the basic pattern of a barrel around 44-48 in (112-121 cm) in length and a ball around .69 in (1.75 cm) in diameter. They differed from the British model in that the barrel was secured to the stock by iron bands instead of the pins used by British gunmakers. Many Americans carried their long, very accurate rifles, many of which were ordinary civilian hunting rifles, although some were produced under contract for the colonists.

The colonists' pistols were also modelled on the British pattern but many of the cavalry were armed with French flintlock pistols.

In 1794 Congress ordered the setting up of two national armouries, which were eventually established at Harper's Ferry in Virginia and Springfield, Massachusetts. The weapons produced were based on French models and when at a later date the percussion system was introduced many of the flintlock models were converted to the new

Single-action model 1861 Army revolver made by Remington, popular during the American Civil War. It was .44 calibre and held six shots. 125,314 were purchased by the US Government.

system. The war between the States (1861-5) increased the demand for firearms beyond all previous expectations and the range of weapons manufactured and imported was enormous. The Confederate weapon makers produced many varieties of carbines and muskets as well as importing many rifles from Austria and Britain. Union forces were armed with a similar range of weapons and both sides were deeply concerned with new forms of repeating weapons.

Following the Civil War the military demands of the Western frontiers ensured that there was continual experimentation and production of new models. In 1878-9 the Hotchkiss magazine rifle was accepted for issue to the troops but it seems to have been supplied

only on a very limited scale. In 1882 the Ordnance Board tested fifty-three weapons and chose three for further examination, the Model 1882 Lee magazine rifle made by Remington, the Hotchkiss and the Chaffee-Reece magazine rifles. These were tested but it was not until 1892 that a .30, five-shot rifle, the Krag-Jorgensen, was selected for issue to the troops. It was modified in 1896 but was to remain in service for many years.

It was in the field of revolvers that the United States led the world. In February 1836 Samuel Colt obtained an American patent for his percussion revolver. The design was good and practical and despite setbacks Colt went from strength to strength and produced a range of revolvers which saw service in the American Civil War and on the frontier.

The United States was also to the fore in the development of metallic cartridges and as early as 1864 the United States Forces were experimenting with cartridge revolvers such as the Bacon Navy model .38 revolver. In 1873 the famous Colt, single-action, cartridge revolver was adopted and Colt revolvers were still being supplied in bulk until World War I. In 1902 Colts produced their first military, self-loading automatic pistol, which fired a .38 cartridge. Further

In 1911 the US Army adopted the .45 Colt self-loading pistol as their official handgun after extensive tests. It was then modified and has remained in service ever since. The barrel is 5 in (12.7 cm) long and the magazine holds seven rounds. This particular example was made by Remington Rand, 1943–5.

developed, the weapon eventually became the famous 1911 .45 automatic which, with modifications, has been used right up until the present.

Germany was another country which played a great part in the history and development of firearms and the names of Peter Mauser and George Luger are known to most collectors and historians. In 1871 the Mauser 11 mm, Model 1871, single-shot rifle was produced, and in 1884 it was modified to take a tubular magazine. The best-known German military rifle was the 1898 model which saw service in World Wars I and II. Mauser also designed handguns, including the Model 1898, which had a quite unusual cylinder rotation system, using a zig-zag groove cut into the cylinder. Possibly the best-known Mauser automatic is the broomstick pistol, with its magazine placed in front of the trigger guard.

In 1908 the German army adopted the 9 mm Pistol Model 08 using the Parabellum cartridge. This remained the standard weapon until 1940, when a Walther P38 was issued. Variants of the Luger automatic were also adopted in other countries.

The famous Mauser 'broomhandle' self-loading pistol with its wooden holster, which could also be clipped on to the butt to make the weapon into a carbine. Patented in 1898 this weapon was popular with officers of many armies and although made originally in 7.63 mm calibre, some, like this model, were made in 9 mm calibre, hence the 9 branded on the butt.

The study of military, breech-loading, cartridge weapons is complex and extensive and almost every country in the world has adopted and adapted a wide range of models. There was a constant striving to produce a robust, accurate, repeating weapon. Ammunition was constantly being varied with the object of being ballistically suited to its task and the power of a bullet to penetrate and maintain an accurate flight was regularly reviewed.

Early firearms had been capable of penetrating most armour and consequently there had been a steady reduction in the amount of armour worn. During the American Civil War some manufacturers experimented and produced a range of body armour designed to offer protection against the rifle ball. There were other attempts to protect troops by using armour during the Franco-Prussian War of 1870, during which the French produced a 'poncho' type of garment with small rectangular plates rivetted to it. During World War I a number of padded and plated body defences were produced by the British whilst the Germans introduced a heavy set of body armour for snipers or machine gunners in exposed situations; this armour weighed around 20 lb (9 kg) and covered most of the front of the body. In World War II and subsequent campaigns interest in body protection increased and a great variety of materials and patterns were used. Most are intended to give protection only against comparatively low velocity projectiles but, though light, they are extremely effective.

Top Ross .303 model 1910 Mk III bolt-action rifle bearing a plaque stating that it was presented to the Rt Hon. W. L. Spencer Churchill on 14 February 1914.

Bottom The Walther P.38 adopted by the German Army from 1938 replacing the old Luger 08 pistol. Both fired the 9 mm cartridge. This pistol is still the official handgun of the modern *Bundeswehr*.

Tomahawk of late 18th century with a Government broad arrow mark. It is also a pipe with the shaft, probably original and stamped BO, pierced for its full length. Tomahawks such as this were distributed to Red Indians during the Revolutionary War and were given as treaty gifts.

COLLECTING, CARE AND DISPLAY

Arms and armour have become very popular over the past twenty years and the number of interested collectors has risen enormously. There is now an increasing demand for a diminishing supply. Prices have climbed consistently and show no signs of decreasing. Most of the large auction houses hold regular sales of arms and armour, usually with a predominance of firearms, in London, Birmingham, Paris, New York, Lucerne and various other centres. Pistols are probably the most sought after, with swords as second favourite.

Firearm collecting is beset by problems not encountered in other fields of antiques. Every firearm, no matter what its age, is potentially a useable weapon and consequently falls under certain prohibitions. These restrictions vary from country to country and collectors interested in this field of collecting should always check on the situation in their particular area. In the United States the general attitude to possession of firearms is far more liberal than most countries but it does vary from state to state and even from town to town. In Britain, at the time of writing, the Firearms Act of 1968 is in force, which excludes antique firearms from its control provided that the pieces are held as 'curios or ornaments'. 'Antique' as a descriptive term is usually taken to mean any item which is over100 years old. In the case of firearms a further distinction is made: if a weapon uses a metallic cartridge it is generally not considered an antique, irrespective of its age. But there are occasional variations even on this basis. Should the owner wish to fire the antique weapon it becomes a 'firearm' within the meaning of the Act, which means the owner must have a current Firearms Certificate granted by the local police, authorizing him to hold such a weapon. It is no easy matter to acquire such a certificate, which must be applied for at the local police station. It is also important to remember that modern reproductions of early firearms, which are intended for use, do not qualify as antiques, since they are less than 100 years old, and consequently their owner must possess a Firearms Certificate.

Every country has its own particular firearms prohibitions and restrictions but, in general, antique weapons may be held without any legal obligation; there are cases when the generalization does not apply, for the interpretation of the term antique may vary from place to place.

If a collector ventures into the field of modern cartridge weapons then security of the collection becomes very important and the local police will insist on high standards of protection. In Britain a request for a Firearms Certificate will not even be considered until local officers are satisfied that the proposed storage space will be very secure. It must also be said that the local police will probably be very reluctant to grant certificates for a collection of modern weapons.

The rising demand for antique firearms has encouraged many dealers to undertake a great deal of repair and restoration. Items which, a few years ago, would have been classed as 'rubbish' are now cleaned, repaired, restored and sold with little trouble. It is possible to purchase first-class replacement parts for virtually any firearm and once these parts have been worked on by a craftsman it is often difficult to distinguish reproduction from original.

It is difficult to decide on what degree of restoration is acceptable. This must be a matter for personal choice, but most collectors would probably agree that an absolute minimum is best. Stripping a firearm is not too difficult but some skill is required. If a collector feels that he is not competent to undertake this job then it is best to pass it on to an expert. Any mishandling could easily damage the piece and so detract from the value quite apart from the physical harm to the weapon. Even with the fine reproduction replacement parts available today it is not recommended that repairs should be attempted by any except a competent craftsman. A poorly restored piece is far worse than a damaged or deficient item.

Firearms are ideal for the location of an identifying mark since there are so many places where it can be conveniently sited. Construction, quality and the material of a weapon must obviously govern the use of such marks, which need be no more than a small label secreted beneath the barrel, under the trigger guard or some similar spot. If something less obvious is wanted than a very *small* scratch mark of an irregular but identifiable shape can be made on the back of the breech, inside the lock or on the back of the hammer. A tiny spot of paint can be used in place of a scratch, with the disadvantage that such a spot can easily be removed.

Records of the firearm should include details of the position of the identifying mark, type of weapon, barrel length, overall length, calibre, any marks or names and the furniture such as trigger guard, ramrod pipes and wooden stock. If it is an official weapon then references giving dates of issue, numbers issued, units to which it was supplied and areas in which it saw service are all relevant. Any illustrations showing it carried or in use should also be noted.

Swords require less restoration than firearms but they are usually more subject to the ravages of rust. The first step on acquiring a new piece must be the removal of any active rust. The weapon should be wiped over with a mixture of oil and paraffin and left to soak. This should effectively loosen much of the rust, which can then be wiped off. Stubborn rusting will have to be removed by some abrasive such as fine steel wool, or jeweler's emery, which is available in many grades. Even the coarsest sheet is relatively fine compared with normal emery cloth and the finest grade is little more than roughened paper. Used one after the other starting with the coarsest, the resultant polish should be very fine. If the blade is etched, blued or otherwise decorated then cleaning is complicated, for removal of rust could also mean removal of decoration. It may be better to leave matters as they are but each case will call for individual decisions. There are chemical rust removers which are effective but they do affect the surface and may give the metal a rather dull, leaden appearance. Once a piece has been cleaned it should, ideally, be oiled

Most armies used small, wide-bored cannon for tossing shells into an enemy position and these mortars were usually cast in bronze. This Spanish mortar bears the cypher of Carlos IV (1788-1808) and the date 1799.

or wiped with one of the silicone dusters. It is possible to dismantle a sword but this is not recommended unless undertaken by a competent craftsman. Grips can also be replaced or recovered but this is not always easy and some skill is required. Metal sheaths can be cleaned in exactly the same manner as the sword but leather ones are rather fragile and need careful handling. They are difficult to repair and if damaged may have to be completely replaced. In order to reduce any bending of the leather scabbard, the sword should always be drawn with the scabbard hanging down in a vertical position. Leather dressing should be applied with care and the fittings, usually gilt or brass, can be carefully polished.

Full dimensions, details of any marks or maker's name, type of hilt, date of issue and units carrying the sword should all be noted. Illustrations are particularly important since swords are usually more difficult to identify than firearms.

Armour can be given the usual metal cleaning treatment: if any of the pieces are loose some re-leathering may be required. This repair involves removing old and perished leather, and replacing the rivets. The job is not one for any but a skilled restorer. Identifying marks are difficult to place on armour and swords since they are not easily concealed, but it may be possible to overcome this difficulty by putting the mark under the guard or perhaps a small label could be pushed into a hilt. Records of the armour present no great problems, but this should include full dimensions, including thickness of plate and weight. Illustrations are very important for, like swords, identification of armour is not always easy.

Swords and firearms, both pistols and longarms, are fairly easy to display and the same system can be used in a variety of ways. Peg board, covered or painted, provides a very convenient base for a display which can be easily varied. Commercial fittings may not always be appropriate but it is not difficult to fashion suitable shapes from thick wire. To prevent scratching or marking the weapons the fittings should be covered with some form of plastic or tape. An alternative method is to use dowelling fixed into wooden blocks or battens, which can be then fixed to a wall or suspended from a hook or picture rail. If swords are suspended then extra care is required to ensure that they are secure, for even a three-hundred year old sword or bayonet can still inflict a nasty cut or slash. Whilst transporting any edged weapon a cork should be pushed over the point for greater safety.

Armour is a little more difficult to display effectively although gauntlets and breastplates are not too awkward since they are complete in themselves; other individual items may prove more problematic. Some form of support of wood or transparent plastic can usually be fashioned to hold the item unobtrusively.

7 Medals and Decorations

One field of military antiques which is especially rewarding, though demanding, is that of medal collecting. Interest in medals has increased enormously over the last few years and, once again, the rising demand has inevitably pushed up prices. One famous firm of London medal dealers has calculated that, on average, most pieces have doubled in price over the last two or three years.

Most antiques are anonymous; they can be classified, described, valued and dated, but little, if anything, is ever known about their 'personal' history. Some medals possess the distinction of being far more identifiable. These can often be traced to a specific person and details of that person can be researched. With some luck, some time and a minimum of research it may be possible to build up a dossier on the life and times of the medal's original owner, which might even include a photograph or print showing the owner. Most medals were issued by official, organized groups which kept detailed records. Many medals carry the name of the recipient together with details of his ship or unit. This is especially true of British campaign medals which were issued only to those who took part in a specific battle or campaign. Such British medals normally have the recipient's name and unit engraved or impressed around the edge. Fortunately the records of the British Navy and Army are fairly complete so it is comparatively easy to check the details of the medal if the regiment or ship and name and number are known.

Campaign medals are probably the most popular of all. The history of these can be traced back to the Romans, or even earlier, when awards were given to members of the army after they had taken part in some memorable victory. From a collecting point of view their real history can be dated from 1588, following on the defeat of King Phillip's Spanish Armada, Queen Elizabeth I, either as a gesture of gratitude or as an indication of her pleasure, issued an Armada medal to a number of her captains. However, it was not until the English Civil War (1642-8) that more general issues were envisaged. In 1643 Charles I authorized a silver medal to be issued to those who served in the 'forlorn hope', the troops who led an attack. After Cromwell's great victory at Dunbar in 1650, Parliament voted that all those who had contributed to the victory, officers and men, should be given a medal.

During the eighteenth century there were very occasional issues of medals but the general attitude of the British Government seems to have been to discourage the soldier from thinking that his service was anything but his duty. But as a result of the Napoleonic Wars the situation changed and during the wars there were a few issues of a semi-private nature. The Honourable East India Company issued a

Silver medal presented by the Honourable East India Company to its troops for their part in the captures of some French-held islands, Isle of France, Bourbon and Rodriguez, 1809–10.

number of medals to its troops; the Highland Society issued a medal for Scots who fought at the battle of Alexandria (Egypt), in 1801. Alexander Davison, Nelson's prize Agent, and Matthew Boulton of Birmingham, both used their own money to purchase medals, which were given to members of the crews of British ships who fought at the Battle of the Nile (1798) and at Trafalgar (1805).

The first general issue of a campaign medal was prompted by the Battle of Waterloo in June 1815. The various rulers were prevailed upon to authorize the issue of a Waterloo Medal. The British issue carried the head of the Prince Regent, later George IV, on one side whilst on the other was Victory, suitably crowned with a laurel wreath. Around the edge was the recipient's name and the regiment in which he served during the glorious battle of Waterloo. It was authorized in March 1816 and was to be given to 'every officer, non-commissioned officer, and soldier of the British Army present on that memorable occasion'.

The issue of the Waterloo medal was made in 1816 but for those who had fought against Napoleon, though not at Waterloo, there was to be a long wait before they received any recognition. In 1847 it was agreed that a Military General Service medal should be made available for those who had served between 1793 and 1814. In 1849 a similar medal, the Naval General Service medal, was issued and this covered battles between 1793 and 1840. The fact that some twenty-five years had elapsed since the coming of peace meant that many of those entitled to the medal were already dead, decrepit or uninterested. However, a large number of these medals were issued and have now become very desirable to the collector. Their overall value has risen quite considerably but the price of a specific medal depends upon a number of factors. First of all there is the campaign for which the medal was awarded. This is indicated by a narrow strip of metal stamped with the name of the particular action and attached to the suspender bar of the medal. The value is increased by the number of bars on the medal and by the combination of such bars, the regiment to which the medal was issued and finally its condition. A four-bar medal is usually, but not inevitably, more desirable than one with a single bar, although there are exceptions to this general rule. The value of any particular Naval or Military General Service medal is particularly affected by the bars for which the medal was awarded. Certain actions were on a comparatively small scale and correspondingly a small number of bars were issued, making them rare. This in turn makes them more desirable, and they will realize a much higher price. Since the period covered by the Naval General Service medals extended right up to 1840, bars for the later actions such as that by the Navy off Syria in 1840, are less sought after. Consequently all other things being equal, a Naval General Service medal with this bar is likely to be comparatively cheap.

Once the idea of issuing medals had been established the practice was repeated many times. The number of campaigns fought during the reign of Victoria (1837-1901) was very high. There were actions in

Africa, China, Canada, India and New Zealand apart from the major wars, the Crimean War (1853-6) and the South African War (1899-1902). As a general rule it may be said that the earlier the campaign the more desirable the medal and the more expensive it is likely to be, although, again, it must be emphasized that there are exceptions. Of all campaign medals those of the two World Wars are the commonest and, apart from some rare examples, are very cheap.

After World War I (1914-18) millions of medals, all named, were issued and there is one very common group of three, The 1914-15 Star, British War Medal and the Victory Medal, known popularly as Pip, Squeak and Wilfrid, after characters in a newspaper cartoon strip. These medals are of very little value because they are so common, a sad comment when one considers the effort, sacrifice and unhappiness that these medals represent.

British World War II campaign medals are, with one exception, of very limited value. One of the most important contributing factors to this lack of interest is the fact that they were issued unnamed, which means that there is absolutely no way in which the authenticity and background details of the recipient can be checked. They were also issued in large numbers and, with the exception of the Aircrew Europe Star, which was the most restricted issue, they fetch little and arouse meagre interest. Many Commonwealth countries issued World War II medals, but again they are mostly unnamed; Canada issued a silver Volunteer Medal which was unnamed as were the New Zealand War Service medal, the South African Medal for War Services and the Southern Rhodesian War Services medal. The Australian Service medal was an exception for it was issued named. Following the end of World War II there were other campaigns. The United Nations issued a medal for those who served in Korea, including British, Canadian, Australian, New Zealand and South African troops. Commonwealth forces were also entitled to the General Service medal with bars for Borneo and the Malay Peninsula but only the Australian troops qualified for the bar for South Vietnam and Australia also issued its own medal for these campaigns.

In addition to campaign medals there are many British orders and decorations awarded for gallantry or in recognition of services. The gallantry awards are probably a little more popular than decorations but the rare ones such as the Victoria Cross are beyond the expectation of most collectors. Others such as the Military Medal, instituted in 1916, are far more common simply because so many more were awarded, especially during World War I. The citation giving the details of the act for which the medal was granted is printed in the official publication *The London Gazette*. There are also medals given only to members of the Royal Air Force which include the Distinguished Flying Cross and the Air Force Medal.

Commemorative medals were often awarded to members of the armed forces and police forces. Coronations, jubilees and royal visits are the kind of occasion marked by such awards. Long Service and

American shooting medal made by John Frick of New York. The three bars are bronze, silver and gold.

Miniatures: (*top*) Mons Star, British War medal and Victory medal, World War I – the oak leaf indicates that the owner was mentioned in dispatches; Star, the Burma Star and Defence medal, World War II; (*middle*) Afghanistan medal, 1878-80; India General Service, 1854–95; token halfpenny; (*bottom*) Hoxne and Hartsmere Suffolk, Loyal Yeomanry Cavalry, 1795; Boer War patriotic medal; French 'brooch' sold to raise money for charities and war effort, World War I.

Good Conduct medals were given to the Royal Navy, Army and Air Force if a man completed a certain number of years exemplary service. These and similar awards are issued named.

There were numerous awards for good shooting, recruiting and sports competitions but they are not greatly sought after and with a few exceptions, such as Georgian shooting medals, they are reasonably priced. Associated with the service awards were those given by various bodies concerned with the welfare of the troops. In 1862 Lt-Colonel Montgomery of the 1st Foot founded a Society in India and called it 'The Soldier's Indian Total Abstinence Association'. Medals were awarded for the number of years of total abstinence. A similar group, the Army Temperance Association, which also presented medals, was formed in Britain in 1893.

Although the cost of collecting early medals has become rather prohibitive there is another way to put together a very comprehensive collection, including such varieties as the Victoria

Cross, at very low prices. Small replicas of the medals were worn by officers in uniform, evening dress and on certain other occasions: these miniatures were apparently introduced sometime around the mid-nineteenth century. All the various campaign medals and decorations were produced and these are available at reasonable prices ranging from £1.00 (approx. $2), to £10.00 (approx. $20) for the rarer ones. This is a very interesting field although, of course, the examples do lack the personal association value of a large, officially issued and named medal.

In America, campaign medals were awarded even less often than in Britain. During the Revolutionary War it seems that only three badges of Military Merit were issued, although four years satisfactory service in the army was recognized by the issue of a strip of white tape on the left sleeve; eight years earned a second stripe. In 1782, three years service was recognized by the awarding of a patch, in the same colour as the regimental facings, worn on the left arm.

British miniature medals and decorations: (*top*) Victoria Cross; Distinguished Service Order; Crimean medal with Sebastopol bar; General Service medal with South Vietnam bar (Australians only); Kaiser-i-Hind medal; (*bottom*) The Most Honourable Order of the Bath; The Most Eminent Order of the Indian Empire; The Most Distinguished Order of St Michael and St George; Russian Order of St Stanislas; Khedives Star, 1882.

American medals: Distinguished Service medal (Army) authorized 1918; Air Force Cross established 1960; Bronze Star medal authorized 1944; Distinguished Flying Cross authorized 1926.

Opposite Daggers of the Third Reich, worn by officers: (*left to right*) Army, Luftwaffe, Sturmabteilungen, and two variant forms of the Navy dagger.

Naturally the Civil War (1861-⌐) encouraged the authorities to consider the awarding of medals. In 1862 the Medal of Honour was authorized by Congress for issue to members of the Army and Navy: its design has been altered over the years. It is still one of the highest United States awards. In the South also the President was authorized to bestow medals on the troops. Little seems to have been done, so that few Confederate medals survive. One, the Southern Cross of Honour, was awarded to veterans in 1900; this was a medal ordered by the Daughters of the Confederacy. The next important US gallantry award is the Distinguished Service Cross, introduced in 1918. These were crosses for the Navy and Air Force. In 1932 the Purple Heart was authorized, based in shape and colouring on the Military Merit badge. Good conduct medals were authorized at various dates.

Service awards during the Civil War were authorized by Congress and also given by individual commanders although, considering the war's length and ferocity, they were few. Battles against the Red Indians were not recognized until 1905, when a medal was authorized by Congress. During the next few decades medals were awarded for service in the Spanish American War (1898), Phillipines (1899-1913), Boxer Rebellion (1900-1), Cuba (1906-9), Nicaragua (1912), Mexico (1911-17), and Dominica (1916).

In World War I the United States authorized a bar for wear with the Victory Medal in much the same way as the British Military General Service medal. In World War II there were numerous awards for service as well as for the occupation of Germany.

Napoleon was well aware of the effect on morale of awards and medals when, in 1802, he instituted the *Légion d'honneur* to supplement the various 'Weapons of Honour' which had been the usual way of rewarding gallantry. The details of the design have altered but basically the same medal is being used today.

Probably the best known of all Europe's medals is the Iron Cross of Germany, which was established by William III in 1813. There is a Grand Cross, which is very rarely awarded, and two classes of the

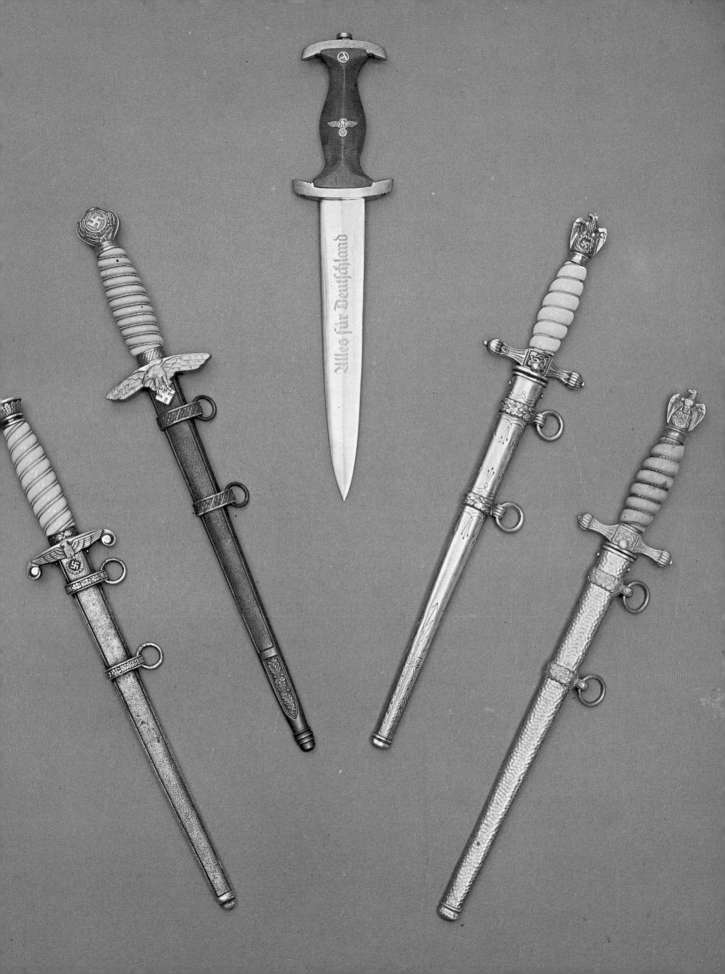

ordinary cross. The medal was given for service in the Franco-Prussian War of 1870-1 and in World War I, a total issue of 720,000. When World War II broke out in 1939, Hitler reinstated the award and although the medal was virtually identical with earlier ones it carried the date 1939. There were a number of divisions; Second Class, First Class, Knight's Cross, Knight's Cross with oak leaves and the Grand Cross. The lower grades were awarded on a fairly liberal standard so that it is not an uncommon medal.

Faced with this bewildering array of material the collector may well wonder on what lines to plan his collection. Some enthusiasts set out to acquire an example of every type of campaign medal issued over a certain period; others will aim to get examples from all the regiments which took part in one particular action. Some will seek to cover one period and acquire specimens of medals bearing the names of every regiment that saw action. Others concentrate on one particular regiment and try to cover the many actions in which it was involved. In some cases it may be the object of the collection to acquire a medal from each ship that took part in a particular action. Some may seek to acquire examples from every country in Europe, indeed the number of alternatives is really very considerable.

Above American medals: (*top*) airman's medal established 1960; Air medal established 1942; Joint Service Commendation medal established 1963; Purple Heart awarded only for combat; (*bottom*) Victory medal, World War I; Asiatic-Pacific Campaign medal established 1942; Korean Service medal authorized 1950; United Services Vietnam Service medal authorized 1965.

Opposite A unique group of medals awarded to Lieutenant-General Sir Colin Campbell, a famous officer of the British Army during the Napoleonic wars, including a rare Army Gold Cross, an Order of the Bath, Waterloo Medal and various Spanish Orders.

COLLECTING, CARE AND DISPLAY

Medals are popular and can be very expensive so that it is important to know as much as possible about them before embarking into this area of collecting. Probably the best sources are the established dealers and auction houses, for they offer some form of guarantee as to authenticity and if there is any question they will normally refund the price. Most medal dealers issue catalogues for postal sales but the demand is very heavy so orders should be sent in without delay. Various auction rooms hold sales and their catalogues are useful reference sources as well as giving some guidance in current values.

The terms describing medals have been formalized and the majority of dealers use the following: *Fleur de Coin*—FDC, Extremely Fine—EF, Very Fine—VF, and Fine—F. Some will also use extra terms such as Fair or Worn. The trouble with all these descriptions is that they are subjective and consequently the same medal may be assessed as EF by one dealer and only F by another. All descriptions should be thought of as approximations only: the collector will make his own decision. Condition obviously affects the price of any medal so it is important that the grading should be correct.

Identification of most medals is not difficult and the books listed in the appendix will readily supply the information required. Collectors of British medals are fortunate in two volumes which are virtually indispensable. Campaign medals are well covered in Gordon's *British Medals and Battles*, which deals with campaigns, lists, regiments involved and, in most cases, the number of medals issued. Another indispensable book is *The Standard Catalogue of British Orders, Decorations and Medals,* issued by the firm of Spink & Son Ltd. This lists virtually every British medal and gives a valuation which is extremely useful as a guide. But it must be remembered that the figure is only a guide, for demand, condition, regiment and even owners name may all affect the price.

Value is very difficult to assess for there are so many variable factors including, among others, condition, regiment, the combination of bars, and whether it is a single medal or one of a group. Groups are even more difficult to value but as a general guide, admittedly only very general, all things being equal, a group is worth the sum total of the individual pieces plus around 20 per cent. In some cases, if an unusual medal is included or the owner is a person of note, then the percentage rise would be much higher. In a few cases a group may fetch less than the equivalent value of the individual pieces but this is only likely to be so for very common groups.

Medals have been the subject of much attention by fakers and it is always as well to check every piece as carefully as possible. In the case of named medals it is important to check the style of naming; whether it is engraved or impressed, which means that the letters are die-stamped in place. Engraved medals are always slightly more suspect than impressed ones simply because it is so much easier to

Opposite Selection of Iron Cross and other medals: (*top*) 1914 issue in its original box; 1870 1st class; 1870 2nd class with oak-leaf cluster for 25th anniversary; (*bottom*) Order of the Red Eagle 4th class; 1914 2nd class Iron Cross; 1914 1st class with unusual screw fitting; Hamburg Cross awarded to all male citizens who served; watch fob fashioned with iron cross motif.

engrave than stamp a name. The style of naming is also important: the reference books will indicate the correct form.

One of the great hazards of medal collecting is re-naming. In the past a soldier may have lost his medal and obtained a spare and had the original name removed and his own inserted. The same thing is still being done today but with less excuse, for its purpose is to change the value of the medal. A Waterloo Medal issued to a member of a reserve regiment which saw little fighting can be turned into one apparently belonging to a member of a famous regiment which saw most of the action. Similarly one of a private could become an officer's. Fortunately it is possible to detect such changes, for in order to remove the original name some metal must be shaved off. The diameter should be measured at several points; if there are variations in the size then the collector should beware.

Since the value of a medal can be determined by the bars attached these may well be altered. Depending on the medal, extra bars may be added, removed or the combination altered. The only way to detect such changes is to examine the rivets very carefully, preferably with a lens. In general, re-named and altered medals are to be avoided but this is a matter for personal choice.

Reproductions are yet another pitfall but with certain exceptions they are fairly obvious. There are many which look absolutely correct but are not heavy enough to deceive. There are others which are more of a problem for they are copies intended to deceive and some skill is needed to spot them. Some, such as the British World War II Air Crew Europe Star differ in detail from the original; but a close examination is required to spot the difference. Some decorations and medals of the Third Reich have also been copied. Specimens such as the Victoria Cross are unlikely to fool anybody!

Having acquired a new medal the next vexed question is whether to clean or not. Some collectors prefer to keep the piece as found but most prefer to do some cleaning. The best advice is to keep it to a minimum, for every rub removes a tiny amount of metal and over a long period this will blur the detail. A wash in soapy water is probably best or, if the medal is silver, then one of the proprietary, long-lasting polishes may be used.

Medal ribbons are attractive. Most collectors prefer to replace old and tattered pieces with new lengths, for almost every design is readily available from dealers.

Having now cleaned the medal the collector will probably want to carry out some research. The first step is usually to verify the medal, a term which needs to be clarified since it is sometimes misunderstood and misused by dealers and collectors. Verification is no guarantee of genuineness since it simply means that the official lists include a man with the same name as that on the medal. It does not automatically mean that the medal is the original, for the name, number and unit may have been altered. Some regiment's medals are more highly prized than others and it is not unknown for collectors and dealers to re-name the medal, substituting a more desirable regiment.

Opposite (*top*) Medal issued to a member of USS *Covington*, torpedoed July 1918; medal for audacity (no. 3121806) with dark blue ribbon (USSR); World War I medal with green, white and red ribbon (Italy); (*bottom*) Colonial medal with silver bar for service in Algeria (France); World War I medal with green, white and red ribbon (Italy); World War I Naval medal, (Italy); Joint Services Commendation medal (USA).

However, assuming that the medal has been verified and appears to be genuine and unaltered, it is possible to search through the records and locate some of the details concerning the recipient. Such documents may contain information as to the physical appearance of the soldier, his trade and whether he was discharged, wounded or whether he died on active service. Once the basic details such as name, place of birth and date of birth have been extracted from the records, it is then possible, should the owner so wish, to continue the search for the family details by reference to the appropriate parish records, if these still exist.

The place to carry out research on British medals is the Public Records Office in Chancery Lane, Holborn, London. Access to these records is restricted and anybody wishing to make use of them must apply for a Reader's ticket. This involves completing a form and the production of some written guarantee of the bona fides and reliability of the applicant. It is as well to apply for the Reader's Ticket in advance of the first research visit, since people without a ticket are not admitted to the search rooms.

It is not possible to be specific for every case but a general procedure applies to the majority of medal searches. The relevant lists and documents are available in the Rolls Room of the Public Records Office and are listed in the War Office and Admiralty indices on shelf R3, identified by the code letter Adm 171 and WO 100. Reference to these volumes will simply indicate what lists of medal holders, known as the Medal Rolls, are available and will give an appropriate reference number. A production slip is then made out and handed in for the document to be produced and this may involve a delay of anything up to an hour or more whilst the documents are brought up to the Rolls Room.

The medal rolls are normally arranged in regimental order and once the required volume is produced it is simply a matter of turning to the appropriate regiment and checking that the name appears. Indices for muster rolls and daybooks are also on R3 shelves and once the man's name and number are known the same procedure is followed to have various documents produced. Photocopies of the documents may be obtained from the Records Office. The procedure described applies to those collectors able to visit the rooms but the Public Records Office offers a service for those who are unable to attend. Overseas or out of town collectors may write to the Records Office giving full details of the medal on a form PS3 and a check for verification will be made. Demands are heavy and quite naturally a charge is made. At the time of writing this was £5.40 (approx. $10.80).

If further research is required the Public Records Office can put applicants in touch with professional researchers. They will follow the instructions of the collector and produce a neatly assembled collection of documents relevant to any particular medal. Again a fee will be payable.

Medal Rolls for Indian Campaigns may not be housed at the Public Records Office but are kept at India House. For campaigns from the

Crimea onwards it is also possible, although by no means certain, that there may be some appropriately relevant photographs in any number of publications. It should not be forgotten that there are a large number of regimental museums dotted about the British Isles and Curators, within the limitations imposed by space, time and money, are prepared to help in answering queries.

It is important to remember that officially a British campaign medal was usually issued on the authority of the monarch and the

Imperial German medals: (*left*) Iron Cross 1st class with oak-leaf cluster for 25th anniversary; (*top*) decoration instituted for women 22 March 1871, *Das Verdienst Orden fur Frauen und Jungfrauen*, and locket of the recipient; (*bottom*) medal for non-combatants during 1870–1 war.

Right British copy of the German medal commemorating the sinking of the RMS *Lusitania* in May 1915 which was sold in its red cardboard box with an explanatory leaflet to raise funds for the blinded of the war.

Please do not destroy this

When you have read it carefully through kindly pass it on to a friend.

A

German Naval Victory

"With joyful pride we contemplate this latest deed of our navy. . . ." —
Kölnische Volkszeitung, 10th May, 1915.

Reproduced . . . issued by the Lusitania Souvenir Medal Com . . . uke Street, Manchester Square W. 1.
All profits accruing to this Committee will be handed to
St. Dunstan's Blinded Soldiers and Sailors Hostel.

Opposite Crimean medal with bar for Alma together with a photocopy of owner's discharge. He was wounded in the shoulder during the battle and was discharged as unfit.

records were, therefore, kept in London. The campaign might be in New Zealand and the troops might include local volunteers but approval for the issue still came from London and somewhere a note was made of the recipient's name. Australians and Canadians were all listed and their deeds of valour recorded in the *London Gazette*.

The Public Records Office holds the documents of officers and other ranks and certain other museums and societies possess copies of the medal rolls. The National Army Museum in Royal Hospital Road, London SW3 has an extensive library and can usually be relied upon to supply information about an officer; but they cannot help very much with details of other rank's service. Some service details about United States personnel can be obtained from local history societies or from the Library of Congress.

The recording of a medal can become very involved indeed. It is entirely a matter of personal preference for the collector just how much information he wishes to amass, but apart from the physical description, size, bars, name and style of naming, the minimum suggested background information would be the present regiment's name, the period that it served in that particular campaign, other bars granted to the regiment and, of course, as described above, some personal details of the recipient. This is not always possible and in

HER MAJESTY'S

Whereof *F. M. H. R. H. Prince Albert K. is Colonel* } *Grenadier* Regiment *of Foot Guards*

[Place and Date] *London 27 February* 18

PROCEEDINGS OF A REGIMENTAL BOARD, held this day, in conformity to the Articles of War, for the purpose of verifying and recording the Services, Conduct, Character, and cause of Discharge of No. *4331, William Fellows Private* of the Regiment above-mentioned.

President.
Colonel Goalburn, Grenguards

Members.
Captain Cooper Gren guards   *Captain Digby Gren guar*

THE BOARD having *examined* and compared the Regimental Records, Soldier's Book, and such other *Documents as* appeared to them to be necessary, report *that William Fellows* by Trade a *Laborer* was BORN in the Parish of *___* in or near the Town of *Oundle* in the *County of Northampton* and was ATTESTED for the *Grenadier* Regiment of *Foot Guards* at *Peterboro* in the County of *Northampton* on the *14 Decr 1841* at the age of *Twenty Years & 7 Mos* that after *the deduction* required by Her Majesty's Regulations, the SERVICE up to this day *allowed to reckon, amounts to __* years *___ 15 ___* days, as shewn by the *Statement* on the 2nd page; during which period, he served Abroad *11 months*

at *with the Army in the East* years,
in *___* years;
" *___*

and further, that his DISCHARGE is proposed *___ Disability*

[In cases of Disability, the Regimental Medical Officer will write his Report on the 3rd Page hereof.] *Stated on ___ page*

With regard to the CHARACTER and CONDUCT of *William Fellows* the Board have to report, that upon reference to the Defaulter Book, and by the Parole testimony that has been given, it appears that *His Character is Very good, He has never been tried by a Court Martial, He is in possession of Two Good Conduct Marks with pay for the same He was present at the Battle of the Alma*

[Give the particulars required by the Adjutant General's Circular Letter, 29th Sept. 1838.]

Austrian medal for service in World War I together with its citation or certificate authorizing its issue. It is of some special interest for the citation is printed in German and Hungarian for at that period the territory was the Austro-Hungarian Empire.

the case of World War II British medals it is impossible, for they were all issued unnamed. If a group includes a Long Service medal or similar award then the recipient's details can be traced, for such medals would be named.

Display methods will depend on a range of factors. The simplest is to use plastic envelopes which hold one medal and can be slotted into the loose leaves of a plastic sheeted album. This system has the advantage of simplicity and ease of re-arrangement. Groups are sometimes described as being mounted as worn. This means they are fixed to some form of backing strip and therefore cannot be slipped into the standard plastic envelope. Some collectors strip down the group and display them separately but if it is desired to keep them together they can be fixed to a strip of card which can then be covered with a piece of thin plastic. Special medal cabinets with shallow drawers can be used although suitable filing cabinets will suffice. The medals can also be mounted on a backing and kept in trays.

More decorative displays can be mounted by using a picture frame with polystyrene or other backing covered with an attractive material such as felt or velvet. The medal is secured to the backing by a staple through the top of the piece of ribbon. The ribbon is then folded back to cover the staple and will hang down without showing how it is secured. If the frame is then glazed the display will look attractive and can very easily be re-arranged should this be desired, and it is also protected from dust.

Medals are small and valuable so that they are vulnerable but they usually carry a name and perhaps a regimental number and so can easily be identified. They should not be scratched or otherwise marked even for reasons of security.

8 Equipment

Ever since armies began the infantryman has been expected to act as a beast of burden as well as a warrior. The Roman legionary marched hundreds of miles with staff, shield, helmet, armour, cooking pots and other items dangling about his person—indeed his nickname was Marius' mule. No doubt the medieval English archer groused and grumbled as he marched along with bow, staff, sword, blankets and provisions. Comparisons made at the beginning of this century showed that the loaded weight of a cavalryman was greater than a fully armoured knight of the Middle Ages! The situation had not changed greatly by World War I, when the infantrymen of all the armies were still festooned with packs and bundles. Mechanized transport in World War II eliminated some of the hard labour, although the infantryman still carried a variety of burdens.

It was necessary to equip the soldier with some means of attaching all the bits and pieces, so a good many belts and straps were developed. Most of the ordinary soldiers carried some sort of sword until the mid-eighteenth century, but examples of early sword belts are very scarce. One of the fine quality slings for a seventeenth-century rapier occasionally appears on the market: they are quite elaborate with velvet, leather and a number of small straps. For the ordinary soldier of the British Army of 1660 there were no such elaborate fittings. Judging by contemporary pictures most of the troops seem to have had a shoulder belt with a simple attachment to hold the leather scabbard. Waist belts were also used. These are shown by contemporary artists, and by the end of the century they seem to have predominated. It seems most likely that they were of plain, untreated leather, fitted with a brass buckle. From about 1680 the infantryman had to carry a plug bayonet as well as the short sword, and a leather, double hanging fitting was fixed to the belt.

For the soldier armed with the musket there was yet another appendage, the cartridge box. As early as the seventeenth century there had been a growing use of paper cartridges in place of the old powder flask with separate bullets. The paper was rolled around a wooden former, filled with powder and a ball and then the ends were twisted to seal it. The troops carried their paper cartridges in a leather box which hung from a cross-belt, at one time apparently secured on the left shoulder by a button and strap arrangement. The cartridge box was used right up to the latter part of the nineteenth century, when the metal cartridge was in use. The majority of the boxes have a metal interior, divided to accommodate the cartridges and many had the regimental badge secured to the leather flap which closed the box. The badge was normally attached by means of threaded lugs and nuts. When the percussion system was introduced another pouch to hold the small metal caps was fitted to the belt, or else incorporated into the design of the cartridge box.

Around the middle of the eighteenth century a double belt made its appearance, one crossing the left shoulder and one the right shoulder. The grenadiers had a very wide cross-belt for the pouch. In contemporary pictures the sword and bayonet are shown suspended from a waist belt, but there appears to have been no standard practice. When the infantryman lost his sword in 1768 the fitting on the belt was changed, since it now only had to hold the bayonet in its scabbard.

Associated with the cross-belt is the piece of equipment known today as the shoulder belt plate, although the contemporary description was the breast plate. These attractive ornaments apparently owe their origin to the buckle of the shoulder belt. The use of cross-belts became more or less standard so that by the 1780s the fitting known as the breast plate had begun to acquire some standard form. Whilst the square buckles were satisfactory at the waist they could be inconvenient on a cross-belt, for the corners rubbed against the belt. So the corners were clipped to reduce the rubbing and eventually the plate became oval. The 'other ranks' pattern was usually very simple, either of stamped brass, bearing no more than the regimental number, or a plain breast brass plate with the numerals attached. The officer's pattern was more elaborate and might be of silver with part of the regimental badge as well as the number. The oval pattern was apparently worn from the latter part of the eighteenth century until the 1815-20 period, when a rectangular shape became more or less universal, probably to create space for the battle honours earned by many regiments. Each regiment developed its own pattern: that of the officer normally consisted of a polished brass or gilt plate to which were fitted a series of extra devices. The

Shoulder belt plates: die-stamped brass plate of the 3rd Notts Local Militia, c.1805; 5th (Northumberland Fusiliers) Regiment of Foot, with gilt plate and battle honours in white metal; 25th (The King's Own Borderers) Regiment of Foot, c.1850, an unusually elaborate example with blue enamel panels; 52nd (Oxfordshire Light Infantry) Regiment, c.1840, brass.

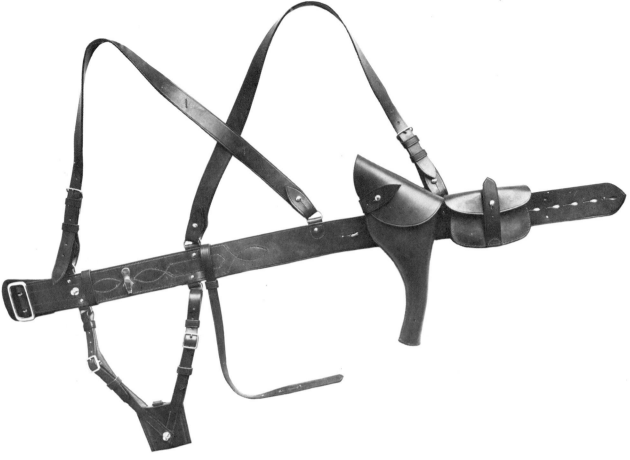

'Sam Browne' belt worn by British
officers. It has two cross braces,
revolver holster, ammunition pouch
and straps with sword scabbard frog.
The long single strap on the left was
to loop through and hold steady the
sword hilt.

component parts have small lugs which pass through the various
pieces and through the plate to be secured by long, thin pins.

There are many gaps in the history of these plates for there were
frequent changes in pattern as battle honours were added and royal
cyphers were changed. There were even differences between those
worn by the first and second battalions in a single regiment. The
innumerable volunteer units of the Napoleonic Wars all had their
own patterns, often with no more than initials to identify them.

Shoulder belt plates were worn by both cavalry and infantry,
although little is known for certain of the cavalry patterns, for they
appear to have been discarded quite early on. Shoulder belt plates
continued to be worn throughout the first half of the nineteenth
century, but when the hardships of the Crimean War forced the
authorities to take a far more realistic view of the whole of the British
uniform, the shoulder belt plate was abolished in 1855. They were,
however, still worn by certain military orders as well as by Scottish
officers, and indeed this practice has continued almost to the present.
The shoulder belt plate was attached to the belt by a system of hooks
and studs. Oval ones normally have two studs and one hook; on the
rectangular ones there are two studs and two hooks.

A new style of officer's belt which first appeared about 1860 was the outcome of an injury suffered by General Sir Samuel Browne VC. He lost an arm and found difficulty with the ordinary belt so he designed his own. The normal waist belt was supported by two cross-braces which passed over the shoulders and ensured a firmer, more secure support for pistol and sword. This style of belt proved popular and more and more officers adopted it. By the 1870-80 period it was in general use by most British officers. The sealed pattern of 1900 was of brown leather, $2\frac{3}{8}$ in (6 cm) wide with braces $1\frac{1}{2}$ in (3.8 cm) and fittings in brass. It could carry a revolver holster—the Dress Regulations 1900 use the term 'pistol case'—an ammunition pouch and the sword and scabbard. Dress Regulations 1900 specify that the brace over the left shoulder could be left off by mounted officers if the revolver was not carried. A less elaborate sword belt of webbing was available for officers to wear beneath their jacket, or under the sash worn around the waist. These crimson sashes with tassels were worn around the waist by Field Marshals, Colonels and Equerries while other officers carried theirs over their left shoulder.

Since the foot soldier was expected to carry most of his personal equipment he had to be fitted with a series of straps, belts, packs, haversacks and sundry other bits and pieces. Early in the nineteenth century he had two straps crossing on the chest and from these, other, shorter straps supported a light brown haversack surmounted by his rolled up blanket. On his right hip hung the cartridge box, which, like the knapsack, was fitted with a brass regimental badge. After 1812 an infantryman had a haversack and circular wooden bottle on his left hip; his knapsack was now black and carried a painted regimental number. By the mid-nineteenth century most belts were of white leather in contrast to the knapsack and cartridge box.

During the late 1860s the equipment was again changed and on the white straps was fixed a large, case-like valise, which hung in the small of the back. On top of the valise was the mess tin and over this the greatcoat which fitted between the shoulders. In the late 1870s the valise was raised to a more comfortable position higher up the back and on the left hip was a haversack; the water bottle was on the right. Most belts of this period have the tongue and slot type of fitting but some had the S, serpent clasp. This style of straps and belt was known as the Slade-Wallace equipment and the cartridge pouches, haversacks and other extras were varied according to the duty on which the soldier was engaged.

Leather, whether natural or treated, was expensive. In the British Army a new, cheaper material was introduced in 1908. This woven material known as webbing was tough and hard wearing and could be easily manufactured into a variety of sizes and shapes. The normal fittings of the type in use during World War I had a wide waistbelt with brass fittings to which could be attached a bayonet frog, shoulder straps, pouches, haversack, pack and a water bottle. This webbing was modified in 1938 but although the waistbelt was made narrower the basic style remained unchanged, though there were changes in the various pouches to hold ammunition. The adoption by

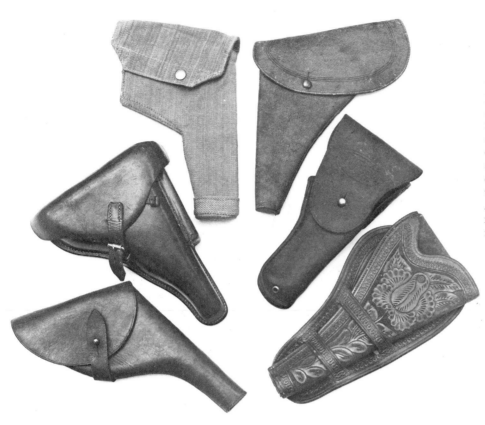

Holsters: (*top*) khaki webbing holster dated 1942 for British Army Webley revolver; leather holster for revolver, probably a privately made one for an early model Webley; (*middle*) brown leather holder for Model 08 Luger pistol bearing Nazi markings and date 1940; brown leather holster for Colt 1911 A1.45, US official issue automatic pistol; (*bottom*) good quality brown leather revolver holster, again privately made for an officer; carved leather holster of the buscadero type, probably for a Colt single-action Army revolver. Unlike standard military holsters it has no covering flap.

the British, in 1938, of the Bren Light Machine Gun, which used a slightly curved metal box magazine meant that special pouches were made to accommodate them. There were pouches to hold various musical instruments, map cases and sundry small items. For officers, certain NCOs and a variety of troops on special duties there were also revolver holsters.

Personal holsters carried at the belt did not generally appear until the mid-nineteenth century. Prior to this date most were fitted to the saddle. Holsters of the seventeenth century are rare and were usually fitted with quite elaborate decorative flaps. Those of the nineteenth century cavalry were of leather, usually brown, and shaped to hold the pistol. When cartridge revolvers became standard issue in 1880 the holsters, normally of leather with a brass fitting, were changed to fit them. Officers were not obliged to carry the standard revolver so long as their chosen weapon took service ammunition. Consequently the range of holsters of this period is likely to be considerable. Most officers' patterns have a large flap but many of the troops carried the later Webley revolver of 1887, in an open topped holster with just a securing strap to prevent the weapon falling out.

Webbing holsters were issued in various styles including some with a series of cartridge loops stitched on the outside. Those for tank crews were designed to hang down much lower than the standard

Collection of American equipment: (*left, top to bottom*) rifleman's leather pouch, *c.*1850; pouch of Civil War period; McKever pouch, 1874; (*right*) small leather pouch to hold percussion caps; support for muzzle of a carbine fitted to a saddle; canteen or water bottle for artillery, *c.*1875; frog for the Springfield bayonet, *c.*1875; belt and buckle, other ranks, Civil War period.

Opposite Group of US items including: tank crewman's helmet, World War II; government issue belt; holster; pouches; bayonet for Model 1 carbine and a cleaning kit for a light machine gun. The Colt .45 automatic is a Japanese-made Replica model.

issue. Although the texture of the material was altered and blackened metal fittings replaced the brass ones, webbing is still used today. British Army webbing was normally khaki coloured but the equipment may be found in light blue—Royal Air Force, dark blue—Royal Navy and white for the Military Police.

American forces also used webbing but theirs was a very different design as well as a different colour. In 1910 the equipment introduced consisted of a cartridge belt with ten pouches, five on either side of the buckle; to this belt was hung a small first-aid pouch as well as a cover to hold a water bottle or canteen. There was a large haversack which opened out flat, to the bottom of which was fixed a pack carrier. One unusual feature was the fitting of the bayonet and scabbard to the side of the haversack. Next came a carrier for a short shovel, the entrenching tool, and then a meal can, knife, fork and spoon went into a pouch. When the entire pack had been assembled by folding over and strapping the various pieces the handle of the shovel hung

down the middle of the back and the pack and haversack sat in between the shoulders with the bayonet on the left. The main infantry equipment of World War II was not greatly different except that the bayonet was attached to the belt. The holster for the Colt automatic pistol M.1911 A1 was of brown leather and was a little unusual in that it had a leather thong at the base so that the holster could be tied down to the thigh. The support for this pistol, for cavalry, General and Corps officers, was the leather waist belt, with a magazine pocket and leather slides to hold the first aid pouch and canteen, or a webbing belt, introduced in 1912, and worn by infantry officers and others.

In Germany the use of leather for personal equipment continued right through World War II. In March 1887 the German army adopted a waist belt with straps which crossed the shoulders and joined in the middle of the back to make a Y-shaped brace. The great majority of the infantry had this equipment in black leather although the Grenadier Battalions of the Prussian Guards and 1st-12th Grenadier Regiments were of leather which was pipeclayed. There were two cartridge pouches, each holding thirty rounds, at the front of the belt, and at the back, suspended from the belt, was a larger pouch holding two packets of twenty cartridges as a reserve supply. On the back was a knapsack of cowhide, strengthened by wooden boards, the hair being left on the skin. Among the many items carried in the pack was a hymn book, spare parts for the rifle and the soldier's clothing. The knapsack, like the reserve ration bag, was secured to the braces by a long metal pin passing through a series of loops. The reserve rations consisted of three tin boxes of preserved meat, a box of preserved vegetables, one of coffee and one of biscuits. On top of the knapsack was placed the forage cap, greatcoat and mess tin. On the right side the soldier carried a brown canvas haversack supported by a canvas strap crossing the left shoulder or, alternatively, it could be secured to the belt. A leather covered, tin water bottle with a cup fitting over the mouth was fixed to the belt and a certain number of men in each battalion carried an entrenching tool—a grand total weight of $64\frac{1}{4}$ lb (29.2 kg). Cuirassiers had a sword belt of white leather with a pouch belt, also white, to support a black leather pouch, holding eighteen rounds of revolver ammunition. On the flap was the regimental badge. The colour of the belt varied with some regiments of Dragoons and Hussars.

There were only a few changes in this type of equipment up to World War II; the cartridge pouches were in two groups of three and the type of canteen was changed; the entrenching tool was held in an open form of leather case; special canvas and leather pouches to hold the Schmeisser machine gun magazines were developed, and there were map cases and binocular cases of various designs. A field service, canvas equivalent of this equipment was produced. The buckle on the field service belt was the usual square shape with twin prongs but most German belts have a rectangular, slightly curved buckle of grey metal which is embossed with a design, normally a

Opposite Group of military items including: shako plate, 20th Middlesex Rifle Volunteers, *c.*1860; Kabul medal, 1842, Crimean medal, Indian General Service medal, 1895; Colt revolver .44 calibre, 1861; badge worn by Observers in the Luftwaffe; RAF officer's cap badge; music sheet, postcard and photograph.

Belt buckles: (*top*) Turkish World War I; US Navy but made to private order in Japan, *c.*1950; Imperial Austrian; (*middle*) German, State Railways; German, early pattern for SS troops of the Essen Gau; Hitler Youth Movement; (*bottom*) German, other ranks, SS troops; German, worn by units serving with International troops in China during the Boxer Rebellion, 1900; German Red Cross.

circular band enclosing the German eagle and carrying the motto *Gott Mit Uns*. Other designs incorporating the Luftwaffe eagle and state symbols were used on various belts for special groups.

In both wars the automatic pistol Luger M 1908 was carried in good quality leather holsters which accommodated a spare magazine as well as a small loading tool. In 1938 the German army adopted the Walther P38 pistol which had a different holster, and included a spare magazine as well as a cleaning rod. Both weapons were carried during the war.

Water bottles or canteens were carried by most troops although on many occasions the contents were rather more spirituous than allowed by Army Regulations. A variety of shapes and materials have been used for this purpose. Many armies made efforts to combine the bottle with a food container or other utensil. Most were covered with some kind of material or enclosed within a fabric carrying case. Wood was commonly used for these canteens until the late nineteenth century.

Entrenching tools of differing patterns have been carried by a proportion of most infantry units. British, German, Polish, Russian, United States and Japanese forces all favoured a spade with a short handle. These tools were attached to the belt or pack in differing ways, but most made some use of a case of leather, canvas or webbing.

The cavalry needed certain special equipment and in Britain this included items such as special leather cases to carry spare shoes for the horse, together with a few spare nails. For lancers there was a special leather fitting into which the butt of the lance was placed and to accommodate the carbine, a short barrelled rifle. There were several styles of leather holster or 'buckets', attached to the harness of the horse. Many cavalrymen carried their ammunition in pouches mounted on a cross shoulder belt, a bandolier, usually of leather but occasionally of canvas. Many mounted troops wore a cross-belt with a large spring clip at the end which engaged with a ring mounted on a bar at the side of the carbine and so prevented its accidental loss.

The spur was an important part of the rider's equipment and can be traced back for centuries, but few appearing on the market will pre-date the fifteenth century. Those from the seventeenth century are recognizable by their acutely angled shank and star-shaped rowel. Eighteenth-century examples are somewhat smaller but still have a down bend on the shank. Nineteenth-century spurs were generally straight-shanked, with a quite small rowel. It is difficult to identify early military spurs, particularly those for other ranks, but there is some guidance when dealing with those worn by officers. Dress Regulations specify the various forms of spurs to be worn with the different uniforms. In 1846 those for Staff Officers in both dress and undress uniform are described as being of yellow metal with a straight neck 2 in (5 cm) long. There were distinctions between the regiments; in the Life Guards spurs for the 1st Regiment were steel whereas those for the 2nd Regiment were gilt. In the Light Dragoons those for dress uniform were to be of yellow metal but for undress they were to be steel with sharp rowels. Hussars in both dress and undress uniforms had gilt spurs with rowels but Lancers in dress uniform wore spurs of yellow metal, 2 in (5 cm) long, with dumb rowels, and in undress, steel, $2\frac{1}{4}$ in (5.7 cm) long with sharp rowels. The Dress Regulations of 1900 were even more specific about the many patterns. Officers' spurs could be supplied in small, padded leather boxes and for high-ranking officers who needed many pairs of spurs, there were long boxes, divided off to hold the various patterns.

The issue spurs for other ranks of the British Army of World War I were steel, with a chain to go under the instep and a leather strap with a large leather tongue to cover the laced part of the boot.

Although many countries had toyed with the concept of aerial warfare it was World War I which saw the emergence of the aeroplane as an important weapon. In Britain balloons had been used for observation but the official British Army Aeroplane No. 1 did not fly until October 1908, the result of the efforts of an American citizen,

Folding saw, British. The two wooden bars served as handles and the tool was for setting the teeth; the saw fits into the leather case, which was attached to a belt. The tool bears the date 1916 and the Government mark of the broad arrow.

Samuel Franklin Cody. In 1911 the Balloon section was expanded to include an Air Battalion which would have its own aircraft and in April 1912 the Royal Flying Corps was formed. Under the pressure of war the force expanded to include all manner of aircraft and all manner of men recruited from the infantry, cavalry and civilian life. On 1 April 1918 the Royal Air Force was created. Following peace in November 1918 its size was greatly reduced although it saw service in many campaigns from then on until World War II.

The men who flew the various planes were given remarkably little extra equipment apart from fur-lined flying helmets, simple goggles and some warm clothing. The uniform was often that of the man's original regiment, although there was an official jacket rather like that of the lancers, with a warm, cross-over front. This coat was known to the men as the 'maternity jacket'. The Royal Flying Corps and the Royal Air Force had, too, their own badges and insignia.

Germany was well aware of the importance of the air and made great use of all forms of flying machines, including airships. At first the flight personnel were part of the army and their uniforms were essentially the same as those of the soldiers, although their service was indicated by badges worn on the left breast pocket. Their flying helmets were rather like those worn by tank crews, with a padded rib running around the brim and across the crown. Following the end of the war Germany was forced to disband most of her armed forces, but in 1933 Herman Goering, a World War I flyer, became Air Minister and the rebuilding of the airforce was accelerated. In February 1935 the *Reichsluftwaffe* was officially and openly made part of the armed forces. This new service adopted new badges and special equipment such as flying suits, fur-lined, zip-sided flying boots, four patterns of flying helmet, including one for jet pilots, and jump smocks for parachutists.

There is a demand for equipment peculiar to the air forces; flying helmets, oxygen masks, compasses and flying instruments are all sought after. A few enthusiasts even collect aircraft engines or the propellers, particularly the wooden ones from earlier aircraft.

Officers, as a general rule, did not carry the same equipment as the other ranks but they had one or two extra items peculiar to their rank. For the cavalryman there were sabretaches which, in effect, were purses or pockets affixed to the sword belt. At first they were essentially practical and useful items but as time passed they became more and more decorative. They appeared in Eastern Europe during the seventeenth century but it was not until the eighteenth century that they are seen on illustrations of British cavalry. They were usually attached to the belt by three long straps. They were finally abolished in 1901.

Another item which started life on a strictly utility basis but became essentially decorative was the small pouch carried on a cross-belt by an officer, which sat in the small of his back. Two forms of these and the sabretaches may be met. There are the dress ones, which are elaborately decorated, and the more functional undress

A.C.S. RADIO SP.

AP MECHANIC

ones, which tend to be much plainer, in leather with perhaps a regimental badge affixed.

Officers normally rode rather than marched and the harness on their horses was usually decorated with regimental badges. The amount of extra equipment for the cavalry was considerable. In the German army of 1885 it included cord, horseshoes, thirty-two nails, nose bag, stirrup leathers and sundry other items. All the extra pieces of horse equipment known as the furniture varied from regiment to regiment and from period to period. The most eye-catching piece was the shabraque, which was the saddle cloth. This normally carried the badge of the regiment as well as other embroidery, all of which added to the weight—7 lb (3.17 kg) in 1815. Saddle holsters of the eighteenth

Air Force badges: (*top*) US Army Air Force technician; Military Observer, Imperial German; (*middle*) Luftwaffe pilot; Polish Observer; Romanian pilot; (*bottom*) Operational flying badge of Italian transport air crew; pilot's badge, Imperial German.

century were fitted with elaborate housings and covers but by the mid-nineteenth century they were of plain leather. Stirrups seldom have any feature to distinguish them as being military except in the case of high-ranking officers. One small item which may not be immediately recognized are the rectangular sliders which fitted on to the stirrup leathers. Like some other pieces of harness they carried the regimental badge.

Officers, certain NCOs and most cavalrymen carried a sword and this was yet another item to hang from the belt or fix to the saddle. Early scabbards were of wood covered with leather and they could be attached to the belt by means of two rings, which engaged with spring clips on the belt straps. Many also had a stud fixed to the top locket which could be slipped into a slit on a leather frog, fitted to a waist or shoulder belt. Later an extra hook was added to the belt so that the top ring of the scabbard could be hooked over this to hold the sword more securely and with less play than when it was on the longer straps. The first all-metal scabbards in Britain appeared at the end of the eighteenth century.

In battle the dangers of being disarmed were obvious and to prevent the loss of the sword it was common practice to fit a leather loop to the hilt. The hand was passed through the loop, known as the sword knot, and should the sword be dropped it was held dangling at the end of the loop. Like so many military accessories the sword knot became decorative with tradition determining the various colours and styles of material used. British knots varied, the earlier ones being of buff leather, but the most common style was of crimson and gold ribbon with a bullion tassel or acorn. Those for Rifle regiments had a black leather strap and a black acorn. The use of sword knots was not limited to the British Army: in the United States forces that of the army was either of gold cord with an acorn or else a gold lace strap with a gold bullion tassel; for the Navy it was blue and gold.

The German army made great use of sword knots in various forms, each with its own peculiarities. The *Troddel* was a loop, which was fitted around the frog for the bayonet and for the dress dagger, worn with the army walking-out uniform. The band was grey or dark green, whilst a knob at the top of a stem-like projection, the slide, varied in colour according to the company, and the stem was in the battalion colour. This combination of colours allowed the owner's unit to be identified with ease. *Faustriemen* were similar but with a strap of grey leather joining directly to a tassel without the stem of the Troddel; it was looped around the hilt of the sword. A third form was the *Portepee* which was worn by senior NCOs and above; it was similar to the Troddel except that it had a silver cord in place of the band and it was worn wrapped around the hilt of a dagger. On the officers' sabre the Portepee took another form, rather like the Faustriemen.

The German army Commanders were well aware of the important, morale-boosting qualities of uniform extras and they made use of the *Ringkragen* for certain troops. There were six main patterns all with different designs, and lettering dependant on the wearer's function.

British Army horse furniture: brass bosses of various patterns which were fitted to the breast plate of straps passing across the chest of the horse; white metal slider for stirrup straps, Victorian.

But all were the same shape, rather like a compressed heart. They were worn suspended on a linked chain around the neck by NCOs, standard bearers, Military Police, Railway Station police, Street Patrols, Honour Guards and a special unit known as *Feldjägerkommandos* whose prime task was to round up any deserters or, in an emergency, any personnel available for service. The Luftwaffe also had one for the *Flugmeister*, an official who observed landings, take-offs and recorded details of flights.

The nearest equivalent in the British service was the gorget, which was originally a piece of armour to protect the throat and top of the chest. Long after it had lost its protective function it was still worn by officers as a decoration. Early examples were fairly large, often of silver, but as the eighteenth century progressed they became smaller. The Royal Warrants of 1743 and 1768 both speak of silver or gilt gorgets, the choice being determined by the colour of the regiment's lace. The gorgets are engraved with the Royal Coat of Arms as well as the number of the Regiment but there is no standard form and examples may vary considerably. Those of the nineteenth century are usually fairly standard, engraved with the Royal Arms, but some examples are quite elaborate with embossed or applied decoration.

For the first half of the eighteenth century it seems fairly certain that the gorget was worn suspended from a ribbon around the neck so that it sat on the chest just below the throat. There were changes after the 1770s and the gorget was suspended by two loops of ribbon which were slipped over the buttons at the throat, on the lapels or even on the shoulders. The ribbons passed through two holes at the corners of the gorget and terminated in a neat little decorative rosette. The inside of the gorget was lined with soft chamois leather.

In 1830 the British Army officially discarded the gorget but it is still remembered by the small patches of red worn on the lapels by Staff Officers. Greece, Belgium, France, Germany and other countries retained gorgets in one form or another long after 1830.

During World War I a new piece of equipment was added to the soldiers load, for on 22 April 1915 the Germans launched their first large-scale poison gas attack. Clouds of chlorine gas rolled across the battlefield at Ypres in France and inflicted ghastly suffering on the French and Canadian troops. In the confusion and real panic a huge gap was torn in the front line and it was the heroism of the Canadians that held the line and prevented a possible breakthrough. Frantic efforts were made to produce some protection for the troops. The earliest were no more than gauze pads and cotton waste. Then a 'smoke helmet' of grey felt with mica eyepieces was produced, but this was useless and often increased the chances of asphyxiation for the wearer. Despite the fact that the Allies were shown an example of the German respirator before the attack took place, it was not until November 1915 that the Allies captured a German rubber respirator which gave them valuable help in producing an effective one of their own. The German and French developed respirators in which the filters were attached to the facepiece whereas the British and Americans concentrated on filters connected to the facepieces by a flexible tube. Apart from improvements in quality the design was not to change very much until World War II, although the increased use of air power increased the possibility of raids on civilians and there were mass issues to all civilians.

The German army respirator was carried in a fluted, cylindrical, grey-coloured can and consisted of a rubber facepiece with two eye glasses and a large filter. It was normally carried slung at the soldiers back but drivers and others who spent much time sitting often changed the position of the can to the chest.

British and Japanese respirators were carried in a haversack which could be slung over the shoulder or, if likely to be used, secured to the chest. American models were fitted with a longer tube which meant that they could be worn with the haversack at the side. There was one type of British respirator issued to those who found the chest position awkward which also had a long tube.

Civilian respirators were simpler. The standard adult British model had a thin, black, rubber facepiece with a large, facial filter

German respirator of World War II and its grey, corrugated case with the spare gelatine-coated discs to prevent misting of the eyepieces, held in a compartment on the inside of the lid.

unit. For younger children a brightly coloured 'Mickey Mouse' model was available, with an escape valve fitted at the front. For very young children there was a helmet into which the baby was placed and supplied with purified air by means of a hand pump. Another type had a thick moulded rubber facepiece and was intended for those whose duties might expose them to greater risk. The trend has been towards the adoption of masks with the filter mounted on the facepiece and most modern respirators are of this pattern.

One other new form of protection which made its appearance during World War I was designed for the crew of tanks. When these new vehicles were introduced in September 1916 their impact was astonishing, for they seemed impervious to bullets. However, one effect was soon noticed by crews and that was the 'splash' of tiny chips of metal from the inside of the tank walls when a missile struck the outside. To protect the faces of crewmen a 'domino-mask' was designed, with a shaped metal half-mask, padded on the inside and leather covered on the outside. A short curtain of mail hung down to

Tank mask of World War I used by British and French crews. It consists of a shaped metal plate covered on the outside with leather and padded on the inside. A short curtain of mail protects the lower part of the face and the mask was secured to the head by the two tapes.

cover the mouth and chin and the vision was through a series of slits. The mask was secured to the head by two long tapes, but it does not appear to have been widely used.

In this chapter it has only been possible to sketch very briefly the wide range of material needed by the soldier. Besides the main items mentioned above there were innumerable smaller items such as compasses, cleaning materials, anti-gas gear, lanyards, first-aid dressings, torches, military issue tools, mess tins—the list could be continued but it would serve little purpose except to show the great range of material awaiting the venturesome collector.

COLLECTING, CARE AND DISPLAY

This is one field where the chances of turning up some unusual pieces is very high indeed for so many of the smaller items fall into the category of 'odds and ends'. The junk box and junk stall, community and jumble sales can provide enough oddments to make visits worthwhile. Second-hand clothing stores may well acquire odd belts, cases, haversacks and similar pieces. Better quality and rarer pieces are, of course, more likely to find their way to the specialist dealers and auction houses, but with the exception of shoulder belt plates most of the pieces discussed above should be quite inexpensive.

The majority of belts are of leather and the best treatment for all such pieces, with a few exceptions detailed below, is a wash in warm water, possibly using a not-too-stiff brush if the dirt is stubborn. When thoroughly dry, (artificial heat should be avoided) the belt can be treated with one of the standard leather dressings. Whilst damp the belt should be hung so that it can dry without any bends or kinks for these can be difficult to remove.

If possible the buckle should be removed but if there is any danger of damaging the belt then it is better to leave it in place during cleaning. If the buckle is very dirty then it will require the same treatment as for badges but care must be taken to avoid marking the belt. Steel buckles will probably require some slightly more robust treatment especially if rust is present.

Officers' dress belts with their dyed leather backing and applied lace decoration present more of a problem. The belt itself may require no more than a gentle wipe over with warm water but if the lace is dirty then one of the proprietary, dry-cleaning fluids may be used, but only after checking that it will not damage the material. Lace can become rather delicate with age and it is wise not to rub too hard. The buckle may be one of those which is made up of several pieces and these can be dismantled for easy cleaning. Heavy tarnish will probably not come off with washing, in which case some stronger cleaning solution may be needed, but try the mildest ones first.

Belt buckles: (*top*) Prussian, other ranks, *c.* 1916; telegraph troops; (*middle*) Württemberg, other ranks; Bavarian, other ranks; (*bottom*) Saxony, other ranks; Essen, other ranks.

British belt buckles: (*top*) gilt, officer's waist-belt plate of the 9th (The East Norfolk) Regiment of Foot, 1837–81; brass, other ranks' waist-belt plate of Royal Marines, Victorian; gilt, officer's waist-belt plate of the 50th (or the Queen's Own) Regiment of Foot, Victorian; (*bottom*) gilt, officer's waist-belt plate of Steam Navigation Company, Victorian; gilt, Indian Army officer's waist-belt plate of 36th Sikhs, Victorian; gilt, Indian Army officer's waist-belt plate of Bengal Staff Corps, Victorian.

Shoulder belt plates are much sought after today. They have become quite expensive and, inevitably, they have been copied. There are one or two pointers to the genuineness of such a plate but if in doubt the collector would be well advised to seek some form of guarantee from the dealer. In general these plates were all of good quality and if a piece is crude and lacking in detail it must be suspect. The lugs and hooks on the back can also help in deciding, for the original lugs were made in one piece and many of the modern reproductions have the pillar and knob in two pieces, a few even have a threaded screw fitting which is certainly incorrect. Many of the brass plates were stamped and if there are indications that the plate is cast it should be examined very closely. Engraving should be crisp and clear.

Officers' plates are usually more elaborate and are often made up of several pieces which are secured to the base plate. To separate these pieces the long securing wires which hold them in position must be removed. These pins are thin and sit fairly tightly in place; removing them can be tricky if the back of the plate is not to be scratched. If the heads of the pin are gripped with taper-nosed pliers there is always the danger that they may slip and leave nasty scratches, so that it may be better to use a small vice to hold the pin and then gently pull it clear. When the pins are removed the pieces may not come away: this may mean that they are slightly deformed, in which case gentle pressure must be applied against the lugs. Some of the component pieces are quite delicate, with numerous odd projections, and they should be treated with care. Any rubbing should be done with great care, since odd pieces can be so easily broken.

When the plate has been stripped down each piece can be washed to remove surface dirt but if this proves insufficient then a mild polish can be tried. When thoroughly cleaned each piece should be dried and then carefully replaced. Missing pins can be replaced by a piece of stiff wire. Some plates still retain the thin piece of leather which slips over the lugs and hooks and covers the wires and lugs, and this must obviously be removed. Great care may be necessary for often this leather becomes very brittle and easily split so that if there is any fear of damage the leather should be treated with a leather dressing before attempting to remove it.

Identification of the regular army plates is fairly simple since most carry the regimental number and name but it is not so easy with the volunteer plates which often carry only the initials of the unit. Sometimes there is no means of certain identification. There are Lists of Volunteer and Militia Units to which reference can be made although copies are difficult to locate.

Webbing is by its nature tough, and except for very old or particularly interesting items, they can usually be scrubbed fairly vigorously with a good detergent solution and stiff brush. Frequently the webbing may be covered with thick layers of old cleaning substances usually known as blanco. This can be difficult to remove, but gentle heat and hard scrubbing will generally work.

The metal fittings, if brass, can be cleaned with polish but the later, darkened metal ones are best just wiped over with a damp cloth and then thoroughly dried.

Leather holsters in good condition will probably require just a wash and dry followed by some leather dressing. Buckles will probably need just a normal cleaning.

German gorgets will probably respond to a wash and little more but the more decorative examples of the eighteenth and nineteenth centuries are normally gilt and silver and consequently need careful treatment. Gilding can be rubbed off so that any cleaning must be the mildest possible.

Respirators and other rubber or rubberized items will probably only need a wipe over with a damp cloth. A dusting of French chalk will help prevent the rubber perishing or sticking but if the facepieces are squashed for any length of time they will become deformed so that it is probably best to remove the respirator from its haversack.

Recording of the multitude of pieces of equipment needs to be as full as possible, detailing material, length, width, purpose and date. Many of the pieces of webbing and leather will be found to have the date stamped or impressed somewhere on the back. Illustrations of the equipment in use will be most useful. Identification marks may be rather difficult to place on most of the equipment. It may be possible to put a very small Indian ink mark at some very inconspicuous position, but, as stressed so many times, this should not be done if it will in any way mar the piece. Gorgets and shoulder belt plates should not be marked except perhaps by some innocuous label which may be tucked behind the lug or behind one of the component pieces.

This field of collecting is one which may well attract the smaller collector, for so many of the pieces are still available at very reasonable prices. Perseverance and good luck may well enable a collector to build up a complete set of equipment for any one of a number of periods.

Imperial German infantry bugle of brass and silver.

9 Military Miscellany

Cowhorn memento engraved with a variation on the badge of the 12th (East Suffolk) Regiment of Foot: the 1st Battalion served in the New Zealand Wars, 1860–6.

Despite his martial air the soldier has, throughout the ages, spent less of his time in fighting than any other military occupation. Most of his time was spent in drilling, marching, guarding and, not least, in enjoying himself. Drink, tobacco and women occupied most of his spare time although he occasionally felt inclined to pass the time in more useful occupations and then he often made things. His materials were necessarily simple; those readily to hand and his tools were also limited to such things as a penknife or a sharpened nail.

Some of the earliest examples of the soldier's art are the simple carved and engraved pieces of horn and ivory usually lumped together under the collective name of scrimshaw. The majority of scrimshaw is naval in origin, often on whales' teeth, with ships and seascapes, sometimes rather crude, and bearing a name and a date. Military examples of scrimshaw are not common; the most highly prized examples are probably the carved powder horns of eighteenth century America. They usually feature a map of part of the east coast of the United States. Powder flasks were not normally carried by troops after the seventeenth century, for paper cartridges replaced them. But flasks were used by British master gunners to place a pinch of priming powder over the touch of the cannon, long after this date. These flasks are a section of cowhorn, the wide end plugged with wood and the tip fitted with a brass nozzle which has a spring clip. Most have two securing eyes screwed into them and some will be found with the WD mark. Since these were 'official issue' it is unlikely that any were ever carved but there are many examples of pieces of horn of various types engraved with appropriate military mottoes, regimental crests, and dedicatory messages, and many carry the carver's name and service details. Gourds were another favourite for the carvers.

Even in battle the soldier found moments of peace which he could spend in making things, and during the nineteenth century there developed a form of soldier/folk art. It appears on a limited scale in the Crimean War, expanded during the Boer War, blossomed during World War I and survived into World War II. This style is usually described as Trench Art but it is very difficult to define. One definition might be that it is the utilization of military items for decorative effect. The majority of pieces which appear on the market are from World War I. They include simple items such as a belt buckle mounted as a matchbox holder, or cap badges set on to a tin lid. More elaborate are the shining, brass shell cases which were strung up as dinner gongs or used as spill or match holders. Larger shell cases were sometimes fitted with lids and turned into boxes or became umbrella stands or similar unlikely items. More elaborate examples

American powder horn with scrimshaw decoration.

World War I Trench Art made great use of the brass shell cases as with these examples.

include rifle butts carved with regimental badges standing on legs of empty cartridge cases and then fitted with an ashtray!

World War II with its more educated soldiers produced far more practical pieces. Empty cartridge cases, especially those from cannons, were converted into cigarette lighters, badges and buttons were fitted to pins and chains to be worn as brooches by wives and sweethearts. In the RAF there was a flourishing trade in brooches and rings fashioned from the transparent plastic, Perspex, used for windows on aircraft; this was a new material for most people and it became very popular, although its private use was discouraged by the authorities. Pieces of shot-down aircraft and similar trophies were occasionally mounted and sent home and these are often found on the market. This too was a practice with a long history: examples dating from the Crimean War are not uncommon. One of the favourite items of this period was a cannonball, solid or hollow, converted into an inkwell and mounted in some way.

Whenever peace came the authorities were faced with vast quantities of surplus material and there were many attempts to find domestic uses for some of it. Hand-grenades were mounted on marble blocks as paper weights and other similar unlikely conversions were tried. But the memory of the horror of war was usually too strong to ensure a good sale.

Crimean Trench Art: inkwell inscribed Sebastopol, Mamelon, Alma and Malakoff fashioned from cannonballs.

Above Soldier's gift boxes.

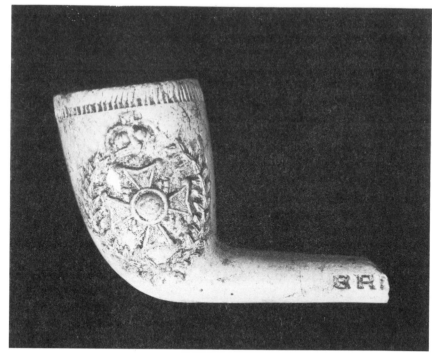

Above right Bowl of a clay pipe embossed with a badge, probably intended to represent that of the Rifle Brigade, late 19th century.

When the off-duty soldier wasn't busy carving or creating trench art, he enjoyed a smoke. Until the appearance of cigarettes in the nineteenth century he would have smoked a clay pipe, popular with the troops from the seventeenth century onwards. During the eighteenth century some pipes were made with the bowls decorated with the Royal Arms. It is possible that some of these too had a military connection but the practice was too widespread to describe them specifically as 'military'. The first pipes that can be so described are those which appeared around the 1830s and 1840s, whose bowls were embossed with various regimental crests. Specimens are not common, for obviously they were expendable and their survival rate was fairly low. It is quite possible that bowls were embossed to celebrate some battles of the nineteenth century, for towards the end of the century it was common practice to produce commemorative pipes.

At the turn of the century, when Queen Victoria felt that her soldiers suffering in South Africa needed some encouragement, she sent to the troops a red and blue painted tin, with a golden embossed bust of her set in the lid, bearing New Year Greetings for the year 1900. Inside were six bars of chocolate wrapped in silver paper, which no doubt brought some comfort to the troops sweating in the African sun. This gesture was repeated during World War I. The tin was well made of gold coloured metal, with Queen Mary's head embossed on the lid, together with the names of the Allies, and at the bottom, in the centre, 'Christmas 1914'. In this gift tin tobacco replaced the chocolate of South Africa.

Penknives figured prominently among the personal belongings of the ordinary soldier. During World War I there were a whole range of welfare funds intended to provide comfort for the troops, if such a thing were possible in the trenches. Some were public charities but others were more personal. Examples of penknives supplied by Lady Wernher at Christmas 1915 may be met. They are sturdy and have all the usual fittings such as button hooks, cork screws and a cap opener. They carry the name of the regiment on the side of' the knife. Occasionally more elaborate knives turn up but these were usually the property of officers and their value was such that the owner considered it worthwhile having their name placed on it. They may carry a range of gadgets such as tweezers, prickers, etc. let into the handle. Troops were issued with cutlery and these were housed in a rolled up, cloth container known as a 'housewife'. Razors were also issue items. The humble value of these items has meant that few survived but an occasional example may turn up.

Another form of knife which was not so pleasant also evolved during World War I. The stagnating, demoralizing, trench warfare was interspaced by raids on enemy positions with the object of gaining prisoners and, above all, information. Such raids needed to be silent, swift and secret and a whole range of practical, if very crude weapons were produced for the grim hand-to-hand combat. Many were made by the troops themselves from bayonets trimmed to

Penknife presented to British Army units at Christmas 1915. It is fitted with two blades, button hook, tin opener and spike; this example lacks its loop for securing it to a lanyard.

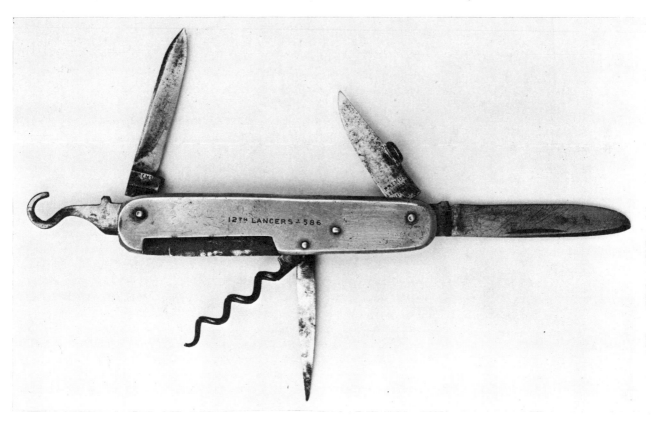

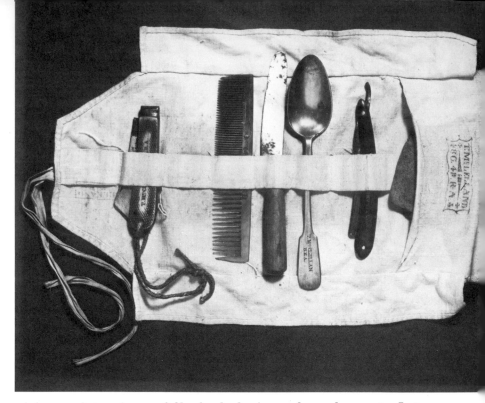

Victorian soldier's 'housewife' holding his personal gear engraved with his name. The holdall is canvas, the comb is of horn as are the grips of the razor and knife, both made in Sheffield. The spoon is stamped on the back with a crowned VR.

vicious points, pieces of file, barbed wire and wooden posts. Later official weapons were supplied, some of these are unusually vicious with large metal knuckle bows in addition to the blade. Perhaps the United States Mark I trench knife was the most eye-catching of all, for the hilt incorporated a metal knuckle duster with spikes. In World War II the Americans produced a variety of fighting knives, including one for the 1st Ranger Battalion. This had a large, cast brass hilt, and a guard which was fitted with a series of lugs so that it could be used as a knuckle duster, whilst the blade was somewhat similar to the old Bowie knife. The British Commando knife of World War II was a slim weapon with a double edged, tapering blade and a single crossguard and turned metal grip. The leather scabbard was so designed that it could be worn in a variety of positions.

In battle the soldier was constantly at risk. One possible fate was capture, in which case the treatment of the prisoner was often barbarous. From the mid-eighteenth century onwards some slight efforts were made to ameliorate the position of the prisoner-of-war. In Britain his treatment, whilst not cruel, was indifferent. As the prisoners arrived in England they were housed in the civilian prisons or on prison hulks. Dartmoor, the most notorious English prison, housed hundreds of French prisoners during the Napoleonic wars. Another very large one was at Norman Cross, near Peterborough, which was unusual in that it was specially built to hold prisoners-of-war.

Apart from his meagre food the prisoner-of-war received no money and very little in the way of clothing and attention. However, the authorities permitted the prisoners to trade in order to raise some money, though, of course, they had little to offer. However, they soon found that the British liked any form of decorated items and their ingenuity sought ways to gratify this market. Every available material was pressed into service including straw, human and animal hair, odd pieces of wood, paper and, above all, bone. Tools were fashioned from nails or any scrap materials and despite the limitations of materials and tools the prisoners produced pieces which ranged from crude to superb. The scope extended from simple bone domino sets to tremendously detailed and complex bone models of men-of-war.

Straw was readily available and was used by the prisoners in a variety of ways. It was soaked and carefully flattened and then used for marquetry, in the same way as wooden veneers. Straw was twisted and built up into patterns of high and low relief; pieces were coloured, cut and used for mosaics, box panels, tea caddies and a whole range of small household items, it was also plaited into hats and bonnets. Human and horsehair were also plaited to make rings, although very few of these seem to have survived.

Paper cutting was another form of decoration; it was cut into strips about $\frac{1}{8}$ in (.3 cm) wide and then worked into patterns which were stuck on to boxes or tea caddies. Spaces were filled in with coloured material or with other forms of decoration.

It was with bone that the prisoners excelled for this material was reasonably plentiful and therefore available to a maximum number of prisoners. The simpler items were small boxes, tobacco stoppers,

Lid of a large box with straw-work decoration done by French prisoners-of-war during the Napoleonic Wars. It is a view of the entrance to Norman Cross Prisoner-of-War Camp.

Napoleonic prisoners-of-war made this large bone model of a British man-of-war, HMS *Royal Sovereign*, early in the 19th century. Items such as this were sold to raise money which the prisoners used to acquire some comforts and extra food.

seals, needle cases, miniature toys, sets of dominoes and even packs of playing cards. Pieces such as these were for the amateurs; for the real craftsmen there were elaborate mechanical toys, work boxes, mirror frames and clock cases. A slightly gruesome and macabre model was the guillotine, which seems to have been quite popular with the prisoners-of-war, whether as an implied threat to their British captors or just as a memory of past glories is not clear! The peak of perfection was reached with the lovingly-made ship models which were often the combined work of several prisoners. They are usually between 12 and 15 in (30 and 37.5 cm) long, with rigging of human hair and sails of paper. Markets were held at the prison, often daily, when local traders and civilians attended to purchase the work. Prisoners used the money they earned to purchase food, clothing, bedding and medicines. It is interesting to note that even at this period, early nineteenth century, the prices of some pieces were very high indeed. It is known that near Portsmouth £40 (approx. $80) was paid for one of the ship models, the equivalent value today would probably be something like £800 (approx. $1,600). Today the cost would be well in excess of that.

During World War I and World War II similar work was carried out by prisoners although the choice of materials was more varied and the items produced reflect contemporary tastes. Tins were carefully hammered out into quite intricate cigarette cases. Rings of plastic Perspex inset with badges, small carvings, toys, and wooden boxes were produced. Italian prisoners of war seem to have particularly excelled, for a good proportion of the surviving pieces are their work.

Among the military souvenir or commemorative items must be included the various pottery figures produced over the last two centuries. Around the mid-eighteenth century some saltglazed stoneware and earthenware jugs in the form of a seated man were produced in the North Staffordshire area of England and some are recognizable as soldiers. Later a more formalized Toby jug became popular and the form was developed and the character changed but not the shape. During the 1914-18 period a series of wartime Toby jug figures was produced by the Royal Stafford Pottery. Modelled by F. Carruthers Gould, the series included Rear Admiral David Beatty, Field Marshal Sir John French, General Sir Douglas Haig, Admiral Sir John Jellicoe, Marshal Joseph Joffre, 1st Earl Kitchener and Lt. General Jan Christian Smuts.

Also from the area of Staffordshire came a number of pottery figures, many with military connections. Some of the earliest figures, dating from the first quarter of the eighteenth century, were by Astbury of Shelton, and these salt-glazed stoneware figures included some soldiers. One most unusual figure by Obadiah Sherratt about

An unusually elaborate piece of prisoner-of-war Trench Art. The barrel of the field gun, which was taken at Cambrai, August 1916, comes from a M.1898 Mauser rifle and the model is over 36 in long (91.5 cm).

1810, shows Lieutenant Monroe meeting his death under a tiger's claws and teeth; a real event which took place in December 1792. Among the more conventional figures are wounded soldiers, members of various regiments and, especially during Victoria's reign, many portrait figures of military figures. These included Nelson, Napoleon I, Napoleon II, Lord Raglan, General Lord Napier of Magdala, General Gordon and the Duke of Wellington. Set pieces had titles such as The Redan, Sebastopol, The Victory and the Soldier's Return.

Plates decorated with military motifs have been produced by potteries in many countries and there was, in the eighteenth century, a flourishing trade to the United States of plates bearing the portraits of American heroes.

In Germany one particular form of china or porcelain ornament flourished. The Germans liked drinking beer from a large mug with a metal cover, known as a *Stein*. Most military steins date from the foundation of Germany as a modern state in 1871, for with this event came conscription. Each of the member states was required to send its young men to serve in the new Imperial German Army. The experience seems to have been enjoyed by the majority of the men, since, when they left, many of them purchased large, ornamental, painted steins which were made to order. Most of them carry at least three main scenes, two side panels and a central one. The majority have, around the top just below the lip, the name of the unit in which the man served, and on the side panel, there may be a list of the names of fellow members of his unit. The owner's name is usually somewhere near the foot of the stein. The metal cover, fixed to the top of the handle and operated by pressing on a thumb lift, is ornate and frequently surmounted by a small metal figure, or a miniature weapon such as the machine gun.

The stein lost its popularity after World War I and very few were subsequently made although the tradition remained and simpler versions were produced during the Third Reich and among the Allied Forces after World War II.

These attractive steins were popular right up until the end of World War I but from then on their popularity seems to have declined and examples from the Third Reich are rare. It seems that a number of Allied personnel serving in Germany after 1945 were rather taken with them and some will be found bearing the designation of American units which served in Germany. A particularly fascinating feature of these steins is that they often have a concealed picture. If the stein is emptied and tilted up to the light a picture becomes visible in the base. This is produced in the manufacturing process and is known as a lithopane. The most usual pictures are of a soldier bidding farewell to a woman or a portrait of the Kaiser or the King of Bavaria. These steins were locally made so that the quality of manufacture, craftsmanship and skill in painting will vary one from another. Another souvenir which the German conscript often purchased at the end of his service was a pipe with a china bowl, which was elaborately decorated with military scenes. There were also fine, flat-sided flasks, often within a metal framework, which were decorated with German military scenes.

Military service, battles and leaders were commemorated in a variety of ways by most countries. Small tin lapel buttons were popular in Britain, especially from the Boer War onwards. Some carried the Union Jack, others the portraits of popular generals of the time. These portraits were also mounted in little brooches, pendants and earrings. They were often sold as a means of raising funds for munitions or for the welfare of the troops. Germany made great use of this system during World War II and, as mentioned in Chapter 6, there are large numbers of these donations badges, some of which have still not been identified.

There are many other items that were of the souvenir commemorative class, including military busts. Events such as Gordon's death at Khartoum in 1885 stimulated the production of his bust, with the fez serving as a match holder and his shoulder as the striker! France and Germany probably dominate the field of popular military sculpture with innumerable busts of Napoleon, Blücher, Hindenburg and Kaiser Wilhelm II. British examples are not so common although the 'Gentleman in Khaki' is possibly the best known. This was modelled by the famous artist Caton Woodville and was reproduced in various sizes and materials.

Medals to mark particular events were another common item. In Britain they can be traced back to the Tudor period, although in Europe they were produced far earlier, even as far back as Ancient Greece. Large numbers were cast or struck and many have survived from the seventeenth century onwards. The English Civil War stimulated both sides to produce quantities of them, bearing the portraits of leaders or celebrating some victory. Many of the commemoration medals of the seventeenth century were of silver, lead or, more rarely, gold. Marlborough's campaigns against the French were celebrated by several medals in gold, silver and copper. The eighteenth century saw a large number of medallions celebrating

Three typical Imperial German
bronzes: Kaiser Wilhelm II;
infantryman; Kaiser Wilhelm I.

battles and in Britain the Society for the Promotion of Arts and
Commerce was responsible for a number of medals relating to the
Seven Years War (1756-63). Victories at Quebec, Montreal and
Plassey were all marked by the issue of medals.

The American War of Independence gave little cause for
celebration on the part of the British but a number of medals were
struck in France to mark the American successes. In Virginia a
propaganda medal supporting the rebellion was issued and on 3
November 1780 The Continental Congress had some eliptical silver
medals struck to mark the capture of the British Agent Major André.
Peace in 1783 also promoted the issue of a number of medals.

The Napoleonic Wars saw the issue of large numbers of medals.
They commemorated victories, the formation of Volunteer Units,
famous leaders and finally peace, in 1815. They were of various sizes
and usually of copper or silver. One of the largest and most elaborate,
over five inches in diameter, was intended to celebrate the victory of
Waterloo, but it was never issued. It was ordered by the Prince
Regent and an Italian, Benedetto Pistrucci, the Chief Engraver at the
Royal Mint and later Chief Medallist, was commissioned. He worked
on the dies until 1849, by which time nearly everybody originally
concerned was dead and the project was dropped. No medals were
ever cast, but just recently a modern copy has become available.

The next great British military events of the nineteenth century
were the Indian Mutiny and the Crimean War and both, especially
the latter, generated a number of medals in copper or, more

popularly, white metal. Some were sold to raise funds for the widows and orphans. One such medallion was issued by Pinches of London to celebrate the Battle of Alma and is of extra interest since it was struck at the Crystal Palace, the original building of the Great Exhibition of 1851. A larger medal was struck to celebrate peace in 1856, and shows Mars laying down his sword.

At the end of the century the South African War promoted a number of issues, some of very good quality but others were cheaper pieces often with a simple red, white and blue ribbon. One such has Pretoria 1900 on one side and a bust of 'F.M. Lord Roberts VC'.

Propaganda was a prime motive behind the issue of World War I commemorative medals and over a thousand different ones are recorded from Germany alone. They celebrated success against the Allies or denounced the Americans for joining in the war: but one had a particularly interesting story attached to it. In May 1915 the British liner Lusitania was sunk by a German submarine. A German medallist, Karl Goetz, issued an iron medal to celebrate this event, blaming the British for allowing the ship to sail, knowing the danger. The British Government issued copies of this medal in a small cardboard box, together with a leaflet condemning German U Boat warfare and its consequences. It was sold to raise funds for charity. The British copy may be recognized by the use of May instead of the German *Mai* for the name of the month. Victory in 1918 was marked by a medal in gilt and copper issued by the famous badge firm J. R. Gaunt.

Two Crimean War mementoes: (*left*) white metal medallion celebrating the British and French victory at the Alma, September 1854. It was struck at the Crystal Palace, London and was sold to raise funds for the widows and orphans of 'our brave soldiers, sailors and marines'. (*right*) Wax impression of the seal of a Russian prince.

Perhaps because of the more 'total' nature of World War II very few commemorative medals appeared between 1939 and 1945; but over the last few years there has been an increase of interest in such items. Sets of medallions commemorating British Regiments and facsimilies of Pistrucci's Waterloo medal are just a few of the recent issues.

Mention has been made of medals awarded as prizes for shooting but there were other forms that such a prize might take. Spoons were popular; in some cases the handle was cast in the form of a rifle and the bowl is inscribed with the details of the winner and his unit. Other items will be found that carry this type of inscription.

Standards of the Third Reich flown on cars; both are 'strengthened' to fly in all weathers.

Yet another slightly unusual area of collecting it that of flags and personal standards. Many units had their own flag, which was flown over the camp, attached to the commander's car, or flown at the mast of a small boat. Some were true flags fashioned from fabric but others were made from a stiffened material so that they 'flew' irrespective of weather. Apart from rarities like Japanese battle flags probably the most collected are again those of the Third Reich. They were re-introduced into the German Army by a decree of 1936 and there was a whole range of different styles, patterns and designs. The full-sized unit banners and standards were either captured or destroyed, but some survived, as did many of the small versions flown on cars and similar vehicles. The standards were carried on poles, fitted at the top with fancy finials. These are also to be found in the market as well as numerous reproductions!

There are many other items of personal military equipment that may well interest the collector. Officers in the eighteenth and nineteenth centuries travelled on duty with as many personal comforts as they could manage and one important part of their gear was a chest. The military chest most often encountered is usually of mahogany with brass fittings and often combines a series of drawers. Many, but not all, carry the owner's name which means that he can be traced from the Army Lists. Cutlery sets in which the various implements fit together into one unit were another item of the officer's gear as were pieces of furniture which folded up.

In addition to all the items mentioned above the venturous will probably find other pieces which by their shape, purpose or inscription will suggest a military origin. There have been, over the years, many patents for inventions designed to help the military man, some of which got as far as the production stage. Some like extending periscopes, were of obvious practical use in the trenches of World War I. Others were less so, but all may be of interest to the military collector.

COLLECTING, CARE AND DISPLAY

Some of the material discussed in this section is just as likely to be found on 'junk' tables as anywhere. Government surplus stores are happy hunting grounds and those magazines which consist primarily of advertisements should always be searched for hopeful leads. Small town auction rooms are always worth checking.

There is very little that can be added on the care of items such as those listed above since the majority are of materials already discussed. Most of the trench art pieces are of brass and will respond to the normal cleaning. Scrimshaw and ivory is probably best treated by washing and a wipe over with a silicone-impregnated material. For clay pipes a wash will probably be sufficient.

The Napoleonic prisoner-of-war material needs to be handled very carefully indeed, the marquetry and inlay is very often fragile. If pieces are missing it is certainly safer to leave things as they are and not attempt to replace them unless, of course, an expert in this type of work is employed. Should the collector be lucky enough to acquire one of the superb bone ship models the best advice about cleaning and restoration is—don't! It is the kind of work that should be undertaken only by an expert who knows exactly what is involved including details of rigging and other naval details.

The china ornaments and steins will almost certainly need little more than a careful washing and drying. This is a reasonably safe process since the items were intended to hold liquids and oil based paints were used so that no paint should come off. The same applies to china pipe bowls. The busts and similar associated material will probably require only gentle rinsing and washing.

Recording of these items should be as full as possible although there is little that one can usefully say about much of the material. Items such as dated pieces of trench art and souvenirs could be related to the events of the time and some information about the regiment could, if mentioned, be included in the entry.

Steins are being reproduced and it may not be easy to distinguish the original from the copy. Its condition may give some guidance, or if the lithopane is of a very unusual nature this too would suggest that the piece is modern. The Staffordshire Pottery figures are also being copied so that care is necessary.

Since the cost of most of these items is very small by present day standards, there is little need for identifying marks.

10 Pay and Mail

From the very beginning armies have always had an administrative problem; no army can exist without some sort of documentation. There are numerous remains of this from the Roman and medieval periods including discharges, testimonials, muster lists, pay accounts and similar material. However, in general, only items post-dating the seventeenth century are available to collectors. Much of this kind of printed material is described as ephemera, the name given to those items that were produced for some transitory purpose, but, against all the odds, have survived.

Most armies have worked the same basic system. A recruit had first to be induced to forsake his civilian life and join the armed forces. The methods adopted to persuade the reluctant recruit to exchange his freedom for the harsh discipline of the armed forces have been commemorated and vilified in plays, documents and booklets. George Farquhar's play *The Recruiting Officer* gives what must be a fairly true account of the techniques employed in 1706. Bribery, threats, trickery and, of course, drink all had their place in the schemes to increase the quota of recruits. The unfortunate recruit was persuaded or tricked into taking the first payment, the Queen's shilling and once this had been accepted he was officially on the army list and subject to military discipline. Eighteenth-century newspapers contain many references to recruiting and deserters, and the Napoleonic period with its heavier naval and military commitments produced a substantial flood of literature. During this period there was an upsurge of patriotic fevour. Groups of local worthies would usually form a committee to start a volunteer unit. Posters or leaflets were printed and distributed, notices were placed in the local newspapers announcing a meeting. At this meeting a group of officers was elected and, after applying for an receiving official approval from London, the unit began training. This procedure was to be repeated in the 1860s and 1870s when there was a similar upsurge of enthusiasm for the part-time military life. The majority of these earlier posters consist of letterpress only. Pictorial ones do not become common until the latter part of the nineteenth century. Similar posters were published in France during the Revolution. Napoleon's rule exhorted men to make sacrifices for 'La Patrie et L'Empereur'.

During the American Civil War leaflets called upon men to volunteer for service with the army. World War I saw a flood of such posters until conscription removed much of the necessity of appealing to the volunteer. Most of the posters required men to protect all that was good; one New York poster of 1915 simply showed a woman holding a baby and the one word Enlist; accusing fingers

Documents giving permission to travel to Pierre Chevinin who served with the forces of Napoleon I. They carry the dates in the revolutionary calendar, which in conventional terms refer to 1797 and 1802.

pointed out from posters where large print stated that 'Your Country' or 'Uncle Sam' needs you. In South Africa, Australia, Germany, indeed all the combatant countries, similar posters appeared, although, since most countries then had conscription, the 'volunteer' was not quite so necessary.

Apart from posters there were exhortations to join up printed in magazines and newspapers, and often these are more interesting because they give more information, albeit somewhat glowing and less than accurate, about life in the various units. In Britain the Honourable East India Company, which had begun as a trading concern and then grown, almost by accident, into the ruling power of much of India, was in competition for recruitment with the regular army. The Company had units of the British army on loan but also maintained its own standing forces and so issued its own recruiting material for European as well as Indian recruits.

Having been inveigled, bullied or coaxed into the forces the recruit had to be documented. Soldiers' personal documents of the seventeenth and eighteenth centuries may not be common but they do turn up and are most interesting. The British Army *Small Book* was a kind of soldier's guide book, full of hints and information,

Right German pay books: Kurt Lucas, Iron Cross 2nd class, Silver Wound badge, Unteroffizier in 52nd Panzer Regiment; Anton Frank, corporal in the Luftwaffe, *4th Gruppe Jagdgeschwader Udet.*

Opposite Collection of Imperial German military documents dating from 1870–1916.

which also gave personal details of the soldier and his service. Like other documents they cannot be described as common but examples do appear on the market. Some of the British examples of the eighteenth century may even be found complete with their small protective metal case. During the American Civil War recruits might also be required to sign an oath of allegiance and this certificate also gave some details of the recruit such as height, hair, complexion and colour of eyes.

The increased size of most European armies and the increased literacy of the period ensured that documents from the mid-nineteenth century onwards stood a better chance of surviving. Pay books of the second half of the nineteenth century are not uncommon. The heyday for the collector of this material is, however, the twentieth century. Material from the Boer War and World War I is still plentiful and relatively cheap, while pay books of World War II, particularly German items, appear on the market in considerable numbers. They are very popular with a large group of collectors and as yet they appear not to have been reproduced or faked. The majority of these documents take the form of a booklet which gives personal details of the individuals, service, pay, promotions and wounds.

Right Three commissions for officers in the British army signed by the sovereign. At the top is one signed by George III on 18 June 1801; next is one signed by George VI in September 1941. The third is of particular interest since it is signed by Edward VII although made out in Victoria's name; it is dated 8 January 1901 and the queen died on 22 January so that this was, presumably, held over because of her illness. The last document grants the dignity of a Companion of the Order of the Bath to a commander in the Royal Naval Reserve.

Opposite Group of bank-notes with military associations, including: German money of World War I; Spanish 'stamp' currency; Confederate States bank-note; Japanese notes overstamped for wartime use; Hungarian notes of World War I and a Dutch note of World War II.

In the case of British officers, the commission granting them their position in the army was received from the sovereign, who signed it personally. Offiers joining the East India Company's forces received their commission signed by the officials of the area in which they were to serve. In the United States such documents were normally signed and sealed by the Governor of the State. During the Civil War officers commanding units signed warrants which promoted and authorized men to hold such ranks as sergeants.

Less common are such items as leave passes; these were normally dealt with internally by the services concerned and once used were eventually consigned to the wastepaper basket. However, an occasional example will appear on the market, probably a permanent pass, which, in the case of the British Army, was often a smallfolder-type warrant with the regimental number and/or badge.

THE NORFOLK REGIMENT

'Shoulder Belt Plate.
1830

Old Cap Badge.
1867

THE MANCHESTER REGIMENT

THE PRINCE OF WALES'S VOLUNTEERS
(SOUTH LANCASHIRE REGIMENT)

Officer's Cap Badge.
40th Regt., 1840

Cap Badge, 82nd Regt.,
1872

A Happy Christmas to you

CAMERON HIGHLANDERS.

CIVIL SERVICE RIFLES.

FRENCH INFANTRY IN ACTION.

If the recruit survived wars, illness, accidents and the hardships of a service life he was eventually discharged and given his papers. Copies of such documents were usually kept in the record depositories of the world but examples of the man's own document may be found. They usually give details and are signed by his commanding officer and the head of a medical board. Those of the American Civil War are often quite elaborate with a decorated heading but otherwise are very similar in content to the British paper. If a soldier survived the holocaust of World War I he received a slightly more elaborate certificate of discharge, especially if he was disabled; in France he might receive a Diploma of Honour and Glory. If the soldier was killed, then, in Britain, his next of kin received a memorial plaque bearing his name, in Germany a memorial print was common.

Far less common are the official returns of various kinds for these were normally trapped in official pipelines and very few escaped. They cover casualties, materials, daily strength, sickness, requests for material and similar necessary but routine administrative matters.

Two other 'forms of documentation' may be found. Most armies issued their troops with some form of identification disc or plate. Imperial German troops were given a 'tin ticket' stamped with number, company, squadron, battery or regiment and this he carried on a cord around his neck, under his clothing. US troops had an identification tag, and in the British forces two were carried, also around the neck. British troops were also issued with a bed plate which was of brass, stamped with the man's name, regimental number and badge. This was displayed by the man's bed in barracks and some bore, in addition, wording stating ON DUTY or ON GUARD.

During his service life pay naturally occupied much of the soldier's thoughts although rates were pretty low and out of his pay there were frequent stoppages for a variety of reasons so that the amount he eventually received was small. Until this century, bank-notes, seldom came his way, except in special circumstances such as sieges which, because of their strangling of supplies, were often responsible for the production of special military money. During the Sudan fighting, General Gordon, the British Commander, was beseiged in Khartoum

Opposite French, Belgium and English coloured postcards, 20th century.

Left American Confederate $10 bank-note showing a horse artillery unit galloping into action.

2d brass taken, the Manchester
Artillery Canteen and on the other
side the inscription *Quo Fas et
Gloria Ducant VIII Jeffs Man^r,
Lancashire* around a field gun, *c.*1800;
copper medallion with Wellington
bust and on the other side Britannia
and Edward Bewley, 1816.

and he had special notes made, usually signed by him, to pay his
troops; they are dated 25 April 1884 but some spurious copies exist.
Gordon was following a precedent established as early as 1807 when
Colberg was besieged and did the same thing. Venice, fighting for its
independence in 1848, also produced a strictly local form of paper
currency. Possibly the best known paper siege money was issued in
1899-1900 during the South African War (1899-1902). The town of
Mafeking was besieged by the Boers and the British Commander
Colonel Baden-Powell, had some one pound notes printed on
notepaper and signed each one, nearly 700. In March 1900 ten shilling
notes were issued and later notes valued at three, two and one
shillings were issued.

Sieges also produced a whole range of peculiar coinage which,
although not strictly military, is of interest; the specialist name for
this coinage is obsidional. There are at least twenty recorded cases of
sieges where conditions forced the commander to issue local coinage
and the usual procedure was for silver plate to be cut up and then
stamped with some identifying mark such as the initials or the arms
of the commander. In some sieges there was not enough plate
available and materials such as card and leather were used. In
England, during the Civil Wars, the forces of Charles I were several
times involved in sieges and emergency coins were struck at Carlisle,
Colchester, Newark, Pontefract and Scarborough. The coins are of
silver, cut roughly round or lozenge-shaped and stamped with
various legends. Much the same sort of procedure was carried out
when a country was occupied. During World War II the Germans
printed notes for circulation in the occupied countries—
Reichskreditkassen ranging in value from 50 pfennigs up
to 50 marks. Troops were also issued with Auxiliary Payment
Certificates—*Behelfszahlungsmittel*. These were primarily intended
for internal use in barracks and canteens. The Allies made some
copies which, on one side, carried derogatory poems and similar
propaganda. Italy and Japan all printed occupation money and those
places of horror, the concentration camps, had locally issued notes.
When the Allies returned to Europe and invaded Japan they too
supplied special forms of currency and vouchers.

Even in time of peace the British soldier could have trouble with
his cash. From the seventeenth century until the early nineteenth
century there was a dearth of low value coinage, which was eased by
issuing (pseudo-coins'. These were not authorized by the mint but had
a face value which was accepted within certain localities. These
tokens were produced by a variety of suppliers and were usually
stamped discs of brass or copper, bearing the suppliers name and
some appropriate design. Their use continued until an Act of
Parliament which became law on 1 January 1818, made the use of
tokens illegal. There were certain exceptions but by the early 1820s
these small tokens were no longer in circulation. The Royal Mint, the
official institution for making money, had finally become modernized
and was capable of supplying the quantities of coins required.

Tokens were issued by a great variety of establishments including shops and coffee houses, but, perhaps of greater interest to the troops were the inns and taverns. Some of these tokens were used in canteens and shops situated in or near the military camps; others, although apparently intended to look like a token, bear no value, but instead are, in fact, seeking recruits for the Honourable East India Company and were probably distributed free, or dropped in likely places, a practice continued in some areas up to this century. A few tokens were not exclusively for the use of the military but carried a martial portrait such as the heads of Charles Marquis of Cornwallis and General Elliott. Survival rate of these military tokens has not been very high and they are comparatively rare and therefore highly prized by the collector.

Among the thousands of soldiers that have served their countries since the seventeenth century there were always a few literate soldiers, although they were, until the nineteenth century, a very small minority. Surviving examples of early letters from soldiers are uncommon, since the number written was small and odds against their survival were very high. A fair number were written by officers, since the rate of literacy among the lower ranks was not high.

Early letters were not carried in envelopes. The sheet was merely folded over and sealed with a blob of sealing wax or gum and the address was written on the outside. There were special arrangements for soldiers' mail. Letters of the mid-eighteenth century bear a postmark AB in a circle and at the end of the century the words 'Army Bag' and 'Post Paid Army Bag' are recorded. Troops were granted privileged rates and their letters were carried for a flat rate of one penny. Letters from troops in India were given a special stamp when they arrived in England 'India Soldier' and the recipient had to pay three pence. Letters from Spain and Portugal during the Peninsular War were handled by an office in Lisbon and the practice of setting up a sort of central post office was started. During the Crimea campaign a Head Post Office was set up in Constantinople. This was the first major war in which envelopes were used. They did not generally come into use until the 1840s. The letters cost the troops one penny, with an extra charge if the letters were carried in French ships. The postmarks used were various and included a crown between two stars and 'Post Office British Army', with a date stamp. This was to be the usual procedure from then on although the wording on the postmark varied and included Field Post Office, Base Army Post Office and Forces Post Office. The number of variations is considerable but it is often possible to identify the particular depot from the various markings. Other specifically military postmarks were used for Prisoner of War mail, army camps, special manoeuvres and barracks. Special 'Soldiers' and 'Seamen's Envelopes' were available to the British forces and each had to be signed by the Commanding Officer on a special space at the side.

The German military post office was very efficient during the Franco-Prussian war, when horsemen collected mail from troops.

Copper recruiting token, Horse Artillery, and on the reverse *Wanted for the East Indias. Apply at No. 35 Soho Square, London, c.1800*; copper token, Gregory Browne tenant by appointment of the War Department, and on the reverse *Royal Artillery Canteen, Woolwich.*

Selection of stamps and postmarks.

During World War I it is said to have handled seventeen thousand million items of correspondence going to the troops and sixteen thousand million going back to the homeland. In World War II the Germans had a *Feldpost* and Italy a *Poste Militaire*. An Army Post Office was the equivalent for the USA.

One method of post which can be said to have developed as a result of military necessity was airmail, for one of its first uses was during the Franco-Prussian War (1870-1). Paris was beseiged by the Prussians and it was virtually impossible to get mail in or out. But on 23 September 1870 a balloon rose into the air carrying 125 kg of mail. The balloon floated to a point sixty miles away where the aerial postman boarded a train and continued his journey. Yet another innovation occurred during this war. Messages going into Paris were photographed on a greatly reduced scale and the film was flown into Paris by pigeon. Airmail developed slowly until July 1933, when Mr D. Gumbley, the Inspector General of Posts under the Iran Government, introduced the special, lightweight Air Mail Letter Card. When World War II was raging the demand on the mail service was enormous. The Armed Forces serving in the Middle East were issued with the Air Mail Letter Cards from April 1941, but still the volume of mail was proving too great for satisfactory handling. It was decided to introduce an 'airgraph' system, whereby the letters themselves did not have to be transported but were photographed on a length of 16 mm film. On arrival the process was reversed and the film was used to print out the letter. The first messages from the UK to the Middle East began in August 1941 and although this form of post was introduced originally for the military it was later extended for civilians.

Associated with postcards and letters home are, of course, the postage stamps. Britain has lagged far behind the rest of the world in the use of pictorials for it was traditional that only the monarch's head should appear on the stamp. Consequently the British pictorial stamp with a military content is unusual. However, Europe and America, particularly during periods of conflict, have been far more ready to produce pictorial stamps which show troops, flags, colours and other militaria. The majority of stamps with military subjects are of comparatively modern production and do not really fall within the scope of this chapter; but for the budding collector of very limited means they offer an interesting field.

COLLECTING, CARE AND DISPLAY

Most of the material dealt with in this chapter can be divided into three main groups, ephemera, money and postal; of all three the first is likely to be the most rewarding and the most fascinating. There are some dealers who specialize in this kind of material but there are not many. Items may well be found in the odds and ends or junk boxes of the booksellers and on the stalls of jumble and community sales. Many dealers will not be very concerned about paybooks, commissions, returns, discharges and similar items and are likely to relegate them to their cheap box; needless to say the specialist dealer will know their value. Larger items such as the posters have had a poor survival rate and older examples are likely to prove elusive. Examples of World War II posters are more available but even these could hardly be called plentiful. Several museums and private concerns have produced some very fine quality copies but most are clearly marked as copies. If any posters are found with traces of tearing along the bottom edge or with part of the bottom border missing they should be avoided for the chances are that they are copies with the identifying legend torn off.

Collectors of bank-notes, coins and postal material are very well catered for with many dealers and several auction houses selling these items. Military tokens are scarce but may be found tucked away in the lists of items in the coin dealers catalogue. The specialist collector may consider it well worth while subscribing to the main dealers for their catalogues in the hopes of finding the odd item. Incidentally those catalogues are often very worthwhile keeping as reference sources.

Storage of these items is of great importance for so many are likely to be rather fragile and so vulnerable to damage. They should be handled as little as possible and for reference it is probably a worthwhile investment to have the pieces photocopied. For many of the pieces plastic envelopes are probably as good a means as any, they are available in many sizes and most pieces can be accommodated. Should a shape prove just too long or too awkward it may be worthwhile making an envelope with the transparent cooking foils now available. Posters can be stored flat between sheets of plastic or, if it is more convenient to store them on end, they should be placed between thin sheets of card or cartridge paper which can then be clipped together. This method will obviate the danger that the weight of the poster may cause it to crease itself. Smaller pieces in their envelopes can be stored in appropriate boxes. But whichever method is used, a good index and location system should be built up as the collection grows, for this will surely save time, trouble and temper.

Stamps can, of course, be mounted in an album using the proper stamp hinges, and envelopes may be mounted with transparent photograph mounting corners.

Cleaning and repair are not easy and inexpert handling can easily cause more damage. Crease marks can sometimes be removed by pressing with a not-too-warm iron over a sheet of thick brown paper. Dirt may be removed by the use of a very soft artist's rubber or stale bread but, as always, check before taking any direct action. One of the biggest enemies of all paper collections is damp and it is important to store the material in a dry room. Any signs of mould developing will call for immediate action.

Foxing, which is the name for the small brown spots which will be found on old paper can be treated by a patent preparation known as Chloramine T. If the writing has faded its legibility may be increased if the document is read under ultra-violet light although it is realized that it may not be easy to locate a suitable source of illumination. Special infra-red film used under a tungsten lamp may also be extremely useful but, unfortunately, there is no way in which the better method can be predicted so it may be necessary to try both.

Records of the pieces should be as full as possible with detailed measurements, type of material, contents and as much background information as possible, relevant to the regiment or unit and biographical details of the original owner.

Identifying marks are probably superfluous, although in some cases it may still be worthwhile considering.

11 Books and Ephemera

The military life has always exerted a very strong fascination for all those not directly concerned with it. From the earliest times stories and pictures of soldiers and their deeds have always been popular. With the development of printing during the sixteenth century there came the beginnings of a larger market for military books, and printers were not slow to take up the opportunity. Much of the earliest output was fictional, and there is still today a big demand for military fiction. Few collectors show much interest in this field though some feel irritation at some of the more glaring errors committed in print.

One very popular market has been for military memoirs, which, from the seventeenth century, have appeared with growing frequency. The majority were written by officers but there has always been a sprinkling by other ranks and NCOs and the number published has grown markedly over the last century. These personal accounts can prove fascinating and should never be ignored since many of the driest and dullest accounts may include some little extra item of information which does not normally appear in the more sophisticated regimental histories or erudite volumes on the subject, whilst those by other ranks often mention details considered unworthy of mention by officers. However reports about the fighting and the conduct of the troops must always be viewed, if not with suspicion, at least with a slight touch of scepticism for it would be very unusual for any soldier to denigrate his own troops.

If basic facts about supplies, numbers of troops, transport and similar items are required then the most useful are probably the official accounts issued by the various governments. These frequently include also much valuable information about dates of sailing and landing, embarkation and a host of other material which can be extremely useful for the collector who seeks to verify and clarify details of his collection. Most of these accounts and memoirs include maps to illustrate the various compaigns. Maps were obviously of great importance to the military man. Quite apart from those in books there were many published maps showing the area of operations and these were produced for every campaign right through to the latest wars of this century. There are, of course, also 'working' maps used by troops in the field; naturally these are much scarcer. Trench maps and 'aircraft' maps of both world wars are not uncommon and are certainly of interest.

In bodies such as the British Army, where the regimental spirit was so strong, there were many regimental histories and these can supply much detailed information. Possibly the best known of the earlier series were those done by Richard Cannon in the second quarter of

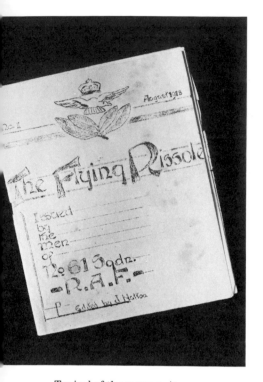

Typical of the many unit newspapers is the six-page, duplicated RAF 61 Squadron magazine of 1918. Most of the contents were topical but one verse expresses a reaction common to troops of all times and places:
Jack Sprat could eat no fat
He could only eat the lean
I'm much afraid he would have starved
If in this squadron he'd been.

the nineteenth century. They have little to recommend them from a literary point of view but they do contain much historical information on the regiment, and most volumes carry one or two coloured illustrations. With the growth of popular interest much more research into regimental histories has been done and the number of such books increases daily. Some are sponsored from regimental funds whilst others are strictly commercial publications. A more recent innovation dating mainly from this century, is the unit magazine. Again most have little literary merit but they can be quite fascinating for the insight which they give into the life and times of the various regiments, divisions or other units. Occasionally, bound volumes of such magazines appear in the booksellers' catalogues and although much of the material is irrelevant to the colletor they usually contain sufficient useful information to make at least a cursory inspection worthwhile.

There have been a number of officially sponsored publications by various governments which deal at length with the histories of various units and these are useful for general background information. The United States Army issues the *Army Historical Series* which are very well produced and illustrated.

A number of publishers have produced military magazines: probably the best known in Britain was the *Navy and Army Illustrated* started in 1895. These are goldmines for they appeared at a time when photography was in common use and their illustrations contain a great deal of information, particularly if they are examined closely with a lens. The articles cover an enormous range of topics including colonial units, police forces and equipment.

The home demand for detailed information on the various British campaigns of the nineteenth and early twentieth century led to a whole series of illustrated histories of the South African Campaign, and World War I and World War II. Again they are always worthy of close examination for although many were produced in wartime and so were subject to censorship, a great range of incidental information can be sifted from the pictures and text.

Although not primarily devoted to the military field such magazines as *The National Geographical Magazine* (United States) and the *Illustrated London News* (Britain) often gave quite comprehensive coverage to various military subjects. In the case of the *Illustrated London News,* which has been printed since the early part of the nineteenth century, there is information to be gleaned about most of the British Colonial Campaigns and conflicts such as the Crimean War, South African Wars and foreign wars from the pages of this magazine. The magazine also carried articles and comments on changes in military equipment and uniform.

During both World Wars there were many official and semi-official leaflets, booklets and magazines devoted to the dissemination of information and propaganda. One such German publication of World War II was *Das Signal* which, although heavily slanted towards propaganda, contained a vast amount of material showing troops of all kinds. Even if the photographs were posed or carefully selected they can still tell much about the differences between what the regulations specified and what the troops actually did and wore.

With a far longer history behind them were the books of instruction for officers and NCOs on the drill and movement of troops. These instruction books date back at least to the sixteenth century but in Britain it was the seventeenth century that saw an enormous increase in production. The English Civil War (1642-9) was responsible for the formation of a citizen army largely officered by people who had virtually no previous military experience at all. Numerous instruction books were written which detailed words of command, sequences of drill, movements for the musketeer and the pikeman as well as the various movements of bodies of troops. Those from the eighteenth century are fairly slim and cover a range of topics such as Manual Exercise, which deals with arms drill, and Platoon Exercises. Probably the best known of this period is *Rules and Regulations for the Sword Exercises of the Cavalry 1796*. This is of particular interest because it is illustrated with nearly thirty plates showing the various positions to hold the Light Dragoon type sabre for attack and defence.

During the nineteenth century, as military life became more and more complex, more and more manuals and instruction books were issued. They now dealt not only with drill but with the new weapons, rifles, percussion carbines and musketry instruction. By the latter part of the nineteenth century these books had acquired a more or less standard form, that of a small pocket book, usually red covered, often with a small metal clasp to keep them closed. As the century progressed the number of such booklets increased and they cover a very wide range of topics including Animal Management, Artillery, Camel Corps Training, German Army, Hygiene, Rifle Ranges, Telegraph Lines and X-Ray Apparatus. For the Royal Navy the books were published with a blue cover. Smaller pamphlets were usual during the period just before and during World War II. Many were devoted to Small Arms Training and dealt with the weapons, rifles, machine guns and mortars.

During the Revolutionary War the numerous volunteer units of the young country sought military guidance; in the early days British manuals were available but soon the demand was being satisfied by volumes produced overseas. One of the earliest American military books was written in 1775 by John Hancock, who pleaded for an increase in the amount of home produced gunpowder. In the same year Thomas Pickering Jnr published his volume *An Easy Plan for a Militia*, which included a number of engavings. One of the most popular military books was *Regulations for the Order and Discipline of the Troops of the United States* by Baron Friedrich Wilhelm Luthalf Gerhard von Steuben, which first appeared in 1782 and was reprinted many times.

The first half of the nineteenth century saw the publication of many military books in the United States dealing with a wide range

One of a set of twenty prints, *Wie die Pflicht es befiehlt,* by Erich Palmowskki issued in 1942 as a propaganda set showing the SS in action.

Selection of military handbooks: (top) 68-page British booklet published in 1914, giving an assessment of the capabilities and organization of the three armies; 152-page guide to British Army ceremonial drill published in 1912; 156-page Field Manual of US Army, 1940, on the Browning machine gun; (bottom) 62-page pamphlet printed in Australia, probably in 1914, although based on information dated 1909; amendments to *Ceremonial Drill Book*; 59-page factory-issued booklet on the Thompson sub-machine gun, 1940.

of topics, including pyrotechnics and naval and military artillery. *Handbook for Infantry* (1812) by William Duane was intended to help in training the troops. Another interesting volume, from which odd plates may be found, contained the report prepared by Colonel Richard Delafield between 1854 and 1856. This report was based on the information gleaned by a commission sent to Europe to study the art of warfare. The plates show the layout of kit, plans of barracks and details of armament. In the second half of the century the Civil War (1861-5) stimulated the market for military books and there were many authors ready to supply the demand.

As weapons and other equipment became more sophisticated the authorities were obliged to issue leaflets and pamphlets on their functions and maintenance. Booklets for weapons such as the Colt single-action Army revolver of 1873 and the Gatling Gun were produced in quantity. In addition to such manuals there were handbooks detailing the various regulations and orders governing uniform, discipline, equipment and similar topics. There developed a whole range of books of varying thickness and complexity known as

Technical Manuals, TMs for short. Collectors and enthusiasts have found these of sufficient interest to convince publishers that it is worthwhile re-issuing them and such reprints are quite common. Military demands since World War II have ensured that modern manuals are still being produced dealing with topics of contemporary interest such as weapons and ammunition of the Vietnam campaigns.

America has been less well served by its military artists and there are comparatively few prints and paintings depicting the country's martial life. One series showing various uniforms up to the late nineteenth century was done by H. G. Ogden and another, issued in 1893 dealt with Militia and National Guard Units and was the work of A. Tholey.

The camera was well established and popular by the period of the American Civil War and consequently this is one of the earliest wars to be well covered photographically. Photographs of members of the various units as well as scenes of battles may be found, but originals are much sought after.

For the collector of medals and researchers into service details of an officer the British Army Lists are invaluable. These volumes were published at various intervals and detailed each regiment with the name of the serving officers and frequently some details of their service. There are two or three varieties of army lists and the earlier ones are very rare. Less common, but full of interest are the official reports assessing an enemy's forces and equipment. In 1888 the British published a thick volume *The Armed Strength of the German Empire* which is invaluable to students of this period. Naturally the same sort of project was undertaken during World War I and one slim pamphlet of 1914 is entitled *Field Notes on the Belgian, French & German Armies*. Similar notes on the Japanese and German armies were prepared during World War II.

It is only in comparatively modern times that the morale of troops has been thought worthy of much care or support. Troops have always been eager for news of events at home and news about their immediate situation. Many armies and sections of the army have produced some sort of newspaper or news sheet. Copies of such publications are scarce because obviously they were intended to be topical, read and then disposed of, but surprisingly copies have survived. During World War II there was among others the *Red Patch* which was concerned with the 1st Canadian Division, Central Mediterranean Forces, *The Chinthe* (12th Army) magazine and, in World War I, there was the *Watch on the Rhine* for the occupation troops.

These were local, but there were also more general ones for all forces, such as *The Stars and Stripes* and the *Union Jack*, which were intended for wider distribution to the armed forces of the United States and Britain; there was even a newspaper for German prisoners of war in England. During World War I the Imperial German Forces did not have its own newspaper, but most towns issued a sort of local newspaper which contained details of casualties and items of essentially local interest that troops of a particular regiment in the field might find of interest.

There were sundry rather special newspapers such as those produced during long sieges. Mafeking in South Africa has already been mentioned as having issued its own siege money; it also issued its own siege newspaper. Copies of these are surprisingly freely available considering the limited number which must have been printed. Newspapers, of course, are not a modern idea and examples dating back to the seventeenth century are not uncommon. One field of collecting for those interested in earlier items is that of newspapers which deal with important military events such as Trafalgar, and Waterloo.

The greater understanding of the importance of morale in modern warfare led to a growing appreciation of propaganda. Most armies at one time or another have employed means which they hoped would undermine the determination of their enemies to continue the fight. With the introduction of aircraft into warfare the dropping of leaflets became a popular method of spreading propaganda. Safe conduct passes, prints of speeches by leaders, threats of vengeance all played their part and were dropped over enemy territory. Generally they all seem to have been fairly ineffective on anything but the smallest scale. During World War II the British indulged in the use of fake newspapers, while Germany produced forged five pound notes, which were to be introduced into Britain as a means of undermining the nation's economy.

Despite the very large number of copies that must have been printed the survival rate of this aerial propaganda has been low and there are no large quantities available on the market although there are still enough around to make it possible to collect them.

Equally ephemeral are locally produced items which were intended for a specific purpose, of which perhaps only a few hundred were printed. Programmes for concerts, social events, and notices from the Occupying Army fall into this group, and these are indeed uncommon. Peacetime programmes for concerts, tattoos and similar events are again rather uncommon and therefore all the more desirable. There are also the thousands of tickets, warrants, requisition notices, advertising material relating to military equipment, leaflets and regulations. A rather specialized, but still interesting study is that of British Acts of Parliament. There were many which dealt specifically with military and naval matters, volunteers and regular forces.

Just as the deeds of warriors figured prominently in the earliest literature so the representation of soldiers had very early beginnings. The Assyrians and the Egyptians all depicted the deeds of their warriors in their wall carvings and paintings. The Roman legions were commemorated on such masterpieces as Trajan's column in Rome which depicts the whole of a legion's activities. Throughout the Middle Ages chroniclers loved to include knights and warriors around the borders of their manuscripts as well as placing little vignettes of them in the main body of the text. For the average collector such treasures as medieval manuscripts are beyond reach, but there are plenty of other pieces for him to look for.

From the fifteenth century onwards there has been a flood of engravings, etchings, paintings, prints, colour prints and photographs which has continued up until the present. It is a field rich in opportunity and with tremendous scope but it is also one beset with dangers for the collector. The issuing of single, separate prints is generally a late eighteenth-century or early nineteenth-century idea. The majority of illustrations on military topics prior to the eighteenth century appeared in books.

During the sixteenth century the majority of engravings were concerned with classical or biblical themes and it must be remembered that the artists of the period clothed their figures in the costume, armour and weapons of their period although the scene might be set in ancient Greece. It is thus not at all unusual to find Homer's *Iliad* peopled by knights in armour and crossbowmen.

The sixteenth century saw the beginning of the flood of military books prompted by the dynastic and religious wars which were then consuming so much of man's time and ingenuity. From the mid-sixteenth to the late seventeenth century the output of books on military topics was considerable, one bibliography listing only books printed prior to 1642, includes nearly a thousand titles, and the English Civil War was responsible for even more. Most of these books

Print of the Battle of Naseby, 1645, fought between Royalists and Roundheads during the British Civil War. It comes from *Historical Collections* by J. Rushworth published in seven volumes, 1659–1701.

A Description of His MAJESTIE'S ARMY of Horse and Foot, and of his Excellencies Sr THOMAS FAIREFAX: as they were drawn into several Bodies at the BATTAIL of NASBIE June the 14th 1645.

A satirical view of military life; engraving after H. Bunbury, published in 1780.

contained only a frontispiece and perhaps one or two inset plates, but a few included a number of smaller pictures. Often they dealt with fortifications and battles and contained a large number of plans and maps. One of the most important and most frequently copied sets of prints of this period were those done by Jacob De Gheyn. They appeared in a book first published in 1607 entitled *The Exercise of Armes for Calivres, Muskettes and Pikes*. There are approximately ninety plates, each showing in detail a movement required for the drill of loading and firing a musket or caliver, or handling the pike. They were copied by lesser artists throughout the whole of the seventeenth century and right up to the early nineteenth century. Original prints from this book very occasionally appear on the market but they are few and far between and as the book has recently been beautifully reproduced it is as well always to check such items very closely.

During the eighteenth century the number of military illustrations published decreased, until the outbreak of the Napoleonic wars, when there was an intense burst of patriotic activity. This, in turn, stimulated a demand for suitable martial illustrations. Some of the best known cartoonists of the periods, such as Thomas Rowlandson (1756-1827) and James Gilray (1757-1815) turned their attention to military matters and produced satirical and sometimes downright libellous illustrations showing the volunteers and regulars in action. A very fine series of coloured prints done by Rowlandson and published by the famous Rudolph Ackerman in 1799, was *The Loyal Volunteers of London and its Environs* which gave details of the volunteer units. Each plate shows a member of the unit performing some drill movement. Exploits of the British troops during the Napoleonic campaigns figured in a number of prints. Probably the best known of these was published in 1819 by Edward Orme and was entitled *Historic and Military Anecdotes*.

A source of single plates was the series of regimental histories published by R. Cannon between about 1830 and 1850. There were over sixty-five of these volumes and most contained a coloured illustration showing the flags and uniforms of that particular regiment. Many of these plates were, and still are, extracted from the bound volume and appear on the market as individual items.

During the nineteenth century there were great improvements in printing technology and consequently the number of military magazines and books increased. There was also a correspondingly larger amount of space in popular magazines devoted to the many campaigns in which Britain became involved. Many magazines included an occasional print, particularly during the middle of the nineteenth century, when volunteers were prominent, for there was an upsurge of patriotism sparked off by the fear of French action. Naturally enough the country was proud of its volunteers and there are a number of colour prints showing their uniforms. Popular magazines such as *Boy's Own Paper* and the *Illustrated London News* carried occasional special supplements which included colour pull-

outs or fold outs of the regiments of the British Army and its standards among others. At the turn of the nineteenth century several multi-volume works dealing with the history of the British Army were published. Two in particular, *Her Majesty's Army* and *His Majesty's Territorial Army*, both by Walter Richards, contained a large number of coloured plates which were done by H. Bunnett, G. Giles and R. Caton-Woodville. These too will be found as individual items.

Conflicts such as the Boer War and World War I produced a veritable flood of coloured illustrations. There were little booklets containing pictures of the commanders of the British Army; there were instruction booklets on how to recognize various units and ranks. There were also a number of large, folded sheets, measuring about 34 in × 22$\frac{1}{2}$ in (87 mm × 57 mm) published by Gale and Polden which show, among other things, Insignia of the United States Army, Crests of The Royal Navy and Badges of the British Army.

The collector of British military prints will very soon become familiar with the names of Richard Simkin, Captain Oakes-Jones and Harry Payne. The output of these artists was very considerable

Engraving from the *Illustrated London News* for 22 March 1862, relating to a report of the Federal Victory at Roanoke Island, North Carolina, 7 February 1862.

and Simkin's name appears on a wide range of material, book illustrations, postcards and prints. Generally their standard of accuracy was high but they should not be taken as being totally and absolutely correct in detail.

Military painting is a very specialized collector's field, although occasionally small sketch books of the late Victorian or Edwardian period do appear on the market. They are usually the work of officers or their wives and are sometimes very competent. They can be most useful and are always interesting. Portraits are not popular with collectors unless the regiment or the sitter can be identified. This is sometimes possible and then the only criterion must be the quality of the painting itself and the price asked. Miniatures of officers dating from the late eighteenth century and the early part of the nineteenth century are very pleasant, and very desirable. But, again, the same problems of identification arises as with the large paintings. Paintings of battles and military scenes seem, by and large, not to attract collectors unless the artist is well known, but in such cases the price is inevitably very high.

Although the output of prints in Britain was considerable, in Europe it was, if anything, higher. The name of Knötel will be familiar to every collector who specializes in European prints. His output was enormous, his accuracy high and his original cards are very desirable. In America the output of military prints has been much smaller. Possibly the best known are those by H. G. Ogden. His series shows the changes in the US military uniform from the War of Independence until the late nineteenth century. There are also a number of prints and books which show in colour all the various details of uniforms. One very useful book of this period is *Croquis de Cavalerie* by L. Vallet, published in Paris in 1893. It deals with the cavalry of Europe and has over 300 engravings and fifty colour plates. Germany, England, Austria, Austro-Hungary, Belgium, Denmark, Spain, France, Holland, Italy, Russia and Sweden are all detailed. The style of the prints is perhaps a little formal but there is a tremendous amount of information in this book.

Picture postcards owe their origin to the Franco-Prussian War of 1870, when a local stationer is reputed to have produced the first cards for the French troops. The idea was popular and an exhibition at Nuremberg was commemorated by an official issue of cards in 1872. Their popularity grew and soon there were numerous issues in many countries. In September 1894 the British General Post Office finally gave permission for picture postcards to be used for inland postage only. There was a limitation in that only the name and address could be written on the card: messages were forbidden. In 1902 the plain side of the card was divided vertically by a line and a message was then permitted in addition to the address.

The majority of cards of this period were half tone but photo-lithography had been developed by German printers and rotary presses were being used more and more, opening the way to a larger supply of coloured cards. British printed cards did not really become

Opposite Cover of sheet music of Victorian period.

"The Services"
Royal Naval & Military Tournament Olympia. 138.

common until the beginning of this century. In November 1899 the firm of Raphael Tuck began to issue sets of cards and of the first thirty sets issued ten were on military subjects. Another firm, Gale and Polden of Aldershot, also specialized in military subjects and in 1908-9 they issued a series illustrating the regiments and badges of the British Army.

During World War I the number of cards published, both coloured and monochrome, drawn and photographic, was really considerable. In Britain over twenty sets of eight cards featuring official war photographs were issued by the *Daily Mail,* a famous British newspaper. Commercially produced cards continued in production and it is interesting to reflect on the differing national attitudes to the war. Those of France suggest a more cosy, glamorous, heroic view of war, British cards are more ironic, confident and frequently take a humorous sardonic view of the whole horrible business.

Similar cards were produced during World War II but many were far more restricted in that they were produced for units, a ship, a regiment or a squadron. Special cards were printed for occasions such as Christmas and the New Year and propaganda versions were printed—the Chinese Forces in action during the Korean War (1950-3) issued one exhorting the United Nations troops to go home.

It is perhaps not inappropriate to mention the humble cigarette card which also had military interest. Tobacco reached Europe late in the sixteenth century and it was largely smoked in pipes except in Spain and Portugal where some cigars were smoked. This fashion was acquired by British troops during the Peninsular War, early in the nineteenth century. The Duke of Wellington disliked the habit intensely and tried, without success, to curtail smoking. It was

Three postcards illustrating the rather sentimental, whimsical approach to the military man prevalent during the early part of this century. The photographer obviously rang the changes with his available models without undue attention to detail, for the Household Cavalryman has been given a lance.

Opposite Selection of British cigarette cards, 1900–35.

during the Crimean War that British and French troops acquired the habit of smoking cigarettes, a practice previously largely limited to Russia and Turkey, and brought them back to Europe. Late in the nineteenth century the cigarette packets had inserts of small coloured pictures. Both British and American manufacturers produced these cigarette cards and the idea was taken up by many European manufacturers.

Military subjects were very popular indeed. Apart from the purely pictorial sets which listed uniforms, famous regiments etc, there were others aimed at informing the smoker and these covered an enormous range of subjects. Many sets illustrate only the national forces of the country of origin; British ones also feature forces from the Empire and many sets covered the world's forces and warriors. Production largely ceased when World War II began although cards of a similar size have been offered with products other than cigarettes. In addition to cards, specialities like silk reproductions of army colours have been issued by British manufacturers.

Another unusual field of military illustration is that of sheet music covers. Most are lithographs, a system of printing which originally used stone but which, from about 1820 used zinc plates in the same way. The system allows a freedom to the artist not found in many other forms of illustration. This style of colouring reached Britain about 1800 and was developed there by Rudolph Ackerman. He produced a whole range of military subjects including articles in his monthly magazine *Repository of Arts, Literature, Fashions etc.* which ran until 1828.

Lithograph permits bright colouring and is a cheap process, ideal for the front covers of music sheets. There are a few rare examples of song sheets with military topics which date from circa 1745 but most examples of covers date from about 1840. The art form reached its peak around 1860-70 but the sheets were still being issued at the end of the century although they were generally less colourful. The Crimea, The Indian Mutiny, and African campaigns figure prominently in titles such as *The Abyssinian Expedition—Grand Divertiments* (1867), *The Battle March,* and the *Triumphal Entry into Delhi* (1857). There were also dedicated pieces of music such as *The Rifle Corps Polka* (1860), and *The Hussars Waltz* (c. 1875).

Another nineteenth-century military oddity is the matchbox label. These were introduced about 1829 and the first pictorial ones appeared soon afterwards, some carrying military decoration. In Belgium between 1914 and 1918 there was one brand called 'Ypres Best Tommy Match' which shows a British soldier. When America entered the war boxes distributed to the troops were labelled 'A Match for the World', and showed the British and American flags with a patriotic verse. During World War II United States troops received 'Independence' brand matches, which showed the clock tower of Independence Hall in Philadelphia. Matchboxes bearing the Philippine and American flags signed by General MacArthur and with his pledge 'I shall return', were dropped over the Philippine

Opposite Selection of postal items from both World Wars: at the top left is a propaganda card with anti-intervention slogan inside used by the Chinese forces in Korea, 1950; the book of stamps on the right was sold to raise funds for comforts for French troops.

Above Typical Boer War photograph beloved by British troops, in this case members of The Queen's Own (Royal West Kent) Regiment.

Islands. Another United States matchbox was khaki in colour and held about 350 matches. This was issued just before 'D' Day, 1944. The matches were specially made water-resistant ones. Between 1943-4 many United States camps and airfields issued boxes, each with their own special label. In Russia a set was issued for the 150th anniversary of the French defeat of 1812. They comprised a container holding sixteen boxes each showing Russian uniform of the period. From Austria came a brown and fawn label with 'Camel' and this held boxes of matches for Rommel's Afrika Korps.

It must always be the regret of all collectors that the camera was not invented at the very least a century earlier but from the mid-nineteenth century onwards it was increasingly used by enthusiasts to record the contemporary scene. Photographs from the Indian Mutiny, The American Civil War, the Crimea and the Franco-Prussian War are not uncommon: but with the growing demand for early photographs the price has shown a corresponding rise. The volunteer movement of the nineteenth century created a demand for photographs of the patriot in his uniform and there are plenty of examples to be found in the odds and ends boxes of some dealers. They should not be ignored but examined closely with a lens, for many of these units lasted for short periods and there are many gaps in our knowledge which could well be filled by these photographs. Albums kept by officers are another very rich field. Many contain some very revealing views of regimental life. There are also a number of 'record' photographs showing scenes in the South African War and the Indian campaigns. Personal photographs of both World Wars are eagerly

Opposite Victorian music sheets, dating from 1857 to 1900. These celebrate British military events except for that in the top right corner, which is French and celebrates the expedition to Syria in 1860.

collected and again can contribute a great deal to our knowledge and understanding. Collections and albums are obviously more desirable than individual odd items and if devoted to a particular unit or station can be very desirable indeed.

Magic lanterns were very popular with Victorian and Edwardian families and slides of naval and military interest were available. These are normally of glass and, of course, are very susceptible to breakage and staining, but a surprisingly large number have survived. Subjects range from 'Life in foreign climes' to 'Our brave lads in action', and mix hand-painted with photographic scenes.

The Victorians delighted in technical innovation and one popular form of home entertainment was the stereoscopic viewer. Experiments with the stereoscopic photograph began with the invention of photography but when Queen Victoria gave it the accolade in 1851 by expressing her own interest, it became very popular. Special cameras photographed the subject from two slightly differing viewpoints: the two prints were mounted side by side and were then viewed through a special device with twin lens. The most popular viewer was the 'Holmes' which had a central slide, with a twin lens, hooded eyepiece at one end and an adjustable holder. Simple, but effective, this model continued in production until the 1930s. From about 1850-65 the stereoscope was immensely popular but then it went out of fashion except for periods around the 1870s

Print from a Victorian magic lantern slide showing British troops in action at the lock of Kassassin in August 1882.

and 1890s. Among the sets of cards for these viewers there are a number dealing with military and naval topics including troops and scenes of battles.

Another popular pastime at the turn of the century was the compiling of scrap books and a whole range of military sheets was published. Recognized artists such as Harry Payne produced material like the embossed series *Victoria Cross Gallery*. Sheets of these scrap book pictures, even individual pieces, are well worth acquiring not so much for their accuracy as for their period flavour.

COLLECTING, CARE AND DISPLAY

Booksellers are today the obvious source for much of the printed matter discussed above but there are still opportunities for acquiring some of the earlier editions from the 'oddments' sources. Manuals, magazines, newspapers and similar ephemera are less easy to locate, apart from the few specialist dealers and auction houses. It is good policy to check all the books for book plates, dedications and signatures for it is by no means unlikely that the book may have belonged to someone of some military importance.

Older books with leather bindings may well need some attention and the use of a good quality leather dressing is recommended: but any re-binding should be left to an expert.

Records of books should include all the obvious information such as size, number of pages, author, place of publication, book title, manuscript additions and perhaps the titles of any other books by the same author.

Technical manuals have been reprinted and the price of an original is obviously going to be greater than for a reprint so the printing date should always be checked.

Newspapers should be stored flat and uncreased and, like posters, need to be protected by placing them between sheets of thin card or thick paper. Stored vertically they should be supported by clips to prevent 'self' creasing and before opening any portfolio or storage folder it should be laid flat. A photocopy will be useful and reduce the number of occasions on which the paper has to be handled.

Prints fall within several collecting fields. They may be collected because of the artist, the date or the content. Prices are today quite high so that it is important to be sure of the piece's authenticity. Modern reprographic processes are very good indeed, and despite assurances it is not always easy to distinguish original and copy. Even with some of the seventeenth-century books, such as that by De Gheyn, high quality modern editions have been produced. For a collector unused to the field it could well be difficult to distinguish the modern one. With coloured prints, particularly those of the late nineteenth century the same problem exists. The best hope is to look at them with a lens to examine the texture of colouring and paper. If possible a similar original print should be examined so that some standard of comparison is obtained.

Part of a larger print showing an event during a siege of the Religious Wars in the late 16th century. It comes from *De Bello Belgico,* 1637–42, but illustrates an army typical of the period up to the latter part of the 17th century.

Uncoloured prints can be cleaned and brightened by a soak in warm water with some very gentle agitation. The wet print needs to be lifted out very carefully, preferably on some flat surface, a sheet of glass or plastic, the surplus water drained off and then allowed to dry flat on a clean surface. Too much soaking is dangerous since the paper might possibly begin to disintegrate. This method is not recommended for any colour print, for the colouring may well suffer. Further cleaning is likely to require more skill and the reader is recommended to the specialist books listed in the Bibliography.

Identification of British military prints has been greatly facilitated by the publication of *The Index of Military Prints*, and every military collector owes a debt of gratitude to the Ogilby Trust for this book. It lists hundreds of prints, giving dates, identification and other details.

Postcards, matchboxes and cigarette cards are handled by many dealers and some of the larger concerns issue catalogues: but no opportunity to turn over the odd pile should be missed. Sometimes the cigarette cards are mounted in the albums sold by the tobacco companies and this adds interest. If the cards are just gummed down on to a scrapbook they may have to be soaked off in warm water. Care should be taken, for too much soaking can harm the card; but no attempt should be made to peel off the backing before the card is thoroughly soaked.

Music covers are fairly uncommon and the search may be long and disappointing especially in the case of early ones. Print and ephemera dealers are probably the best hope although booksellers occasionally have them in stock.

Photograph collecting is one of the few fields in which it is still quite possible to find a treasure. Many dealers do not consider old photographs to be worthwhile and may well bundle them into a bargain box at a fixed price. Any such boxes should be carefully sorted through: the result may be a treasure—or perhaps just a stiff neck. Specialist dealers, of course, know their stock and will sort and price it with care and skill. Booksellers may occasionally handle the odd bundle of photographs so it is as well to let local dealers know of your interest.

Early photographs have recently become very collectable and it is not uncommon for the auction houses to hold sales of good specimens. Prices are quite high, especially if the photographs are known to be the work of some well-established pioneer in the field.

Many of the photographs are difficult to date and it is often possible to allocate them only to a general period. Some, though not enough for the enthusiast, bear a date and often the name of the sitter and the place where it was taken. These can be very useful indeed in pinpointing details of uniform and equipment.

Lantern slides and scrapbook material are fragile and luck is an important component in the collectors equipment. Junk boxes are one of the happy hunting grounds and prices are likely to be reasonable.

The recording of all these items is fairly straightforward but full details as to size, mounting if any, source, date and a brief description of the subject should be included. Identifying marks are probably superfluous on the majority of the pieces.

This is part of a rare set of twenty-eight aquatints by H. Alken and G. A. Sala published in March 1853 to mark the funeral of the Duke of Wellington. This is number twenty-three and shows the funeral car.

12 Model Soldiers

Model soldiers have been found in some Ancient Egyptian tombs but it is probable that they had a spiritual significance and were, perhaps, intended to serve as an escort for the soul in the world of the dead. Miniature soldiers have been found in Etruscan and Roman tombs but again they may well have some religious significance. Early examples of model soldiers intended purely for play occur first in the Middle Ages. They took the form of wheeled horses, on whose back sat a model knight, complete with couched lance. Two such knights were set face to face and pushed together and a good hit with the lance tumbled one knight from his saddle.

Miniatures of lead were probably made as early as the fourteenth century but it is certain, at least, that French manufacturers were making them in the seventeenth century. Louis XIII of France (1610-43) was an enthusiast, who amassed a large collection of models, some in silver and others in cardboard. In Germany during the sixteenth century *Zinnsoldaten*, or tin soldiers, were fashioned from a mixture of lead and tin. Their popularity increased and by the eighteenth century they were a popular and common feature of German life.

It was in Nuremberg that the first steps were taken to turn them into a really popular item, when a family named Hilpert began to mass produce them. Early Hilpert miniatures were of tin but they were too soft and pliable for satisfactory use and various cheaper alloys of lead were substituted. As the sale of these miniatures expanded other manufacturers entered the market.

The German figures were 'flats', which means that they were two-dimensional. It was apparently in France that 'solids', three dimensional figures, were re-introduced in the late eighteenth

German made 'flats' of ancient warriors. This type of figure is the older form pre-dating the solid three-dimensional style. Today they are still produced and commonly used for war-games.

54 mm figure of a 15th-century Swiss mercenary Landsknecht; 54 mm figure of a soldier of the Continental Army of American Revolutionary War.

century, and by 1820 several Paris firms were producing them. These solid figures were heavier and more expensive than the flats but were so much more satisfactory. Cheaper versions were cast in one piece and the more expensive figures were built up in sections, torso, limbs and head. A few solids in lead were produced in Germany but the major output was still of flats. Some semi-flats were also made but these were essentially 'swollen' flats.

Britain was not to show any interest in the manufacture of military miniatures except for one notable exception in the early nineteenth century, when a Captain William Siborne was commissioned to supervise the construction of a model of the Battle of Waterloo. The finished model contained 190,000 figures! Wooden soldiers enjoyed a great popularity in Victorian Britain but very large numbers of the German flats were imported and France and Germany dominated the world markets. It was not until 1893 that the situation changed. An English manufacturer, William Britain, experimented in using an alloy cheaper than lead, and produced a lighter, cheaper model than the 'solids'. The molten alloy was poured into the mould, swirled round to ensure that a thin layer of metal settled on to the walls, and the excess alloy poured out of the mould, leaving just a shell. British reaction was, at first, cool but gradually the new product gained acceptance and by the early twentieth century Germany, the home of

Three figures of the Napoleonic period by Charles Stadden: officer of Highland Regiment; private of the 51st (2nd Yorkshire, West Riding) Light Infantry Regiment; officer of the same regiment.

toy soldiers, was importing Britain's hollow casts. This firm concentrated on English troops, beginning with the Life Guards in 1873. By 1904 there were over 100 different models. Some guidance in dating these early figures is given by details of the markings, for in 1900 the figures carry 'Copyright Wm Britain Jun'. From 1905 the labels on the foot figures were embossed. Prior to 1906 the figures were fitted on oval bases which, in that year, were changed to a rectangular base.

New figures became more and more popular and Britain's range grew and grew. Equipment such as artillery, ambulances and searchlights became available, his range of models probably reaching a peak around 1939-40. Although the emphasis was on troops of Britain and her Empire the firm also produced model soldiers of armies ranging from Abyssinia to the USA as well as Zulus, Knights, Arabs, Cowboys and Indians. The models were produced in scales from 00 in which the figures stood $\frac{7}{8}$ in (2.2 cm) high, up to HH at $3\frac{1}{4}$ in (8.25 cm) high.

Production of Britain's metal figures ceased in 1967 but after seventy years the total number must have been enormous. The models were varied over the years and many of the figures can be dated by details of construction. Despite their charm these were toy soldiers made to be played with. Britain's cannon fired matchsticks, peas or similar ammunition which was frequently aimed at the models and breakage rates were fairly high. But despite the undoubtedly high wastage significant numbers have survived and today Britain's figures fetch good prices at auctions. His models were supplied either individually or in sets, in a fine, red, shiny, cardboard box, which was a familiar feature of many homes forty years ago. Much time has been devoted to the study of Britain's figures and details of the relevant books will be found in the appendices.

Britain's figures were soldiers to be used and played with but a new trend had been started and there was a demand for models which were detailed and accurate and of a sufficiently high quality to be appreciated in their own right. One of the first of the British modellers to supply this market was Richard Courtenay, who specialized in models of armoured knights which were always finely modelled and beautifully accurate. Examples of his work are highly prized by collectors. The number of specialist artists in this field gradually increased and today J.A. Greenwood and Miss K.M. Ball, Russell Gammage (Rose Miniatures), Hinton Hunt and W. Y. Carman are, among others, subjects for eager collecting.

Present-day collectors all have their favourite makers but few would dispute that Charles Stadden stands high among all makers. His range of figures is considerable and all are superb.

The great majority of the miniatures are in the 54 mm range but there is at present a move towards larger scales which offer the possibility of adding much greater detail. Of course, they are slightly easier to paint, simply because of their size. Another change has been in the greater use of kits, when the figure is supplied in pieces, which are assembled by the modeller. Most models are moulded in varying compositions of white metal but a new material, plastic, has been gaining in popularity. There is still some suspicion and reluctance by modellers to accept the new material but this attitude is gradually changing and in Britain the firms of Airfix and Historex are making great strides in encouraging modellers to accept the change.

As so many models are now available the amount of research into all details of uniform and equipment has been enormous. Several firms issue sheets or booklets giving details in words and pictures of the more popular figures. It is possible to purchase the figures ready painted but most enthusiasts prefer to paint their own.

Many modellers like to adapt the figures and change the stance, uniform or weapons of the original model. In the hands of an expert a plastic or metal Indian can become a Zulu, a hussar or a Confederate cavalryman. A variety of commercially produced materials is available for use in these conversions but the true enthusiast presses a whole range of everyday items into service, including tooth-paste tubes, card, tops from milk bottles and a mixture of adhesive and plastic filings. Methods of painting and adapting these models do not fall within the scope of this chapter but reference to the appropriate books will provide the details.

There are two other types of miniature soldiers, the flat and the war-game pieces. Flats, though two dimensional, are still very finely

Another Stadden figure of a Prussian Life Guard Hussar, *c*.1912.

modelled and have long been popular. They are still produced today and owing to the smaller amount of material required are cheaper than the solid figures. They are almost invariably of the smaller scales. The war-game figures are again small-scale, solid or flat and are usually less detailed than the larger figures. They are produced for the enthusiast who requires an army of hundreds of figures in order to fight out table top battles. These do not really count as collector's pieces.

Besides the metal figures described above there have been models in many other materials including plaster, plastic, wood, papier mâché and, of course, paper and card. In the eighteenth century large quantities of sheets, covered with brightly coloured soldiers, were made, and early in the nineteenth century, when lithograph reduced the costs of printing the number of sheets available increased greatly. Few of the early sheets have survived but there are numerous modern sheets.

Wooden figures were popular from the seventeenth century onwards but they were usually fairly crude, being more representational than accurate. There were exceptions though, and some very finely modelled pieces have been produced, such as the eighty-three wooden figures carved by C.d'O Pilkington Jackson which are in the Scottish United Services Museum in Edinburgh.

Papier mâché has been used since the late seventeenth century, but such models never became really popular, although firms like O. & K. Hausser produced them from 1836 right up to 1939. The firm also produced a wide range of models of German troops and prominent members of the Nazi Party and, although comparatively few have survived the war, the figures are highly prized by collectors. The firm was restarted after World War II and still produces a large number of models, though now in plastic.

The United States had very few manufacturers of model soldiers although quantities were imported from Europe. It was only at the end of the nineteenth century and the beginning of this century that home-produced items appeared. Today there are a number of firms making good quality items.

In addition to the models described above a number of museums and collections issue figures based on items in their collections. The quality of such pieces is usually very high indeed. This practice seems to be spreading and some institutions are also issuing larger figures which are correctly dressed in uniform.

Models are collected for a variety of reasons including rarity, special interest, or, in the case of the better quality items, for their intrinsic beauty. Although most of the pieces are hardly old enough to qualify for the definition of antique there seems to be little doubt that they will certainly be valued as such in the future.

An associated field of growing modern interest is that of miniature arms. A number are of some age but most are modern and are the work of a number of enthusiasts working in Italy, Britain and America. These craftsmen produce superb miniature facsimilies of automatic Colts, modern rifles, wheellocks, crossbows, bowie knives, and Kentucky rifles, all copied lovingly, and usually capable of operation. There is no standard scale, so that examples on the market

French 'doll' by C. D. C. Société Mollard of Paris of a Carabinier of Napoleon's Army; British Action Man model of infantryman of World War II; Action Man of German infantryman of World War II.

Above One of the new series of 54 mm plastic kits by the British firm of Airfix. This figure has thirty-four separate pieces and is of a British Hussar of Waterloo.

vary considerably. The degree of skill, time and knowledge required to produce each piece ensures that they are expensive but it is certain that their value will not only be maintained but will surely increase over the years. These miniature masterpieces are, like model soldiers, the antiques of the future.

A few enthusiasts are also producing miniature replicas of armour. The quality varies but those from the top craftsmen have every detail correct with straps, buckles, swords which will draw from the scabbard, moveable visors; indeed the whole suit of armour can usually be stripped down, just like the genuine item.

During the nineteenth century the Victorians delighted in armour and all things which were associated with, to their mind, the romantic Middle Ages and some miniature armours were produced. They are, to say the least, of questionable quality. Many were produced in Italy and they are collectable, but for the prices paid for one of these it is almost possible to obtain one of the superbly made modern reproductions.

Occasionally the collector may encounter a weapon, a sword, a pistol or musket which seems to be of some age but is much smaller than the standard specimen. Such items were frequently produced for sons of wealthy families or for use by page boys and attendants at weddings. They are very desirable and certainly worth colleting. In Japan the Festival of Boys was an occasion when small armours and weapons were produced. These may occasionally be found in the market and are an interesting association with the Samurai, the warrior class of Japan.

Miniatures of a different kind were the mementoes popular during and after World War I. There were many varieties, including small copies of steel helmets fashioned as inkwells or powder boxes. At about this period there was also a spate of small china ornaments with a military connection, they were very similar to the small souvenirs of a visit to a holiday town. They were usually of white china lined with gold paint and may be found in a variety of shapes. A very large number were produced by the firm of W. H. Goss of Stoke-on-Trent, which had specialized before the war in heraldic china souvenirs. Some pieces were simply the firm's normal peacetime products, decorated with regimental or unit badges; more than 130 army, and over forty-five different ship's badges. Goss produced a small number of specific military mementoes in the shape of two bombs, two shells, a tank and a contact mine. Although Goss was a leader in this field a number of competitors produced similar pieces. These were mostly military models such as tanks, including one which was fashioned as a money box, armoured cars, war memorials, machine guns, busts of military leaders, shells, gas masks, grenades, tents, ships and aircraft are all to be found in this series. The quality varies greatly and some are undoubtedly crude, whilst others are very fine indeed.

Military toys, apart from model soldiers, have always been very popular but few of any great antiquity have survived. Most of those which appear on the market are likely to date only from the latter part of the nineteenth century. Wooden forts, a great favourite in the Victorian nursery, occasionally turn up, as do some of the early tin toys such as lorries, tanks with rubber caterpillar tracks or even a mounted soldier, whose horse moved along with somewhat jerky gallops. These tin toys were very popular between the wars, especially in Germany, and included models of motorized infantry, searchlights as well as individual figures. Clockwork mechanisms were used to power devices as far back as the eighteenth century but they were not fitted into toys until the middle of the nineteenth century. A whole series of die-cast metal toys, were produced many of which were military in nature including some of the series of Matchbox and Dinky Toys. There are also many tanks and craft currently in production. A few years ago Triang produced a range of 'waterline' models of warships. Although not strictly toys, models of aircraft used during World War II were made for use with aircraft recognition classes. These were often reduced to a 'solid silhouette' with details such as aerials and landing gear removed and the whole painted black. No doubt all these unconsidered toys will be collectable in the future.

Toy guns were widely produced after the American Civil War and have always been popular. Quality varies from the cheap tin, cap-firing pistol to the very fine, modern, die-cast metal replicas produced in Japan.

Soldier dolls became especially popular during World War I, and stuffed, soft toys of the soldier in khaki were produced as a finished toy or as a cut out pattern to be assembled. The tradition has been maintained and today finely detailed plastic 'dolls' under a variety of trade names such as Action Man, offer a wide range of military accessories. Complete German, British, Russian, naval and air force uniforms are available, together with a number of weapons and items of equipment. Again such pieces will eventually be collectors' items.

Military games have long been popular. Some are basically a shooting game including missile weapons and target, such as the American Soldier Company version called 'At the Front', which included a toy pistol to shoot the troops. Following World War II there have been a number of far more complex board games involving all manner of complicated rules and decisions by the player.

There is no doubt that the fringe items such as Dinky toys and games have only a comparatively small following of collectors at the moment. But if trends in other areas of antiques are any guide then they will certainly become more popular.

COLLECTING, CARE AND DISPLAY

The model soldier enthusiast is well catered for today for there are many first-class firms supplying models which range from the earliest ancients to the present and even look ahead to imaginary wars of the future. There are several magazines and societies devoted to the

Above Plastic Historex 54 mm figure of a Napoleonic artilleryman.

Metal British infantryman of mid-18th century; Napoleonic Hussar with dolmen at his shoulder. Both are 54 mm scale.

needs of the model enthusiast and a tremendous range of paints, modelling materials and tools are available. The techniques of painting and conversions are very well dealt with and full details are available in many of the publications listed in the appendix.

The collector of the earlier pieces will also find that he is reasonably well catered for. Several auction houses hold sales of model soldiers and similar items, and many of the shops which handle the modern miniature also deal in the earlier pieces. Most pieces are not very expensive, although, as in every field of antiques, prices are rising steadily. Fakes are few and in general one may buy with confidence.

The greatest dangers for the miniature model soldier are, of course, wear and damage. Many enthusiasts like to mount their figures on a wooden base so that when the piece is examined the base can be held without any risk of harming the actual figure or rubbing the paint. The other technique is to varnish the figures. This is a method favoured by some and rejected wholeheartedly by others.

There are many ways of displaying the miniatures but one of the best effects can be obtained by setting them in a small glass cabinet with a strip light to give direct frontal illumination. Dioramas and set pieces are always very effective, or the individual figures can be protected from dust by means of small plastic or glass cases.

Model soldiers can be recorded in exactly the same way as any antique. Size, manufacturer, scale, details and any information about the regiment can be noted. Identification marks are rather superfluous on these items.

There are a few dealers who specialize in toys and one or two of the auction houses include such items in their periodic sales. Much has been published on the history of toys and in consequence most dealers are aware of the rarity of their pieces. 'Sleepers' are unlikely but it is always possible that some long-neglected toy may turn up at one of the odd jumble sales or on the junk stalls.

The clockwork toy may be found to lack some of its parts or the spring may be broken, but fortunately there are a number of restorers and repairers who will undertake such work. Repainting, like so many other aspects of collecting is a matter of personal preference; some collectors like to keep the pieces as found, others prefer to return them to their original state.

The miniature arms are not widely available at the moment but the British Miniature Arms Society exhibits regularly at the London Arms Fair held in April and September. Their output is limited since the work involved is very considerable and prices are high. For those anxious to acquire examples the best method is to contact the society direct. The care of such pieces is, of course, virtually the same as would be required for any miniature work of art—that is they should be protected from damp, dirt and excessive handling.

13 Police

Until the latter part of the nineteenth century the distinction between soldier and policeman was often blurred. In Britain and throughout her Empire, indeed in most countries, the soldier was expected to fight not only the enemies from without but to preserve order within. In times of crisis local officials could call upon the army for support in supressing riots. In Britain the Riot Act had to be read to the crowd but once this formality had been carried out then the troops could be ordered into action by the magistrate. In other countries such as France and Russia there was seldom such restraint. In Imperial Russia the Cossacks were one of the instruments of suppression, ready to ride down any crowd.

British people, as a whole, have always exhibited a marked reluctance to accept outside interference in their personal life, but, equally, they expected the king to maintain peace and order in the land. The most that the rulers were able to do was to set out laws which were then, hopefully, to be enforced by the local authorities.

Prior to the Norman invasion fines were the chief form of punishment and murder was not a capital crime but the person responsible had to pay three fines, one to the king, one to the lord and one to the victim's next-of-kin. All men were made responsible for each other's good behaviour and freemen were banded together in groups of ten, a tything, with one member chosen to be the headborough. The tythings were united into tens to form a hundred and all men were bound to report any crime and to ensure that any of their members who committed an offence was produced for trial. If they failed to do this then the tything and the hundred were liable to a fine.

The system was continued under the Normans. An official went on circuit at Michaelmas (in September) to hold a series of trials called the Court of Tourn. Other local courts, as Courts Leet, dealt with minor offences.

In 1258 Henry III approved the appointment of four knights by each county to keep an eye on the sheriff. In 1285 the Statute of Winchester restated the group responsibility of the district in which a crime occurred and it also started the rule of Watch and Ward. A guard of twelve men, the Watch, were to guard the gates of the town which were to be shut from sunset to daybreak. London was a special case. In 1285 an Act of Parliament divided the city into twenty-four areas called Wards, each with six watchmen. There was also a semi-military group known as the 'marching watch' who patrolled and generally guarded the entire city. Early in the thirteenth century there occurred the first mention of the 'constable', and in 1285 the Statute of Winchester ordered that there should be two constables for each hundred, to inspect the arms and armour held for the defence of the king's realm. The constable was responsible to the local judge—the Justice of the Peace—and had to arrange watch and ward, start a hue and cry after a criminal, enquire into and prosecute offences, as well as serving warrants and summonses. The job was unpaid, it exposed him to danger and it made heavy demands upon his time. Men could be excused for serving in the office of constable, normally held for one year, by paying a fine or offering a substitute, and many took advantage of this clause. The magistrate would issue a warrant and it was up to the local constable to execute this and bring the person for trial or see that they reported at the circuit court. In the event of serious disturbance obviously the local constable was totally inadequate and it was then that the army was called upon to back up the local judge. A message was sent to the local barracks and the troops were called out to follow the Justice's instructions.

During the Protectorate (1653-60) following the English Civil War, the army played a very active part in maintaining law and order. Under Cromwell's guidance the country was divided into twelve districts each under the command of a Major-General and his troops were, in effect, the police for that area. The entire force comprised a group of militia some 6,500 strong, mostly mounted. One of their jobs was to ensure that nobody had too good a time and many traditional pastimes were abolished while heavy fines were imposed for a variety of offences. The system was not popular and with the Restoration in 1660 it disappeared.

Throughout the whole of the country the parish constable continued to do his thankless job but life was violent and dangerous and after the Restoration the London Watchmen were instituted. In honour, or derision, of the king, they were known as 'Charlies'. The idea was workable: 1,000 men were supposed to patrol the streets, maintain observation and in the event of fire or other emergency to call out assistance. Unfortunately the job was not well paid and it became a sinecure for old and decrepit members of the parish whose sole aim was to avoid trouble rather than prevent it. It became a popular pastime to harass and embarrass the local Charlie and they achieved little, if any, improvement in law and order. Troops were still called upon to help when riots occurred.

So poor was the law enforcement in London, indeed in most of Britain, that men like Jonathan Wild (1659-1731) made a good living selling stolen property back to the owners. During the rebellion of Bonnie Prince Charles in 1745 the fear of an attack on London caused the authorities to call out the Trained Bands. There were some 10,000 men in six regiments and they were used as a kind of para-military police. After Culloden in 1746 the threat of Prince Charles disappeared and the militia/police were stood down.

Conditions in London may well have continued to be as bad had it not been for the efforts of two brothers, both London Magistrates. They were not satisfied merely to draw their money and their proportion of the fines but were actively concerned with reducing and preventing crime in London. The two Fielding Brothers, Henry and John, were not professional law men but they took an active interest and instituted a small group of law enforcement officers. Originally they were known as Henry Fielding's people but became better known as Bow Street Runners, and this small group, seldom numbering more than about ten, all volunteers, made a remarkable impact on the horrifying crime figures in London. The Runners were really in the nature of private investigators. When a crime was reported to Fielding at his court in Bow Street they would circulate a description of the person concerned and the property stolen. The Fieldings would swear out a warrant for the arrest of the criminal and the Runners would then do their best to arrest him.

Although the Runners had a remarkable effect they were obviously unable to contain serious disturbances. In times of serious revolt the army was still called out. In June 1780 the Gordon Riots broke out in London and for nearly a week the capital was at the mercy of the mob. Hundreds of troops were drafted in and London took on the appearance of an armed camp. The final cost in human lives was at least 210 killed by the troops. This was one of the worst manifestations of mob rule but it was by no means the only one. If trained troops were used in such situations things were not too bad but if volunteers, lacking the discipline of the regular troops, were involved the results could be disastrous. Probably the best known incident occurred in 1819, in Manchester, when a large crowd, assembled at St Peter's Field, was charged by a group of local yeomanry and some of the 15th Hussars. When their charge was over a number of people lay dead and wounded on the square.

In the meantime the government, in the face of strong opposition from many interests, had taken a very small faltering step along the path of establishing a genuine and useful police force in London. In 1792 the Middlesex Justices Bill was passed and this set up seven Public or Police Offices in London. Each was staffed with three magistrates who were to be in daily attendance and, more important, they were to be paid a salary and receive no part of the fines taken by the office. They were backed up by the magnificent strength of six or perhaps as many as a dozen paid constables; this for a city with a population of several million. Bow Street continued to be the prime office and the Runners were still considered to be the élite of the force. Reluctantly the public accepted that the Act had some value and a number of subsidiary groups of offices were set up, The Foot Patrol, The Dismounted Horse Patrol and the Horse Patrol. Most of these officers were armed with pistols and many carried a sword; but the usual weapon was a truncheon.

The truncheon was the standard symbol of a constable and the tipstaff was his badge of authority. Truncheons in various forms date back to antiquity but the majority of those surviving are usually of eighteenth- and nineteenth-century origin. As befits something conferring authority on its holder truncheons were often quite decorative. They vary in length between 10 in (25.4 cm) and 20 in (50.8 cm)

(*left*) The letters MP in gold on a red background identify this truncheon as having belonged to London's Metropolitan Police. The royal arms are those adopted in 1837 but the truncheon dates from *c.* 1850. (*right*) Elaborate truncheon from Jersey, Channel Islands. One end is fashioned into a crown and the truncheon was probably used as a badge of office rather than a weapon, *c.*1850.

(*top*) Solid brass tipstaff carried by a constable attached to the Police Office Whitechapel in London. This office was one of a group which were the forerunners of the Metropolitan Police Force from 1792 to 1829. (*bottom*) Hollow, brass tubular tipstaff, *c.*1880, engraved *Metropolitan Police Constable employed in plain clothes*. It was carried as a means of identification in the same way as a modern warrant or identity cards.

and those intended to be used primarily as a weapon were usually much plainer. The decoration on the truncheons is extremely varied but most have a base colour of black or dark blue whilst the coat of arms, district name or other applied decoration is usually bright and of a fairly high standard. Identification can be a problem for, like the volunteer shoulder belt plates, often no more than the initials are given and these may refer to a town, a village or a parish so that the number of possibilities is depressingly large. Whilst the majority of truncheons are cylindrical with perhaps just a slight widening towards the tip, some are more elaborate with one end carved as a crown. Others have a metal end and a few were made in the form of a flail with a central leather hinge.

Truncheons ordered in bulk to meet a particular emergency such as a forthcoming political meeting, were invariably simple and plain. The custom of painting truncheons continued right up to the latter part of the nineteenth century. Examples bearing dates as late as the 1920s were, as a rule, made for civic functions.

Truncheons were one form of authority, the other was the tipstaff, which was frequently merely a short truncheon. Most of the earlier examples are of wood, with a tapering shaft and a thicker, cylindrical section at the top. During the nineteenth century a whole range of tipstaffs were produced, some entirely of metal, others part wood and part metal. Tipstaffs were sometimes given as a mark of respect or remembrance and such are inscribed with some dedication. They frequently include the name of the donor or recipient and often the place and the date of presentation. A few are of silver and may be found complete with their velvet-lined presentation case.

It is often claimed that tipstaffs were used to carry the warrant, the paper giving the constable authority to arrest. It is difficult to know quite where this idea grew up but it is suspect for a variety of reasons. Most of the tipstaffs are solid and could, therefore, hold nothing. Some which do unscrew might possibly hold a warrant, but surviving warrants show no signs of having been rolled as they would have been in order to fit into the body of the tipstaff. It is also difficult to see why it should be necessary to put the warrant inside the tipstaff. The business of unscrewing the tipstaff, removing the warrant and, opening it to show the offender would have taken too long, possibly giving the prisoner time and opportunity to make off.

At the base of the truncheon handle there is often imprinted the name of the supplier. Tipstaffs are less often marked although some makers supplied both truncheons and tipstaffs and occasionally the maker's name may be found impressed on the metal part of the tipstaff.

The situation in London showed little or no signs of improvement as far as law and order were concerned. In 1798 one of the magistrates from the police courts, Patrick Colquhoun, was approached by West Indian merchants who suffered heavily from the depredations of the river pirates, and as a result of this meeting, he set up the Water Police. The rate of pilferage dropped dramatically.

Sir Robert Peel, the Home Secretary, knew that a full, professional police force was the only answer. In 1786 The Dublin Police had been formed and they had shown their capability. Peel was determined to introduce a similar force to London but he had not reckoned on the strong opposition that he would meet. By dint of persuasion and bullying he was able to get his Bill passed and in September 1829 the Metropolitan Police was formed and the New Police became a fact. About 3,000 men were employed at a wage of nineteen shillings (95p, $1.90) a week. The uniform was specifically non-military, with a strengthened top hat, a blue frock coat with a high neck and drill trousers and boots. Their appearance was greeted not with enthusiasm but with scorn, ridicule and downright hostility. Some of this criticism was justified for a number of the men had seen the job as a fine opportunity to make an easy living and many were dismissed in the first few months for drunkenness. Despite this handicap the force gradually established a reputation for itself. The men were not armed: the only equipment carried was a wooden rattle, the head weighted by small lead inserts, and this was sprung to summon assistance. The only weapon was a wooden truncheon carried in a leather truncheon case suspended from a black leather waist belt. Later versions of the truncheon case were spring loaded so that when the top was opened a spring at the base pushed the truncheon upwards and so offered a ready grip for a quick withdrawal. Cutlasses were also available although these were not normally carried. The old watchmen, parish constables and watch were pensioned off and the old system disappeared. The old police offices of 1792 continued but they became police courts until 1839.

The numbers of the police increased and despite hostility and opposition the success of the force was such that provincial magistrates were unable to ignore it. In 1839 the Permissive Act was passed which gave Justices of the Peace the right to set up a paid police force in their own county. A number took advantage of this fact and created their own police forces but most of the Justices of Peace felt that the expense was unjustified so the Act was not really successful. In 1856 the Rural Police Act, The Obligatory Act, was passed which placed an obligation on the authorities to create a professional force so that the majority of British police forces date from this period.

Most armies have had their own special police forces. In the British army the military police have long been known as the Redcaps for those on duty have a red cover over the top of their caps. There has been an official known as the Provost Marshall in the British Army since the sixteenth century and he has always been responsible for enforcing the law among the troops. He obviously had staff to help him and in 1809 the Corps of Mounted Guards was raised and they also had some police duties in addition to interpreting and delivering dispatches. In 1813 the Staff Corps of Cavalry was formed and one of their tasks was to assist the Provost Marshall.

During the nineteenth century there were Military policemen as well as Garrison police who were local to specific military areas. In 1855 a branch of Mounted Police was formed which was designated the Corps of Military Mounted Police in 1877 and in 1885 the Corps of Military Foot Police was raised. In 1928 both were united into the Corps of Military Police.

The middle period of the nineteenth century was one of change for the Metropolitan Police Force in particular, the old top hat was abandoned and replaced by the helmet, the rattle was replaced by a whistle and the truncheon case was abolished. This last move was welcomed by the constables for it is on record that the truncheon case was a thorough hindrance, getting between the men's legs and tripping them up when chasing suspects: it also provided a very convenient holding point for an assailant. The truncheon disappeared from view and was carried in a long narrow pocket in the right hand trouser leg. From the 1860s onwards there were no major changes in the uniform or equipment of the London policeman until a collar and tie were introduced and the old high collar abandoned.

The success of the Metropolitan Police and the fame of its officers spread over great areas of the world. The records of Scotland Yard at this period contain numerous requests from parts of the British Empire asking for the loan or transfer of London police officers to assist in the formation of their own police forces.

The British system of police was often exported, as those who emigrated took the basic idea with them. However, a number of forces were created in situations and areas which were virtually on a war footing and this meant that many of the forces were of a para-military nature. In the eighteenth and early nineteenth century Australia had a very high percentage of criminals who had been transported from England and a number of volunteer groups were formed to assist in maintaining law and order. In 1825 the Mounted Police were formed and in 1839 the Border Police were created, whose job was to deal with any trouble from the natives.

The discovery of gold raised a great many problems and was responsible, in December 1854, for the only battle to be fought on Australian soil. This was at the famous 'Eureka Stockade', when 124 policemen and colonials, supported by 152 men of the 12th and 14th Regiments, set out to attack the gold miners who had rebelled over the licensing laws. It was not by any standards a very serious affair

although some thirty to forty men were killed. Today there is a Commonwealth Police Force concerned with enforcing the Commonwealth Laws rather than State ones and they are also responsible for the territories of Papua and New Guinea.

In New Zealand the first general constabulary was created in 1846 but the provinces were able to control the men. In 1867 a National Police Force was raised under the Armed Constabulary Ordnance but again they were essentially a para-military force. It was in 1886 that the islands were given a national civil police force.

In Canada there were several smaller forces but the most famous is the Royal Canadian Mounted Police which was formed in 1873 as the North West Mounted Police, essentially a para-military force. Their job was to control the Indians and they had to police enormous areas which they did very satisfactorily. On occasions they still wear the ceremonial uniform of red jacket, breeches and campaign hat. During the South African War the Second Canadian Mounted Rifles was composed of 245 members of the force. The name was changed to The Royal Canadian Mounted Police in 1920. There are, in addition to the RCMP, a number of provincial forces and municipal forces throughout Canada. The position is not dissimilar from that in the United States.

It is interesting to note that in many ways the American system parallels that in force in Britain until the nineteenth century. Many of the police officers are elected to their posts and are therefore political appointments, something which the British force has

Folding coloured plate from *Boy's Own Paper* showing some of the varied uniforms of the world's police forces at the turn of the century.

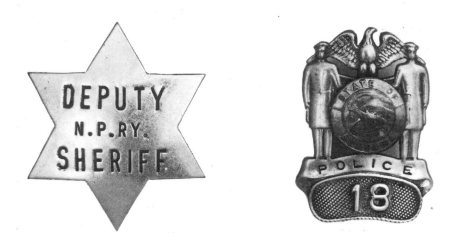

American police badges: (*top*) gilded
badge of Police Commissioner of
Winchester, Mass., *c*.1935; white
metal badge of Deputy Sheriff of
Northern Pacific Railway; cap badge
of Alabama Police; (*bottom*) breast
badge of patrolman of State of
Missouri.

always managed to avoid. There are many police forces throughout
the whole of the United States and they all have their own uniforms
and badges. The forces fall into five main groups; Federal
Government Forces (Treasury, FBI and Post Office), the State police
forces, sheriffs and deputies for the counties and the police forces of
the towns and cities. There are also hundreds of separate
independent forces making a total of over 40,000 separate police
agencies. 15,000 villages, boroughs and incorporated towns of the
USA have police forces, some of them very small. One of the best
known is the famous Texas Rangers, founded in 1823 by a citizen,
Stephen Austin, who hired ten volunteers. It is still a very small
force numbering only seventy men. In 1874 they were split into two
groups, one to patrol and deal with the bandits along the Rio Grande
and the other to be a Frontier battalion to suppress cattle thefts. In
1935 they were placed under the control of the Texas Department of
Public Safety.

Other famous forces are The Pennsylvanian State Police which
was formed in 1908, the Californian Highway Patrol, 1929, and The
New York State Police, 1917. The largest city force in the USA is the
New York Police Department. This was formed in 1845 but uniforms
were not introduced until 1853.

Every country in the world has at least one police force, whilst
some, like the United States, have very large numbers of them. Each
has its own badge and the collecting of police badges has become very
popular indeed and there is now a considerable traffic in them. In
Britain many of the forces wear the large, cork helmet and these have
the helmet plate which is not greatly different from those worn on the
1879 army helmet. They have a sunburst and some sort of centre
device bearing the county arms or the name of the police force.
These plates are mostly die-stamped and fixed to the helmet by lugs.
The variety of patterns is very considerable and examples are not
difficult to obtain. In most forces inspectors and ranks above wear a
flat cap, as do constables in cars, and these caps have a different,

British and Colonial police badges:
(*top*) silver star of Federated Malay
States Police, 1926; helmet plate
worn by Metropolitan Police, 1938–52;
white metal cap badge of the East
Suffolk Police; (*bottom*) helmet plate
worn up to the mid-1930s by constables
of the Metropolitan Police; helmet
plate of the City of London Police;
Inspector's helmet plate of Royal
Irish Constabulary worn until 1922.

Handcuffs of a design which remained largely unaltered throughout the 19th century. These pairs date from the middle of the century and were opened by means of a screw key.

smaller form of badge. There is also the Special Constabulary which is a part-time volunteer force and members have their own badges of which there have been various patterns. Some, but not all of the forces also have lapel badges.

In the United States the vast majority of officers wear flat caps and although it is obviously impossible to do more than generalize over such an enormous number of forces, most wear a breast badge which is usually shield-shaped, with a number, and perhaps an indication of rank on it and probably the name of the force. This is worn clipped to the breast of the shirt or jacket and there is also a cap badge of a different design. In addition to this most of the forces wear shoulder flashes, large embroidered insignia, which are stitched to the top of the arm or the coat or shirt and, obviously, the number of different designs and patterns is really quite considerable. During World War II some of the military police forces wore specially-painted steel helmets—the United States wore white—as well as a variety of arm-bands bearing many cryptic abbreviations such as RTO (Rail Transport Officer).

In addition to badges there is a great deal of interest in the collecting of police helmets and hats but their acquisition is not always easy. It can be of great help if contact can be made with a member of one of the police forces for there is an international camaraderie and, in fact, an International Police Association and quite often swops and purchases can be arranged. The same applies, of course, to badges and even parts of uniforms. There is, however, understandably, a certain reluctance on the part of many authorities to part with uniforms and hats for fear that they should fall into the wrong hands, but they do turn up on the market. Belts are popular and in the case of the many forces of a para-military nature these are quite complex with handcuff cases, containers for chemical agents, revolver holsters and truncheons.

In addition to uniform and equipment there is a great deal of ephemera. In Britain early warrants authorizing the arrest or transport of people may turn up and there are a large number of books devoted to the early history of the police as well as quite a number of official publications dealing with different aspects of police work.

There are pieces of equipment that can be collected such as handcuffs, and these too are commonly found on the market. Some of these may be found to carry military markings including the BO sign or the abbreviated title of a unit.

It must be remembered that quite a number of the early forces such as the British South Africa Police were of a para-military nature and therefore it is not uncommon to find medals, particularly of the latter part of the nineteenth century, awarded to members of the various police forces for they often served in local campaigns. There are also a number of British Commemorative medals awarded to officers on duty at the Coronation and Jubilee parades. There was one for 1887, one for 1897, one for the coronation of Edward VII and one for each of the subsequent coronations. There are also long-service medals both for regular and special police. In 1900, when Queen Victoria visited Ireland, the Dublin Metropolitan police who were on duty at the time were issued with a medal in commemoration of this event.

The collecting of police material is an expanding interest and, because the items are still comparatively cheap, one that will tend to expand more as prices in other fields rise. There are gaps in present day knowledge about many of the details of the various forces and there is a great need for a definitive book on police material.

COLLECTING, CARE AND DISPLAY

British police badges are in approximately the same position as military badges were some ten of fifteen years ago. Nobody is producing fakes and consequently all badges on the market are genuine and they are still comparatively cheap. There have been one or two occasions when a local police force have claimed that the sale of these badges is in contravention of the Police Act, which indicates that all police equipment is 'restricted'. But so far this attitude has not been stressed so that it seems unlikely that a collector would find himself in trouble over this matter. Single badges can be found in many of the smaller general antique shops, those of the reigns of George V, George VI and Elizabeth II are not uncommon, but Edwardian and Victorian ones are highly prized and consequently more expensive.

The biggest problem facing the collector of police badges is the lack of a quick and reliable means of identification. As yet there is no comprehensive source book dealing with the considerable range of badges available. Fortunately those from the USA are usually identified, as far as the place is concerned, since most bear the name of the Force, and this also applies to many other countries, though by no means all. Dating is another difficult matter. The design of many badges has remained virtually unaltered since they were first introduced. Several of the British forces have small museums and can sometimes advise as to the date a badge was worn.

The early badges of Sheriffs, US Marshals and the Texas Rangers have been reproduced in quantity as have those of the railway special agents. On the whole they are fairly obvious reproductions but genuine examples are extremely rare.

The price of truncheons and tipstaffs has risen over the past few years. They are still the sort of item that may occasionally be found in the odds and ends box but most dealers are now familiar with them. Prices depend very much on condition. In general, if they are in poor condition they are really not worth adding to the collection. One of the main reasons for collecting them is their painting and if this is in poor condition then the piece is best left alone, unless there is some very special reason, such as extreme rarity, for making an exception. Identification is very often a matter of luck. Many of the pieces are clearly marked with the name of the place of origin but some will bear only a coat of arms. In these cases a search of the heraldry books is

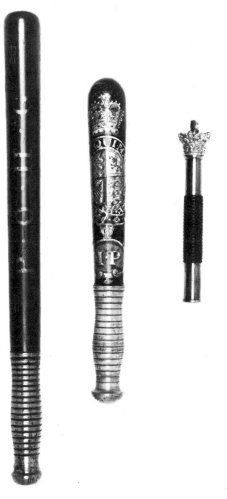

19th-century British truncheons and tipstaff: plain black staff bearing in gold letters POHG, Police Office Hatton Garden, 1792–1829; short painted truncheon bearing the letters MP, Metropolitan Police, c.1850; brass and ebony tipstaff, carried by Inspectors of the Metropolitan Police c.1860.

Pass of 1807 issued by Napoleonic French Police Department. A description of the owner is given on the left.

necessary and this can be a long, tedious business, with no guarantee of success. Some truncheons carry initials which may refer to any one of a range of divisions such as parish, town, hundred or tything and it is impossible to identify these with any certainty.

The care of truncheons is best limited to a wash with a mild detergent, after checking that the paint will not suffer. A rub with a good quality wood polish or one of the silicone impregnated cloths will then usually be sufficient. Dents and bruises in the wood can sometimes be removed by steam but this is a matter of experience and luck and the technique is probably best practised on a useless item first. A damp cloth is placed over the bruise and then covered with a piece of stout brown paper. These are then pressed with a hot iron. The steam generated should then enter the wood and cause it to swell and so close up the bruise. This technique can be used on any wooden item but, as always, check the possibility of damage before trying it: success is not guaranteed.

Tipstaffs are not highly prized: the silver examples will obviously be quite expensive whilst more ordinary ones are still quite reasonably priced. As with truncheons there are difficulties in identifying these items unless there is some inscription or other feature. Dating is also very difficult. Their chief interest lies in the great variety of styles and designs.

Early police weapons are rare and difficult to identify with certainty. Flintlock and percussion pistols may be found with markings which clearly indicate their police origins but these are rare and unusual. Certain patterns of British weapons were officially issued to units such as the Police Force in Ireland. The most common example is a percussion carbine, which has a bayonet with a spring-locking device: 209 flintlock carbines were ordered in 1840 for the Revenue Police. For officers of the Irish Constabulary serving in plain clothes, a simple, almost crude percussion pistol was produced in 1847-8. They bear only the word 'Tower', and usually the date 1848, but no 'police' marking. Colt percussion revolvers were issued to a number of the Mounted Staff Corps and certain of the police forces of Britain but only on a limited scale. In Britain, police have seldom carried firearms, but some are usually held at the local station. Early this century a Webley automatic was officially adopted and examples of these, bearing the letters MP (Metropolitan Police) do appear on the market. But they are, of course, modern cartridge weapons and in Britain require a firearms certificate.

In the United States most forces do not specify a standard weapon. Consequently modern weapons of all types are carried: they do not carry any special markings to distinguish them as official police weapons.

Many swords are described in auction catalogues as being British police swords of the nineteenth century. This description is usually applied to a slightly curved, short sword, with a brass or steel stirrup hilt. Some were indeed carried by the nineteenth-century police but they were also supplied to a variety of civil and commercial concerns and they cannot, therefore, all be ascribed to the police unless so marked in some way. Those which were carried by police and warders in prisons often have a name etched onto the flat of the blade. The sheath is usually of black leather with steel or brass fittings: these may also be found to carry engraved details of their service.

Handcuffs and similar restraining devices often appear among the dealers' stock. Some bear dates but otherwise they are very difficult to identify with certainty for the design has altered little in the past century. Most of the very early fetters were not locked but were rivetted in place and some had separate padlocks. The most common pattern of British handcuffs has a screw-type key which is inserted into the pivotted section of the cuff and turned to lock them. Lacking the key the handcuffs have little to recommend them unless they are of some very unusual pattern. There are three main styles: heavy, light and figure of eight; the heavy and light have a small chain joining the two wrist pieces whilst the figure of eight opens on a central hinge. Modern ones usually have a ratchet and key locking device and are fairly common, since they are readily available from many firms.

Police forces have been featured in all the usual media such as cigarette cards, and forces such as the British, Italian and Royal Canadian Mounted Police have often been featured on postcards. The *Boy's Own Paper* and the *Navy and Army Illustrated* carried articles on various police forces, including some of the old colonial forces. Most were well illustrated including one or two colour plates.

Books on the police are very common but, unfortunately for the collector, the majority are concerned with the job rather than the details of uniform and equipment. Useful references may occur in the text but they must be searched for. In Britain a number of local forces have celebrated their centenaries and have issued histories, often with numerous old photographs. Circulation of these pamphlets has been limited and they are rather difficulte to locate. Some of the early 'memoirs' are often the most rewarding to comb for tit-bits of information.

During the eighteenth and nineteenth centuries there was a great deal of public correspondence on the question of law and order and among this wealth of material there are several which give details of various police activities. Rarer, but more desirable, are the instruction books issued to units of the police. Posters calling upon the public to assist the law, and reward notices are likewise uncommon, although numbers have been reproduced and some 'created'.

Crime has always exercised a fascination for the reading public and details of various crimes have always been popular. In Britain there have been a series of 'Newgate Calendars' which are collections of brief reports of trials. The earlier editions are of particular interest and some were illustrated with fine line engravings.

The care and display of these police items is, of course, no different from the equivalent military items.

14 Naval Collecting

Naval buttons showing two variants of the anchor, plain and fouled, a device used by many navies.

Although there is obviously a difference between the navy and army, as far as collectors are concerned the two are rather lumped together under the general heading of militaria. There are far more collectors interested in military than in naval items and obviously in a book such as this the emphasis has to be on the military side. Interest in naval material is just as keen but the number of collectors is smaller. The situation is perhaps explained by the fact that the range of material is generally more limited and the opportunities are consequently more restricted. Uniform throughout the Royal Navy, in fact most navies of the world, is surprisingly similar. The changes during the centuries have been comparatively slight and apart from the very early pieces there is not a great deal of interest in naval uniforms as a whole.

Naval uniform lagged behind that of the army. Before the seventeenth century civilian dress was standard on board ship, apart from a few special crews. The officers began to adopt a formal uniform around the mid-eighteenth century; as a general rule the coat was of blue with white facings. High-ranking officers naturally had extensive decoration in the way of gold lace and rank distinctions were indicated by minor variations such as the spacing of button holes. Epaulettes were introduced in 1795 and the design indicated rank—an admiral had two gold epaulettes each with three silver stars, a commander had one plain epaulette on his left shoulder. One common item of naval gear which may be found on the market is the japanned case, which holds the cocked hat, epaulettes and belt worn by so many naval officers.

In 1825 the *Description of Uniform, which in pursuance of His Majesty's pleasure, is to be worn by officers of the Royal Navy* illustrated the tendency towards a far more sober, restrained uniform, with a type of frock coat and ordinary trousers forming the basis. Epaulettes were worn by more ranks and the cuffs were used to indicate rank by rings, buttons and embroidered panels. Shoulder straps could also indicate rank.

Officers' hats of the eighteenth century were usually three-cornered, although of slightly differing styles and there was an increasing use of the flatter, cocked hat for certain officers. In 1827 a plain round hat, rather like a top hat, was authorized for certain warrant officers and in 1856 they were given the peaked cap which commissioned officers had had from the 1820s. Seamen wore a form of straw hat known as a sennet hat with the No. 1 Dress until 1927. The round cap was also worn and in 1868 cap ribbons with the ship's name embroidered on them were introduced to replace the old practice of painting on the names.

Japanned metal box for shoulder boards, hat and belt of a British naval officer. The telescope of brass and mahogany is typical of 18th- and 19th-century examples.

Sword belts were graded according to rank and varied over the years. In 1829 officers wore a black leather frog waist belt but 1832 saw the introduction of a gold embroidered waist belt—flag officers had acorn and oak leaf decoration, captains and commanders three gold lines and lieutenants two. Undress belts were still of black patent leather.

Distinctions of trade—signaller, stoker, armourer, telegraphist, gunner and numerous others—were made by arm badges. Cap badges were fairly standard unlike those of the army.

Officers of the Royal Navy Reserve and the Royal Naval Volunteer Reserve had rank distinctions which differed in detail from those of regular officers.

Naval buttons lack the variety of those of the army and the majority carry only the anchor with a cable twisted around the shank—the fouled anchor. Rank was indicated on some by extra decoration such as oak leaves and crowns.

Weapons for the navy were seldom different from those of the army although in the case of swords there were special patterns peculiar to the Royal Navy. Certainly by 1805 there was a regulation pattern sword with a straight blade, ivory grip and a lion's head pommel. In 1827 the Royal Navy adopted a sword with a solid half basket guard and a blade strengthened by a rib running along its back edge: but in 1847 a flat blade was adopted. Early in the eighteenth century the

Miniature of Lady Hamilton by S. Shelley, mounted in a locket, and worn by Lord Nelson.

Lloyds Patriotic Fund £100 sword and
sheath presented to the Captain of
HMS *Britannia*, Charles Bullen, for
his service at the Battle of Trafalgar,
1805.

ordinary seaman had a fairly crude, but substantial cutlass with
broad, rigid blade and a simple guard, although there were changes
later. Dirks were short, dagger-like weapons carried by many officers,
although popular belief arms only the midshipman with them.
Eighteenth-century and early nineteenth-century examples are often
quite delicate, with blades blued and gilt and hilts of turned ivory.

In 1803 it was agreed by the Lloyds Patriotic Fund that swords
should be presented to those who performed some deed of particular
note. There were three types of sword, graded in value £30, £50 and
£100 (approx. $60, $100 and $200). After Trafalgar 1805 a special £100
pattern was given to the captains who served in the battle. These
swords were similar to the Light Dragoon pattern of 1796 with a
broad, slightly curved blade which was blued and gilt and carried a
description detailing the action for which it was presented.
Decoration on the hilt and scabbard was very florid. Since only 176
were ever presented they are extremely rare and very expensive.

Flintlock pistols for the Royal Navy of the late eighteenth and
early nineteenth century are recognizable by the belt hook, which is
a flattened bar set on the left hand side of the stock. This was thrust
under the belt so that the pistol hung ready for use.

Apart from the specifically naval medals already mentioned—including the Naval General Service (1793-1840) with its
231 bars, there are Long Service and Good Conduct medals first
instituted in 1831 by William IV, Naval Engineers Medal (1842-6),
Naval Good Shooting Medal (1903-14) and the Naval General Service
Medal (1915-64). In addition there are many commemorative naval
medals celebrating such events as the Anglo-Dutch wars of the
seventeenth century, battles with the French and voyages around the
world.

Navigation instruments are rather a specialist taste as are such
items as telescopes, although there are collectors who specialize in
the various patterns.

Scrimshaw with a specific naval connection is uncommon since
most of it appears to be the work of merchant seamen; but pieces
bearing names of naval ships do come onto the market.

There are a number of specifically naval china ornaments dating
from World War I mostly produced by the firm of W. H. Goss who
specialized in this type of ornament. The range of naval ornaments
manufactured by the other British firms includes pieces decorated
with the crests of famous warships, models of battleships,
submarines, a contact mine, Admiral Jellicoe and cannon. Some of
the Victorian Staffordshire figures are of naval personalities such as
Admiral Blake and Lord Nelson. Some of the early Toby jug figures
are apparently of midshipmen and seamen of the Napoleonic period.

Ship models are fascinating and, as already mentioned, the
prisoner-of-war bone models are extremely expensive. Other models
were made by both Royal Navy and Merchant Seamen and
occasionally these appear on the market but they are far from
common. The vast majority of ships in bottles are of modern

Part of a British naval inventory of stores on board HMS Edgar in 1801, witnessed by three independent gunners from other ships of the British Navy.

manufacture and do not merit a great deal of attention.

In the field of ephemera there are not nearly as many opportunities as for military enthusiasts but there are commissions and naval wills of the Napoleonic and later periods. Unfortunately it is not as easy to trace details of a person in the navy since lists of naval officers are not quite so readily available as those for the army. There are also muster rolls for the ships which can be referred to but the job is not as simple as for the army. One specifically naval piece of ephemera of particular interest is the list of the stores carried by a ship.

There are numerous paintings of seascapes and naval battles and, on the whole, they are more popular than an equivalent military picture, possibly because it is often possible to identify the particular ships. Naval prints are not quite so plentiful as for the army. There are a fair number of prints of ships but only a minority are concerned with the navy and fighting ships. Ackerman did some prints showing uniforms and George Cruikshank also did a number of cartoons on naval subjects.

Above Will made by William Frampton who served on several British ships but who was, at the time of making the will, a patient in hospital. The other will is that of Lt John Rutherford serving on the Rock of Gibraltar.

There are many books dealing with the story of ships, naval life, navigation and the sea but again the total number is far less than those dealing with the army. There are a few, published in the nineteenth century, which are extremely useful in providing general background information—one such is Captain J. Boyd's *Manual for Naval Cadets*, 1860. There are also a number of Naval annuals giving full details of the various ships in the Royal Navy. For late nineteenth-century enthusiasts the *Navy and Army Illustrated* will prove most useful.

Postmarks and letters of the Royal Navy are of interest and it seems that special naval post offices were set up at the main ports from an early date. In time of war it was important not to reveal a ship's position and letters were cancelled with a circle enclosing the date and 'Fleet Post Office' or 'Fleet PO'. Some letters were cancelled on board the ship of origin in which case some simple pattern only was used. During World War II all naval mail for Britain passed through London and Edinburgh and at first they were cancelled with 'HM Ships' or 'Received from HM Ships', late in 1942 the wording was changed to 'Maritime Mail'. Another mark used between 1944 and 1945 was one bearing 'British Fleet Mail'.

Cigarette cards, picture postcards, lantern slides and stereo photographs all deal with various naval topics.

One fact of interest that emerges from a study of the navies of the world is the surprising similarities in uniforms, swords and badges. The insignia of rank worn at various times on the cuffs of the jacket in the following countries are amazingly similar; Argentine, Brazil, Chile, Nationalist China, Cuba, Finland, Germany, Greece, Italy, Japan, Mexico, Netherlands, Norway, Paraguay, Peru, Poland and Turkey.

Those of the United States are similar to the British but use stars on the cuffs in place of the curl on the top stripe and there are a large number of devices worn on the arm to indicate trade and grade.

In the navy of the Third Reich there were many metal breast badges awarded for service in different capacities including destroyers, E Boats, Coastal artillery and, of course, U Boats.

Specialized offshoots of naval study are those concerned with services like the British Royal Naval Air Service, formed just before World War I, and reformed as the Fleet Air Arm in 1924, or the US Naval Air Force, and the Marine, who combine army and navy life in a unique way. Each group has its own special badges, uniforms and traditions.

Sources of supply, care and display and research will obviously be much the same for naval items as for the equivalent military material.

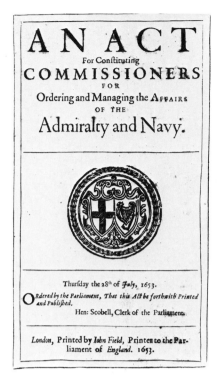

The affairs of the Royal Navy were controlled by the Admiralty, which, in turn, received its authority from the British Government. This Act of Parliament was passed during the Commonwealth, 1649–53.

Select Bibliography

The following list of books is a selection from the very large number dealing with various relevant topics. There are many other titles just as worthy of inclusion but selection has been made on the basis of reliability, usefulness and, with one or two exceptions, availability. Many of the books listed contain extensive bibliographies which give many of the earlier, and less accessible volumes.

General

Frederick, J. *Lineage Book of the British Army*, London, 1969

Higham, R. *A Guide to the Sources of British Military History*, London, 1972

Hutchinson & Co. *The Army in India*, London, 1968

Johnson, S. *Chats on Military Curios*, London, 1915

Lord, F. A. *Civil War Collectors' Encyclopedia*, Harrisburg, 1965

Matloff, M. (ed.) *American Military History*, Washington DC, 1969

Plenderleith, H. J. *The Conservation of Antiquities and Works of Art*, London, 1971

Stewart, C. H. *The Concise Lineage of the Canadian Army,* Toronto, n.d.

Wilkinson, F. *Militaria*, London, 1969

Windrow, M. and Mason, F. *Concise Dictionary of Military Biography*, London, 1975

Wise, T. *A Guide to Military Museums*, Hemel Hempstead, 1971

Wright, R. J. *Collecting Volunteer Militaria*, Newton Abbot, 1974

Uniform

Adair, R. *British Eighth Army in North Africa 1940-43*, London, 1974

Alastair Campbell, D. *The Dress of the Royal Artillery*, London, 1971

Anderson, D. *Scots in Uniform*, Edinburgh, 1972

Barker, A. J. *Red Army Uniform*, London, 1976

Blake, M. *American Civil War Infantry*, London, 1973

Bowling, A. H. *Scottish Regiments 1660-1914*, London, 1970

Bucquoy, E. L. *Les Uniformes de L'Armée Française*, Paris, 1935

Carman, W. Y. *Indian Army Uniforms—Cavalry*, London, 1961

British Military Uniforms from Contemporary Pictures, London, 1968

Indian Army Uniforms—Infantry, London, 1969

Davies, H. P. *British Parachute Forces 1940-45*, London, 1974

Davis, B. *German Army Uniforms and Insignia 1933-48*, London, 1971

Luftwaffe Air Crews, Battle of Britain 1940, London, 1974

Davis, B. L. *German Parachute Forces 1935-45*, London, 1974

US Army Airborne Forces Europe 1942-45, London, 1974

Dilley, R. *Japanese Army Uniforms and Equipment*, London, 1970

Dress Regulations 1846, reprinted, London, 1971

Dress Regulations 1857, reprinted, London, 1976

Dress Regulations 1900, reprinted, London, 1969

Goggins, J. *Arms and Equipment of the Civil War*, New York, 1962

Harris, R. G. *50 Years of Yeomanry Uniforms*, London, 1972

Haythornwaite, P. *Uniforms of the Napoleonic Wars*, London, 1973

Hoffschmidt, E. J. *German Army Uniforms and Insignia 1871-1918*, Connecticut, 1972

Kannik, P. *Military Uniforms in Colour*, London, 1967

Katcher, P. *American Provincial Corps 1775-1784*, Reading, 1973

King George's Army 1775-1783, London, 1973

Knötel, H. *Handbuch der Uniformkunde,* Hamburg, 1966

Lachouque, H. *Dix Siècles de Costume Militaire,* Paris, 1963

Lachouque, H. and Brown, A. *Anatomy of Glory*, London, 1962

Lawson, H. *A History of the Uniforms of the British Army*, London, 1962-67 (5 vols)

Lefferts, C. M. *Uniforms of the War of the American Revolution 1775-1783*, reprinted, London, 1971

Mollo, A. *Army Uniforms of World War II*, London, 1973

Mollo, J. and McGregor, M. *Uniforms of the American Revolution*, London, 1975

Mollo, L. *Military Fashion*, London, 1972

Pietsch, von P. *Formations Und Uniformierungsgeschichte des Preussischen Heeres 1808 bis 1914*, Vol. 1 1963, Vol. 2 1966

Simkin, R. and Archer, L. *British Yeomanry Uniforms*, London, 1971

Strachan, H. *British Military Uniforms 1768-1796*, London, 1975

Thorburn, W. T. *French Army Regiments and Uniforms*, London, 1969

Helmets and Headdress

Carman, W. Y. *Headdress of the British Army—Cavalry*, Sandhurst, 1968
Headdress of the British Army—Yeomanry, London, 1970
Müller, H. and Kunter, F. *Europäische Helme*, E. Germany, 1971
Rankin, R. H. *Helmets and Headdress of the Imperial German Army 1870-1918*, Connecticut, 1965
The Illustrated History of Military Headdress 1660-1918, London, 1976
Tubbs, F. *Stahlhelm*, USA, 1971

Badges and Buttons

Bloomer, W. H. and K. D. *Scottish Regimental Badges 1793-1971*, London, 1973
Carman, W. *Glengarry Badges of the British Line Regiments*, London, 1973
Chichester, H. and Burgess Short, G. *Records and Badges of Every Regiment and Corps in the British Army*, reprinted, London, 1970
Cole, H. *Formation Badges of World War II*, London, 1973
Cole, H. N. *Badges on Battledress*, London, 1953
Edwards, T. *Regimental Badges* (5th edition), London, 1968
Gaylor, J. *Military Badge Collecting*, London, 1971
Kahl, R. *Insignia, Decorations and Badges of the Third Reich*, Holland, n.d.
Kerksis, S. C. *Plates and Buckles of the American Military 1795-1874*, Georgia, 1974
Kerrigan, E. *American Badges and Insignia*, New York, 1967
Kipling, A. and King, H. *Headdress Badges of the British Army*, London, 1973
May, W. and Carman, W. Y. *Badges and Insignia of the British Armed Services*, London, 1974
Parkyn, H. G. *Shoulder Belt Plates and Buttons*, London, 1956
Ripley, H. *Buttons of the British Army 1855-1970*, London, 1971
Rosignoli, G. *Army Badges and Insignia of World War II*, London, 1972
Army Badges and Insignia since 1945, London, 1973
Stockton, E. and Charlton, M. *Reproduction Nazi Insignia*, London, 1971
Stubbs, M. L. and Connor, S. R. *The Army Lineage Series*
Armor-Cavalry: *Part I Regular Army and Army Reserve*
Part II Army National Guard
Infantry: *Part I The Regular Army*, Washington DC, 1969
Wilkinson, F. *Badges of the British Army*, London, 1971

Arms and Armour

Atwood, J. *The Daggers and Edged Weapons of Hitler's Germany*, Berlin, 1965
Bailey, D. W. *British Military Longarms 1715-1815*, London, 1971
Percussion Guns and Rifles, London, 1972

Blackmore, H. *British Military Firearms*, London, 1961
Guns and Rifles of the World, London, 1965
Blair, C. *European Armour*, London, 1958
Pistols of the World, London, 1968
Carter, A. and Walter, J. *The Bayonet*, London, 1974
Carter, J. A. *Allied Bayonets of World War II*, London, 1969
Hicks, J. E. *French Military Weapons*, London, 1964
Hobart, F. (ed.) *Jane's Infantry Weapons, 1975,* London, 1974
Hughes, G. and Fox, C. *A Compendium of British and German Regimental Marks*, Brighton, 1975
Lindsay, M. *Miniature Arms*, New York, 1970
Nadolski, A. *Polish Arms*, Warsaw, 1974
Neumann, G. *The History of Weapons of the American Revolution*, New York and London, 1967
Peterson, H. (ed.) *Encyclopaedia of Firearms*, London, 1964
Roads, C. H. *The British Soldiers' Firearm 1850-64*, London, 1964
Robson, B. *Swords of the British Army*, London, 1975
Smith, J. E. *Small Arms of the World* (10th Edition), London, 1974
Taylerson, A. *The Revolver 1865-1888*, London, 1966
The Revolver 1889-1914, London, 1970
Webster, D. *American Socket Bayonets*, Ottawa, 1964
Wilkinson, F. *Small Arms*, London, 1965
Swords and Daggers, London, 1967
Edged Weapons, London, 1970
Guns, London, 1970
Arms and Armour, London, 1971

Medals and Decorations

Abbott, P. E. and Tamplin, J. M. A. *British Gallantry Awards*, London, 1971
Augustus Steward, W. *The ABC of War Medals and Decorations*, London, 1915
Carter, T. *War Medals of the British Army*, reprinted, London, 1972
Cole, H. N. *Coronation and Commemorative Medals 1887-1953*, Aldershot, 1953
Gordon, L. L. *British Battles and Medals*, London, 1971
Hieronymussen, P. *Orders, Medals and Decorations of Britain and Europe in Colour*, London, 1967
Joslin, E. C. *The Standard Catalogue of British Orders and Decorations* (3rd Edition), London, 1976
Observer's Book of British Awards and Medals, London, 1974
Kerrigan, E. *American War Medals and Decorations*, London, 1973
Littlejohn, D. and Dodkins, C. *Orders, Decorations, Medals and Badges of the Third Reich*, London, 1968
Mericka, V. *Orders and Decorations*, London, 1967
Narbeth, C. *Collecting Military Medals*, London, 1971
Neville, D. G. *Medal Ribbons and Orders of Imperial Germany and Austria*, London, 1974
Purves, A. *Collecting Medals and Decorations*, London, 1968
Risk, J. C. *British Orders and Decorations*, London, 1973
Taprell Dorling, T. *Ribbons and Medals*, London, 1974

Werlich, R. *Russian Orders, Decorations and Medals*, London, 1968

Military Miscellany
Balston, T. *Staffordshire Portrait Figures of the Victorian Age*, London, 1958
Bender, R. J. *The Luftwaffe*, California, 1972
Davis, B. *Flags and Standards of the Third Reich*, London, 1975
Freeston, E. C. *Prisoner-of-War Ship Models*, London, 1973
Harrel, J. *Regimental Steins of Bavarian and Imperial German Armies*, Wurzburg, 1971
Hogg, I. *Gas*, New York, 1975
Jones, B. and Howell, B. *Popular Arts of the First World War*, London, 1972
Rickards, M. and Moody, M. *The First World War*, London, 1975
Toller, J. *Prisoners-of-War Work 1765-1815*, Cambridge, 1965
Tylden, G. *Horses and Saddlery*, London, 1965

Money; Postal Items
Alcock, R. C. and Holland, F. C. *British Postmarks*, Cheltenham, 1960
Angus, I. *Stamps, Posts and Postmarks*, London, 1973
Auckland, R. G. *Air-dropped Propaganda Currency*, Sandridge, 1972
Beresiner, Y. and Narbeth, C. *The Story of Paper Money*, Newton Abbot, 1973
Dalton, R. and Hamer, S. *Provincial Token Coinage of the Eighteenth Century*, reprinted, London, 1967
Davis, W. J. *Nineteenth Century Token Coinage*, reprinted, London, 1969
Jennings, P. *Aerogrammes*, Chippenham, 1973
Kandaouroff, Prince Dimitry, *Collecting Postal History*, Holland, 1973
Mackay, J. *Commemorative Medals*, London, 1970
Porteus, J. *Coins in History*, London, 1969
Raynor, P. E. *A Reference List of British Army Post Marks used in the Great War 1914-18*, n.d.
Rendell, Joan *Collecting Matchbox Labels*, London, 1963
Whiting, J. R. S. *Trade Tokens*, Newton Abbot, 1971
Commemorative Medals, Newton Abbot, 1972

Books and Ephemera
Cockle, M. J. *Bibliography of Books Relating to the Military History of India*, Simla, 1901
Bibliography of English Military Books up to 1642, reprinted, London, 1960
Crookshank, C. de W. *Prints of British Military Operations*, London, 1921
Denny, Rev. A. H. *Militaria—Collecting Print and Manuscript*, St Ives, 1973
Gunn, M. J. *Print Restoration and Picture Cleaning*, London, 1911
Haswell-Miller, A. and Dawnay, N. *Military Drawings and Paintings in the Royal Collection*, London, Vol. I 1966, II 1970

Holt, T. and V. *Picture Postcards of the Golden Age*, London, 1972
Howarth-Loomes, B. E. C. *Victorian Photography*, London, 1974
Judd, D. *Posters of World War II*, London, 1972
Nevil, R. *British Military Prints*, London, 1909
Ogilby Trust, *Index to British Military Costume Prints 1500-1914*, London, 1972
Pearsall, R. *Victorian Sheet Music Covers*, Newton Abbot, 1972
Rickards, M. and Moody, M. *The First World War*, London, 1975
Staff, F. *The Picture Postcard and its Origins*, London, 1966
White, A. S. *Bibliography of Regimental Histories of the British Army*, London, 1965
Wilder, F. *How to Identify Old Prints*, London, 1969

Model Soldiers
Britains Ltd. Toy and Model Catalogue 1940, reprinted, London, 1972
Carman, W. Y. *Model Soldiers*, London, 1973
Garratt, J. G. *Model Soldiers*, London, 1962
Collecting Model Soldiers, London, 1975
Harris, H. *How to Go Collecting Model Soldiers*, London, 1969
Nicollier, J. *Collecting Toy Soldiers*, Fribourg, 1967
Richards, L. W. *Old British Model Soldiers 1893-1918*, London, 1970
Scrine, J. *History of Britains Ltd.*, 1955

Police
Cramer, J. *The World's Police*, London, 1964
Uniforms of the World's Police, Illinois, n.d.
Critchley, T. A. *A History of the Police in England and Wales*, London, 1967
Dicken, E. *The History of Truncheons*, Ilfracombe, 1952
Hallett, H. V. D. *Survey of the Present and Former Police Forces of England, Wales and Channel Islands*, West Bridgford, 1975
Hibbert, C. *The Roots of Evil*, London, 1966
Joy, W. and Prior, T. *The Bushrangers*, London, 1963
Lovell Knight, A. V. *A History of the Office of The Provost Marshal and the Corps of Military Police*, Aldershot, 1945
Reith, C. *New Study of Police History*, London, 1956
Shaw, A. G. *Convicts and Colonies*, London, 1958

Naval Collecting
Frere-Cook, G. *The Decorative Arts of the Mariner*, London, 1966
Goggins, J. *Ships and Seamen of the American Revolution*, London, n.d.
Jarrett, D. *British Naval Dress*, London, 1960
Keble Chatterton, E. *Old Ship Prints*, reprinted London, 1965
Long, W. H. *Medals of the British Navy*, London, 1895
May, W. and Annis, P. *Swords for Sea Service*, London, 1970 (2 vols)

Military Museums and Collections

The following list is just a selection from the extremely large number of museums in the English speaking world which specialize in, or hold a reasonable number of, military items.

Readers who wish to find further details, such as times of opening, full addresses and an idea of contents, are referred to:

Hudson, Kenneth & Nicholls, Ann (eds.), *The Directory of Museums*, New York, 1975

Wise, T. *A Guide to Military Museums*, Hemel Hempstead, 1971

Index Publications; ABC Travel Guides

Australia
Albany
Albany Old Jail
Ballarat
Montrose Cottage & Eureka Military Museum
Canberra
Australian War Memorial
Sydney
Fort Denison
Our Yesterday's Museum

Canada
Borden
Canadian Forces Intelligence & Security Museum
Royal Canadian Army Service Corps Museum
Calgary
Glenbow Foundation, Alberta Government Museum
Regimental Museum of Princess Patricia's Canadian Lt Infantry
The Queen's Own Rifles of Canada Regimental Museum
Duck Lake
Duck Lake Historical Museum
Edmonton
Princess Pat's Light Infantry Regimental Museum
Elk Point
Fort George Museum
Fort Macleod
Fort Macleod Historical Museum
Fredericton
The Guard House
Military Compound
York Sunbury Historical Museum
Halifax
The Army Museum
Kingston
Old Fort Henry

Royal Canadian Signals Museum
Royal Military College Museum
Montreal
Museum of The Military and Maritime Society of Montreal
Royal Canadian Ordnance Corps Museum
Niagara-on-the-Lake
Navy Hall
Oromocto
Canadian Forces Base, Gagetown Museum
Fort Hughes Blockhouse
Ottawa
Canadian War Museum
Governor General's Footguards Museum
Public Archives of Canada
Penetanguishene
British Naval and Military Establishment Museum
Regina
Royal Canadian Mounted Police Museum
Rocky Point
Fort Amherst Nat. Historic Park
Saint-Jean
Royal Military College
Saint-John
Martello Tower
The New Brunswick Museum
St Johns
Newfoundland Naval and Military Museum
Shilo
Royal Canadian Artillery Museum
Toronto
HMCS 'Haida'
Historic Fort York
Royal Canadian Military Institute
Vedder Crossing
RCE Military Museum

Ireland
Curragh
Curragh Camp Military Museum
Mullingar
Museum of the 4th Artillery Regt

New Zealand
Auckland
Auckland War Memorial Museum
Burnham
Medical Corps Museum
Greymouth
Greymouth Returned Services Association War Museum
Waiouru
Army Museum

United Kingdom

England
Aldershot (Hants)
Army Catering Corps Museum
Army Physical Training Corps Museum
Museum of the Airborne Forces
Queen Alexandra's Royal Army Nursing Corps Museum
Royal Army Dental Corps Museum
Royal Army Veterinary Corps Museum
Regimental Museum of Royal Corps of Transport
Alnwick (Northumb)
The Fifth or Royal Northumberland Fusiliers Regimental Museum
Arborfield (Berks)
Corps Museum REME
Ashford (Kent)
Intelligence Corps Museum
Ash Vale (Hants)
Royal Army Medical Corps Historical Museum

Bagshot (Surrey)
Museum of the Royal Army Chaplain's Department
Barnsley (S. Yorks)
Cannon Hall Museum and Art Gallery (13/18th Royal Hussars)
Beaconsfield (Bucks)
Royal Army Educational Corps Museum
Berwick-upon-Tweed (Northumb)
King's Own Scottish Borderers Regimental Museum
Beverley (Humberside)
East Yorkshire (The Prince of Wales' Own Regiment of Yorkshire) Regiment Museum
Biggleswade (Beds)
The Shuttleworth Collection (Aircraft)
Blackburn (Lancs)
East Lancashire Regimental Museum
Blandford Forum (Dorset)
Royal Signals Museum
Bodmin (Cornwall)
The Duke of Cornwall's Light Infantry Regimental Museum
Brentwood (Essex)
The Essex Regiment Museum
Bury (Greater Manchester)
Regimental Museum XX The Lancashire Fusiliers
Bury St Edmunds (Suffolk)
Suffolk Regiment Museum
Camberley (Surrey)
National Army Museum (Part)
Royal Army Ordnance Corps Museum
Canterbury (Kent)
The Buffs Regimental Museum
The Queens Regimental Museum
Carlisle (Cumbria)
The Border Regiment Museum
Chatham (Kent)
Museum of the Corps of Royal Engineers
Chelmsford (Essex)
Chelmsford & Essex Museum
Chester
The 22nd (Cheshire) Regiment Museum
Regimental Museum 3rd Carabiniers (Prince of Wales' Dragoon Guards)
Chichester (Sussex)
Corps of Royal Military Police Museum
The Royal Sussex Regiment Museum

Devizes (Wilts)
Wiltshire Regiment Museum
Dorchester (Dorset)
Dorset Military Museum
Durham
Durham Light Infantry Museum and Arts Centre
Exeter (Devon)
The Devonshire Regiment Museum
Gloucester
Regimental Museum of the Gloucestershire Regiment
Gosport (Hants)
Submarine Museum
Grantham (Lincs)
Regimental Museum 17th/21st Lancers
Guildford (Surrey)
Women's Royal Army Corps Museum
Halifax (W. Yorks)
Bankfield Museum, Duke of Wellington's Regiment & 4th/7th Royal Dragoon Guards
Hereford
Hereford Light Infantry Museum
Hull (Humberside)
3rd Battalion The Prince of Wales' Own Regiment of Yorkshire
Kingston-upon-Thames (Surrey)
Museum of the Queen's Royal Surrey Regiment
Lancaster
Lancaster Museum, King's Own Royal (Lancaster) Regiment 4th Foot
Leicester
9th/12th Royal Lancers Museum
Royal Leicestershire Regimental Museum
Lichfield (Staffs)
The Regimental Museum. The Staffordshire Regiment (Prince of Wales)
Lincoln
Regimental Museum, Royal Lincolnshire Regiment
Liss (Hants)
Royal Corps of Transport Railway Model Room and Museum
Liverpool (Merseyside)
Museum of the King's Regiment (Liverpool)
London
Honourable Artillery Company Museum (EC1)
Museum of the Order of St John of Jerusalem (EC1)

Her Majesty's Tower of London Armouries (EC3)
The Royal Fusiliers Museum (EC3)
Middlesex Regimental Museum (N17)
Imperial War Museum (SE1)
Royal Military School of Music (Twickenham)
National Maritime Museum (SE10)
Museum of Artillery (SE18)
Royal Artillery Regimental Museum (SE18)
Berkshire & Westminster Dragoons Museum (SW1)
Guards Museum (SW1)
London Scottish Regimental Museum (SW3)
London Irish Rifles Regimental Museum (SW3)
National Army Museum (SW3)
RAF Museum, Hendon
21st Special Air Service Regiment (Artists) Museum (SW3)
Wellington Museum (W1)
Maidstone (Kent)
Queen's Own Royal West Kent Museum
Manchester
Queen's Park Museum & Art Gallery, Manchester Regiment & 14th/20th King's Hussars
Middle Wallop (Hants)
Army Aviation Museum
Newcastle-upon-Tyne (Tyne and Wear)
Regimental Museum 15th/19th The King's Royal Hussars
Northampton
Museum of the Northamptonshire Regiment
Norwich
The Royal Norfolk Regiment Museum
Nottingham
The Sherwood Foresters Regimental Museum
Pontefract (W. Yorks)
The King's Own Yorkshire Light Infantry Regimental Museum
Portsmouth (Hants)
The Victory Museum
Preston (Lancs)
Regimental Museum, The Queens Lancashire Regiment
Reading (Berks)
Royal Berkshire Regiment Museum
Richmond (N. Yorks)
The Green Howards Museum

Sheffield (S. Yorks)
Sheffield Regimental Museum, The York & Lancaster Regiment
Shrewsbury (Salop)
The King's Shropshire Light Infantry Regimental Museum
The King's Shropshire Light Infantry (Territorial) Museum
The Light Infantry Museum
1st The Queen's Dragoon Guards Regimental Museum
The Shropshire Yeomanry and Shropshire RHA Museum
Southsea (Hants)
Royal Marines Museum
Stratford-on-Avon (War)
Queen's Own Warwickshire and Worcestershire Yeomanry
Strensall (N. Yorks)
The Yorkshire Regiments Museum
Taunton (Somerset)
Somerset Light Infantry Military Museum
Wareham (Dorset)
Royal Armoured Corps Tank Museum and Royal Tank Regiment Museum
Warminster (Wilts)
School of Infantry Museum
Warrington (Lancs)
The Queen's Lancashire Regiment Museum
Warwick (War)
Regimental Museum of the Queen's Own Hussars
The Royal Warwickshire Regimental Museum
Westerham (Kent)
Quebec House
Squerryes Court
Winchester (Hants)
Royal Army Pay Corps Museum
The Royal Green Jackets Museum
The Royal Hampshire Regimental Museum
Windsor (Berks)
The Household Cavalry Museum
Wootton (Northants)
Royal Pioneer Corps Museum
Worcester
The Worcestershire Regimental Museum
Yeovilton (Somerset)
Fleet Air Arm Museum
York
Castle Museum
Prince of Wales' Own Regiment of Yorkshire Museum

Scotland
Aberdeen (Grampian)
The Gordon Highlanders Regimental Museum
Ayr (Strathclyde)
Ayrshire Yeomanry Museum
Dunkeld (Tayside)
The Scottish Horse Museum
Edinburgh
National Museum of Antiquities
The Royal Scots Regimental Museum
Scottish United Services Museum
Fort George (Highland)
Regimental Museum of Seaforth Highlanders, The Queen's Own Cameron Highlanders & Queen's Own Highlanders
Glasgow
The Royal Highland Fusiliers Museum
Hamilton (Strathclyde)
Regimental Museum, The Cameronians (Scottish Rifles)
Penicuik (Lothian)
Scottish Infantry Depot (Glencourse) Museum
Perth
The Black Watch Museum
Stirling (Strathclyde)
Regimental Museum, Argyll & Sutherland Highlanders

Wales
Brecon (Powys)
Regimental Museum, The South Wales Borderers & Monmouthshire Regiment
Caernarvon
Regimental Museum, The Royal Welch Fusiliers
Cardiff (Glam)
Regimental Museum, The Welch Regiment
Crickhowell (Mon)
Welsh Brigade Museum

Northern Ireland
Armagh
Regimental Museum, The Royal Irish Fusiliers
Belfast
The Royal Ulster Rifles
Carrickfergus (Co Antrim)
Museum of the Irish Cavalry Regiments
Enniskillen (Co Fermanagh)
Regimental Museum The Royal Inniskilling Fusiliers

USA
Abercrombie (N. Dak.)
Fort Abercrombie State Park Museum
Acton (Mass.)
Historical Museum of the North and South
Albany (N.Y.)
New York State Museum, History Collection
State Capitol
Alexandria (Va.)
Ford Ward Museum
Annapolis (Md.)
US Naval Academy Museum
Appomatox (Va.)
Museum of Appomatox Court House National Historic Park
Austin (Tex.)
Texas Confederate Museum
Baton Rouge (La.)
Old Arsenal Museum
Bennington (Vt.)
Bennington Museum
Boalsburg (Pa.)
Pennsylvania Military Museum
Boston (Mass.)
Museum of Ancient and Honourable Artillery Company of Mass.
USS Constitution
Bremerton (Wash.)
Naval Shipyard Museum
Bucksport (Me.)
Bucksport Historical Society Museum
Carlisle (Pa.)
Hessian Guardhouse Museum
Charleston (Mo.)
Citadel Museum
Cheyenne (Wyo.)
Warren Military Museum
Columbia (S.C.)
South Carolina Confederate Relic Room and Museum
Columbus (Ga.)
Confederate Naval Museum
Cordele (Ga.)
World War I & II Museum
Dayton (Ohio)
United States Air Force Museum
Detroit (Mich.)
Fort Wayne Military Museum
Durant (Okla.)
Oklahoma Historical Society Museum
East Greenwhich (R.I.)
Varnum Military and Naval Museum

Eureka (Calif.)
Fort Humboldt State Historic Park
Evanston (Ill.)
Evanston Historical Society Museum
Fairfield (Utah)
Stage Coach Inn
Fort Belvoir (Va.)
US Army Corps of Engineers Museum
Fort Benning (Ga.)
US Army Infantry Museum
Fort Bragg (N.C.)
82nd Airborne Division War Memorial
Fort Campbell (Ken.)
Fort Campbell Museum
Fort Carson (Col.)
Fort Carson Museum
Fort Eustis (Va.)
US Army Transportation Museum
Fort Knox (Ken.)
Patton Museum of Cavalry and Armor
Fort Leavenworth (Kan.)
Fort Leavenworth Museum
Fort Lee (Va.)
US Army Quartermaster Corps Museum
Fort Lewis (Wash.)
Fort Lewis Military Museum
Fort McClellan (Ala.)
Edith Nourse Rogers Museum
Fort George G. Meade (Md.)
First US Army Museum
Fort Monmouth (N.J.)
US Army Signal Corps Museum
Fort Oglethorpe (Ga.)
Chickamauga-Chattanooga National Military Park
Fort Riley (Kan.)
US Cavalry Museum
Fort Sill (Okla.)
Fort Sill Museum
Franklin (Tenn.)
Carter House
Gettysburg (Pa.)
Gettysburg National Museum
Greensboro (N.C.)
Guilford Courthouse National Military Park
Harlingen (Tex.)
Confederate Air Force Flying Museum
Hartford (Conn.)
Connecticut State Library Museum
Jeanette (Pa.)

Bushy Run Battlefield Museum
Kanapolis (Kan.)
Fort Harker Museum
Kansas City (Mo.)
Liberty Memorial
Key West (Fla.)
Lighthouse Military Museum
Kings Mountain (N.C.)
Museum of Kings Mountain National Military Park
Lebec (Calif.)
Fort Tejon State Historic Park
Lexington (Va.)
Virginia Military Institute, Jackson Memorial Hall
Lone Jack (Mo.)
Jackson County Civil War Museum and Battlefield
Madison (Wis.)
Grand Army of the Republic, Memorial Hall
Manassas (Va.)
Manassas National Battlefield Park Museum
Monterey (Calif.)
US Army Museum
Morristown (N.J.)
Morristown National Historical Park
Murfreesboro (Tenn.)
Oaklands
Newburgh (N.Y.)
Jonathan Hasbrouck House
New Haven (Conn.)
Winchester Gun Museum
New Orleans (La.)
Confederate Museum
Historic New Orleans Collection
Newport New (Va.)
War Memorial Museum of Virginia
New York (N.Y.)
Aeroflex Museum
Fort Wadsworth Museum
Museum of the American Numismatic Society
Police Academy and Museum
Norfolk (Va.)
Hotel Nanseamond
Ogden (Utah)
Browning Gun Collection
Oswego (N.Y.)
Fort Ontario
Pea Ridge (Ark.)
Pea Ridge National Military Park
Pensacola (Fla.)
Naval Aviation Museum
Petersberg (Va.)
Quartermaster Museum

Philadelphia (Pa.)
Perelman Antique Toy Museum
War Library and Museum of the Military Order of the 'Loyal Legion of the United States
Port Gibson (Miss.)
Grand Gulf Military Park
Prairie Du Rocher (Ill.)
Fort de Chartres State Park Museum
Prospect (Me.)
Fort Knox State Park
Quantico (Va.)
US Marine Corps Museum
Raleigh (N.C.)
North Carolina Museum of History
Richmond (Va.)
Museum of the Confederacy
Rockford (Ill.)
Memorial Hall
St Louis (Mo.)
Soldiers Memorial
San Antonio (Tex.)
Hanger 9, Edward H. White II Memorial Museum
San Diego (Calif.)
San Diego Aerospace Museum
San Francisco (Calif.)
Fort Point Museum
San Juan (Puerto Rico)
Museum of Military and Naval History
Santa Fe (N. Mex.)
New Mexico Military Museum
Savannah (Ga.)
Factors Walk Military Museum
Sharpsburg (Md.)
Antietam National Battlefield Site
Springfield (Mass.)
Springfield Armoury Museum
Starke (Fla.)
Museum of the North and South
Vicksburg (Miss.)
Vicksburg National Military Park
Warren (Wyo.)
Warren Military Museum
Washington (D.C.)
National Museum of History and Technology
National Rifle Association Firearms Museum
United States Navy Memorial Museum
West Point (N.Y.)
Museum of United States Military Academy
Wheaton (Ill.)
Cantigny War Memorial Museum of the First Division

Specialist Publications and Societies

As most of the Societies are run by volunteer, unpaid officers, addresses change, so that it is as well to check with current lists of Associations and Societies.

Agrupación de Miniaturistas Militares
La Boletín
Señor M. Almirall
Fuste, Avenida José Antonio 595, Cupala de Coliseum Barcelona, Spain

Airfix Magazine
Bar Hill, Cambridge CB3 8EL

Arms & Armour Society
Publishes a journal twice yearly
Secretary R. Whittaker
30 Alderney Street, London SW1

Battle Magazine
M.A.P. Ltd, PO Box 35, Bridge Street, Hemel Hempstead, Herts HP1 1EE

British Model Soldier Society
Publishes a bulletin
Mr H. Middleton
169 Queens Road, Cheadle Hume, Cheadle, Cheshire

Deutsches Waffen-Journal
Journal-Verlag Schwend GmbH, 7170 Schwab. Hall, In den Herrenackern 5-7, West Germany

Diana Armi
Vide Milton 7, SO 129 Firenze, Italy

Dispatch
Journal of the Scottish Military Collectors Society
Secretary Mr M. S. Davidson
Findon Croft, Findon, Portlethen, Aberdeen AB1 4RN

Figarina Helvetica
Dr E. Diefenbacher
Via Bellavista 17 6977, Ruvigliana, Switzerland

Forces Postal History Society
Address not known

Gazette des Armes
Gazette des Uniformes
Sera, BP 24, 92603 Asnières, France

Gun Report
PO Box 111, Aledo, Illinois 61231, USA

Guns Review
Standard House, Bonhill Street, London EC2

Historical Breech Loading Small Arms Society
Imperial War Museum, Lambeth Road, London SE1 6HZ

Historical Firearms Society of South Africa
The Secretary, 'Minden', 11 Buchan Road, Newlands, Cape, South Africa

Irish Model Soldiers Group
Mr F. Glenn Thompson
6 Greenlea Park, Terenune, Dublin, Ireland

Journal of Imperial German Military Collectors Assoc.
PO Box 651, Shawnee Mission, Kansas 66201, USA

Military Historical Society
Hon. Secretary A. E. Bowell
16 Sweetwater Close, Shamley Green, Guildford, Surrey

Military Historical Society
Adjutants Call
Mr Peter Blum
PO Box 39, Times Square, New York, USA

Military Historical Society of Australia
La Sabretache
262 Tucker Road, Ormond East SE 14, Victoria, Australia

Miniature AFV Collectors Association (GB)
Mr G. E. G. Williams
15 Berwich Avenue, Heaton Mersey, Stockport, Cheshire

Miniature Warfare
Box 005 61, Benares Road, London SE18

Orders and Medals Research Society
Mr N. G. Gooding
11 Maresfield, Chepstow Road, Croydon CRO 5UA

Shooting Times and Country Magazine
Cornwallis Estate, Clivemont Road, Maidenhead, Berks

Shooting Times
News Plaza, Peoria, Illinois 61601 USA

Société des Belges
Coll. de Figurines,
La Figurine
75 rue de Prince Royal Brussels 5, Belgium

Soc. des Collectionneurs de Figurines Historiques
Publishes a journal
Madame Simone Gayda
38 rue de Lubeck, Paris 16eme France

Society for Army Historical Research
Publishes a journal quarterly
c/o Library, Old War Office Building, Whitehall, London SW1

Society Napoleonic
Publishes a journal quarterly
Mr R. Leighton
49 Brampton Road, Kenton, Middx

Soldier Magazine
HMSO, Atlantic House, Holborn Viaduct, London EC1

Tac Armi
Via Leonardo da Vinci 169, Milano, Italy

The Canadian Journal of Arms Collecting
Museum Restoration Service, PO Box 2140, Picton, Ontario, Canada KOK 2TO

Tradition
44 Dover Street, London W1

Unione Nazionale Collezionnista d'Italia
La Voce del Collezionnista
Signor M. Fasparinette
Via Lattanzio, 15a Rome, Italy

Index